Good-bye, Union Square

ALSO BY ALBERT HALPER:

by Albert Halper

Good-bye, Union Square

A WRITER'S MEMOIR OF THE THIRTIES

CHICAGO

QUADRANGLE BOOKS

1970

Contents

08275

Good-bye, Union Square

An Afternoon
Phone Call

A person who has truly lived and loved in New York during the 1930's hesitates to discuss that decade before strangers at a cocktail party. That time for him has become a buried thing, an epoch for dedicated scholars engaged in research on the hieroglyphics of that era.

"America," an international, aging, night-club super-star complained bitterly in one of her rare interviews recently, "is simply not the same place any more." She added: "Neither is New York." And one night on a television interview show, a man with a gray face looked into the camera and said to ten million people: "There used to be a rose on every cafeteria table, during the Depression, when coffee was five cents." Theirs is not my lament. That long gone age for me, I knew, had indeed vanished into the vaults.

But one sunny afternoon the telephone in my apartment in New York rang; and the loud ringing on that June summer day sent my thoughts whirling back to the embalmed past. The memories I'd thought had been buried forever trembled and came to half-life, then to life, and I was confronted with what I had thought the years had sodded over forever—the suddenly resurrected image of myself during a restless, troubled time.

Over the wire came the inquiring voice of a stranger, an utter stranger. "Is this Albert Halper?" It was a man's voice, hearty, warm, yet a trifle ill at ease, I thought. "Is this Albert?"

"Yes," I replied. "This is he."

"Do you know who this is?" The voice, still hearty, grew very pleasant indeed, more confident now.

"Well," I stalled politely, "you do sound very familiar . . ." the lie every one of us tells over the phone, in response to an inquiry like this one.

"Think back sixteen years," the hearty voice continued, very, very friendly now. "Don't you know me?"

I racked my brain for a couple of seconds, and drew a blank. "No," I said, turning honest. "I don't think I do."

There was a slight, self-conscious pause, followed by an explosive comradely laugh, then a name came over the wire, a name I never thought I would ever hear again over any phone. It was my former literary agent and, of course, with a shock I well remembered his voice now. In the old days I had heard it frequently, whenever he had sold pieces of mine to Mencken at the old *American Mercury,* to George Leighton up at *Harper's,* to the editors at *The Atlantic Monthly, The New Yorker, Yale Review, Commentary,* and all the others, including book publishers.

"How are you, Albert?" his familiar voice boomed warmly, now that he had established himself in my life again, sixteen years later, on this sunny June afternoon.

I was still shocked, but I managed to say, dishonestly, "I'm fine, it's good to hear your voice after all this time . . ." How I envied, at that moment, those quick-thinking people who knew how to rise to such occasions, curtly cutting off such conversations with, "Look, I'm sorry, I'm really busy now, I'll call you back." As I yearned, in that split second to have so agile a personality, the voice over the phone boomed on.

"Albert, I'm now living in Europe, and I'm over here on a visit, to meet publishers and get some books for translations for various firms I represent there. It would be nice to see you again."

"How long are you going to be here? . . ."

"Until August. But I'm going to the west coast soon so I won't be in New York too long. I'd certainly like to see you."

I was still a bit dazed and my silence must have troubled him a bit. "I might as well confess, it was Junior who told me to call you. You remember my son, don't you, Albert?" Of course I did. I'd known him since he was six years old. "Junior told me to call you. He said, 'You've simply got to phone Albert Halper and ask him to dinner.' I'm staying with him during my visit."

"How old is Junior now? . . ."

"He's forty."

"What?"

"Certainly, time marches on," he laughed. "Remember the summer when you, Pauline, I, Minna, and Junior spent two weeks together up at Lake George, swimming and boating?" I recalled that time at once. "And how he played his clarinet up in his room, and in the morning slipped his short stories under your door for you to read and criticize?"

"What's he doing now?"

"He's married. He's a doctor, specializing in research in one of the big hospitals here. He told me I had to call you, Albert . . ."

Five minutes later, after promising to phone Junior for a

dinner date the following week, I hung up, my face a little damp, my hands weak.

Lorna came from her studio, a room in our apartment she uses for her painting; with brushes in her hands and the sun shining on her hair, she asked, "You look sort of funny, who was that calling?"

I told her. Years ago I had spoken to her about my former literary agent. At the time, her eyes widened as I mentioned his involvement with a secret Communist underground activity that came to light during a major espionage trial held sixteen years ago, which had ruined his literary agency and had driven him from the city.

Lorna looked at me in silence for a while. "Will you call back next week?"

I stared toward the windows. I was in no condition to make a decision. "It all happened so long ago. Junior used to be a wonderful kid and it would be nice to see *him* after all these years. But I don't know if I'll phone . . ."

The sunlight poured into the room through the two windows. I was still a trifle weak. This man had not only been my literary agent but also my close friend. He had sustained me with constant encouragement when, as a fledgling writer, I had first handed him my short stories to read. As my agent he had argued vehemently with dozens of editors until he had finally placed my work. During the ensuing years we had eaten together in small restaurants countless times. Then one day he had betrayed me, almost ruining my life. It had been a terrifying experience for me then; and all the painful details of that agonizing episode now returned. "Well," Lorna said gently, "what will you do?"

"I don't know," I said again. "I don't know yet." I watched her turn thoughtfully and go into her studio to resume her painting. Sitting alone in the room my memories of the thirties swept over me with a rush. Somehow I half-yearned to see my agent again, yet I didn't know if I wanted to initiate the move for a meeting. What were the advantages, or disadvantages, for such a confrontation? It turned out to be a long, long afternoon for me. That telephone call had peeled away the years . . .

The Pullman
Gets You There

A young writer's life really begins when he leaves home. There is no other distant city but New York for him and, if he has just sold his first story, the long journey east can be unforgettable, epochal. Let me begin at the beginning. I had just quit my job as a mail-sorter on the night shift in Chicago's big Central Post Office. I had quit on the very day I was promoted from substitute clerk to a regular clerkship with increased pay. With my short story accepted, and three hundred dollars saved up, I felt, at twenty-four, it was time to try writing in a room in Manhattan instead of typing away in a dull flat on Chicago's West Side.

I arrived in New York in the fall of 1929, a month before the big stock market crash. I didn't hitch a ride or make the trip on a jolting bus. I traveled smoothly by Pullman, having been tipped off by a fellow postal clerk about a cheap yet luxurious way to journey to New York. While my father, a short, stocky, irascible, lonely man who had just given up his little grocery, stood bewildered in the living room watching me pack my suitcase, I looked up from my packing and told him I was leaving Chicago "for a few months." My mother having died six months earlier, my job now thrown over, I felt there were no further ties holding me to Chicago. Avoiding my father's troubled, beseeching stare, I shook hands with him briefly and, to conceal my own emotion, made a clumsy quip about "trying my luck east." As I was about to depart, the phone rang—one of my brothers (the oldest, the forty-year-old) was calling hurriedly to dissuade me from imminent disaster. "Al, don't go to New York. Get into advertising if you want to write. Today I phoned my close friend Morrie Lowitz who runs an ad agency and I told him about you and he wants to see you. Don't try and be a *poet* or anything, for crissake. There's no money in it."

After he hung up, screaming, another concerned brother called immediately; this was the quiet one, about thirty-seven, who worked as office manager in a mail-order clothing firm. "Al, I can get you into the company as a correspondent. I'll talk to the boss. You'll earn a steady salary writing letters to customers, there's a chance for advancement. . . ." After he hung up, frustrated, it was my sister's turn to phone. "Albert, don't you think you're acting hastily, giving up your Post Office job?" she asked tactfully. "You were in civil service, Albert, and there are *five* million unemployed, I read it in the *Tribune* today. . . ." Another brother did not phone; a traveling salesman, he was selling sweaters and raincoats on the road, in Iowa or somewhere. And as for Louis, the baby brother, he didn't call either; a dental student, he was working nights as a clerk in a United Cigar store in the Loop.

An hour later I stood under the stars of the deserted South Side platform of the B & O—I had been instructed over the phone by a mysterious caller not to board downtown—waiting for the train that would take me east. It was a chilly night and above the freight sheds floated the smoke from busy locomotives shunting coal cars under the arc lights. When a passenger train arrived for this South Side stop, I headed briskly with my suit-case and portable typewriter for the last car where a conducter stood waiting on the lower step. He gave me no nod of recogni-tion. As I shook hands with him, he took the white envelope in my palm that contained my twenty-five dollars. A Negro porter greeted me solemnly as I got into the sleeping car. He was out-wardly the epitome of all black Pullman porters, about sixty, heavy, wise, and tactful; he gave me a slow smile, his honest, re-liable eyes sizing me up as I struggled with my bag and type-writer. "I'll take those, son," he said, and put them away for me.

I wasn't alone on the trip. Behind me puffed a fat young man of about twenty-two carrying a cheap brown suitcase and two thick brief-cases, followed by a stunning looking girl of twenty or so with two expensive bags. I knew at once they were also in on the deal. The locomotive let fly a sharp whistle, and soon the long train, picking up speed, began thrumming across the plain, bound for the east coast.

While we three sat waiting for the porter to make up our berths, we suddenly turned to each other and introduced our-selves. In a remarkably short time we exchanged biographies, as soldiers do when riding in trucks toward the front. I learned that Pembroke, the plump young man, had batches of manu-scripts in his bulging brief-cases; he was on his way to Broadway, he explained, to become a playwright. "I just finished a new play Friday that will simply be great for Mae West," he confided. He added that he also had a "strong script" about a big gangster, and he described the obligatory scene in the last act, a shoot-out between two rival gang leaders on the West Side Elevated plat-form which took place while expresses and locals roared in and out of the station.

As for Joan, the attractive looking girl, she was headed for New York to pursue a career as a dramatic actress; and in a low, pleasant voice she suggested, after listening to us and perhaps deciding Pembroke and I were gentlemen, that for the sake of economy we three might share an apartment together. "Of course, we'd occupy separate rooms." Because of her undeniable charms, this struck me as being an interesting possibility, and as the porter appeared to inform us that our berths were ready I said I'd certainly give the matter of our living together, for economic reasons, my deepest consideration. "It sounds very feasible," I stated. We climbed into our separate berths, an aura of intense friendship hovering over our part of the car.

When, almost twenty-four hours later, the train pulled into the B & O terminal in Newark, I saw my friend Melvin Epstein waiting loyally at the gate for me. Big and hulking, he stood there with his long, sad nose catching beams of light from the ceiling chandeliers, his hand outstretched in warm greeting. "Hey, you made it. I was afraid for a while you weren't coming to New York." We had been co-workers on the night shift in the Chicago Post Office, until he'd moved to Brooklyn with his family eight months ago. He kept pressing me to come east in his letters, especially after he learned that Marianne Moore, editor of the *Dial,* had accepted my first story. In his eyes there was no envy, and his British accent—he and his family had emigrated from Manchester only a few years before—fell agreeably upon my ears. For two years he had been writing humorous sketches (this had been our bond at the night-time mail cases), composing them in the style of Stephen Leacock. He had written them secretly at home, without his family's knowledge, and week after week the editors he had sent them to returned them, until, in his last letter to me, he admitted he had thrown in the sponge. Now he took up my bag while I carried my typewriter. Turning, I waved and called out to Pembroke and Joan: "I'll keep in touch."

We rode a subway under the river to Manhattan, then transferred to a train that took us on a long ride. When we at last emerged from the subway I found myself in the Brownsville section of Brooklyn, a drab area of low houses that seemed to stretch for miles into the night. The buildings, even the street lamps, were different than those in Chicago, and I told myself: "Well, you're here, for better or for worse; you're not throwing mail any more."

Although it was rather late, Melvin's family had sat up for my arrival. As soon as we opened the door I knew I had stepped into a home I liked, into a warm, lively world. The Epstein family consisted of Melvin's parents, his three brothers and his two sisters. The oldest sister, twenty-six, married to an Italian furrier who was present, shook my hand warmly. I learned later her husband had once organized migrant fruit pickers in California and had worked with Big Bill Haywood, the legendary head of the I.W.W. A small, dark, handsome man, Carlo quietly smoked cigarette after cigarette and regarded me with thoughtful, friendly eyes. Louie, tall and thin, two years older than Melvin, the family comedian, gripped my hand and with a grin announced: "Welcome to the next floor show of the evening!" He then proceeded to rock the room into laughter with two-liners and an imitation of Al Jolson singing "Mammy." The second sister, who was a year younger than Melvin, ignored me as well as Louie's performance; she sat silently reading a book, relenting every now and then to throw a suspicious glance my way. "Don't mind Sadie," Melvin whispered to me. "She's a snob, a member of the Communist Party."

Mrs. Epstein, a small and friendly woman who seemed overworked, set a plate of food before me. Although I explained that I had dined on the train, she wouldn't take no for an answer and practically forced me to eat while the others looked me over. Melvin's two younger brothers, twelve and ten years old, sat grinning at me foolishly, in that warm way kids do when a stranger is welcomed into the family circle. Mr. Epstein, a big, heavy man who drank shot glasses of whiskey alone in a corner, listened to his oldest son's monologue in sullen silence; and after he had laughed grudgingly, once, at Louie's act, he began to stare at me fixedly, evidently trying to figure me out. In Chicago Melvin had confided to me that his father was a lecher who disappeared two or three nights a week, had women on the outside and was hated by all the children.

For forty minutes Louie continued performing with his two-liners and imitations, ending with an impersonation of Harry Richman. Suddenly Sadie, the sister who was a Communist, put down her book and addressed me abruptly. "I understand you're a writer." Conversation elsewhere in the room stopped. "Melvin told me you worked in a foundry before you got a job in the Post Office. Is that right?"

"Yes."

"How long did you work in the foundry?"

"Four years." The others were listening.

"And where else did you work in Chicago?"

"In a mail-order house as an order filler, for a year."

"Did you ever hear of the Agit-Prop Players?"

"No. Who are they?"

"They go around giving plays and skits in union halls all over the city, for the workers. Haven't you heard of them?"

"No," I admitted. I was somewhat taken aback by this type of questioning.

"My God. With your background, they need you. You can write proletarian plays for them. I know someone who's a member of the company . . ." She picked up a piece of paper and scribbled the address where the Agit-Prop Players rehearsed, without ascertaining whether or not I was interested in producing material for them.

"Please, he just got here," Mrs. Epstein admonished Sadie. Her daughter flung up her hands.

"So what? My God. The movement needs people like him."

"Oh, leave him alone!" Tillie, the older sister, cried. "Always carrying the banner, for Christ's sake! Like Ma said, he just got here!"

"Shut up, you Wobbly! Why don't you and Carlo belong to a real party!"

Everybody started yelling and arguing, except Mr. Epstein who rose from his chair with a grunt and carried his bottle off into another room away from the tumult. Their British accents entranced me. What a wonderful family!

"All right," Carlo said quietly, at last. "The dog and cat fight is over."

"Communist!" Tillie screeched at Sadie, her face livid, before subsiding into silence.

Mrs. Epstein opened the sofa and made a bed for me. "You're very welcome here, stay as long as you like."

"I'll look for a room tomorrow, or the next day for sure."

"No, no. Stay a week, a month, you're welcome here."

"Sure, Ma," Melvin smiled. "Can't you see he likes your cooking?"

Later, when the flat was dark—Tillie and Carlo had departed for their own apartment a few blocks away—I lay alone in the living room staring up at the ceiling. Someone flushed the toilet. I listened to Mr. Epstein, grumbling, get into bed beside his wife in the room down the hall. No, I wouldn't stay here more than a few days. No point wearing out my welcome. Still it was good to be in this flat tonight.

Will You Write
Skits for Us?

In the cold evening Pembroke and I stood before the big building on the east side of Union Square, trying to make up our minds about entering it. On the ground floor was a very large cafeteria through whose plate glass windows we saw many people sitting at tables or moving about. The gray building rearing up above us in the cold air was the headquarters of the Communist Party of America; we hesitated, but, because the patrons inside the cafeteria looked colorfully interesting, we decided to investigate the place.

As we entered, the aromas of east European cooking together with blasts of conversations hurled themselves toward us. The high ceiling had no sound-proofing and the din was overwhelming. On the walls were gigantic murals, executed in the Soviet style, depicting heroic workmen with huge muscular arms marching with banners toward victory. These murals bore the signature of Hugo Gellert, whose "proletarian" efforts I was soon to

15

see in many Party publications. Along the wall the cafeteria's lengthy steam table offered simmering dishes at modest prices.

But no one, Pembroke and I noticed, was eating. The customers, crouched over cups of coffee or tea, were arguing, gesticulating, shouting. "But comrade, you don't understand Lunacharsky!" "No, no, according to Marx, who says . . ." "Excuse me, the Party did *not* mean such a thing at all!" "I tell you he's no good, he has become a lousy Lovestoneite! . . ."

My first impression, which was to remain with me permanently, exploded inside me. *These people, they'll never create a revolution.*

No one paid any attention to us as we moved between the crowded tables. A few young people were present but most of the clientele were middle-aged men and women whose speech ranged from a volatile mixture of Yiddish-English to harangues in truncated Italian, Russian and Ukrainian. Making our way to the counter, we bought cups of coffee and sat hunched over a table, sipping, and listening. "As Stalin said in the second Congress!" "You are mistaken, comrade, it was Kamenev who made that point! . . ."

"This place confuses me," Pembroke whispered.

"I've seen similar types before on Roosevelt Road in Chicago."

A half hour later we finished our cold coffee and wandered up among the upper floors. No one stopped us or asked us to identify ourselves. In contrast to the uproar in the cafeteria, the upper floors were quiet. We passed offices and lofts where men were typing or girls were sitting around smoking and conversing. Unlike the grossly drawn characters of Communists depicted in the cartoons of the commercial press, these people looked thoughtful and intelligent. On one floor we glimpsed cases of Chinese hand-set type with Cyrillic lettering printed on the wooden boxes indicating the shipment had come from the Soviet

Union, which made me wonder if a left-wing Chinese newspaper was to set up here in America.

After climbing another stairway we stumbled into a large room where a meeting was taking place. Men and women were sitting on folding chairs listening attentively to a middle-aged, sturdily built man who was speaking with great earnestness. Two or three people glanced at us, but again we were not asked to identify ourselves. Working up courage, I turned to a woman as I sat down in an empty seat and inquired who the speaker was. The woman whispered, "That's comrade William Z. Foster."

Foster was speaking persuasively, describing a strike now taking place in some mills in Passaic and Paterson, New Jersey. In language utterly devoid of forensic fireworks and avoiding exhortations—a contrast to the shouting in the cafeteria downstairs —he attempted to forecast the probable success or failure of the striking workers. It was a forthright, well-organized speech. In ensuing years I was to listen to Foster roar empty bombast at many public meetings where hollow Party cliches were used to arouse audiences already partisan to the cause. This, I was to learn, was the schizophrenic role of a Party leader.

Fifteen minutes later, with comrade Foster still talking, Pembroke and I slipped out of the room. We continued our wandering among the upper floors till at last we came to a large room where members of the Agit-Prop group were rehearsing. When we opened the door they were shouting in unison with fists upraised in the middle of a run-through of a scene of protest. Instantly the rehearsal stopped and the members stared at us, some of them glaring. A young man in a sweat-shirt, evidently the group director, shouted at us.

"What do you want? Who are you?"

I tried to explain. I said we were writers who had been told to come here with the idea of possibly doing scripts for the company.

"Are you from Chicago?" a girl suddenly asked.

When I said I was, she turned to the director and told him about Melvin's sister who had suggested our visit here. The director's harshness softened immediately.

"Fine, glad you came. Sit down until we complete our run-through, then we can talk."

The rehearsal resumed, lasting a half hour. Watching and listening to the awkward movements of the players and their noisy repetitive exhortations, "Strike, strike strike!," I envisioned cheering workers in seedy union halls who were hungry for this kind of entertainment. After the run-through the cast took a breather, and the director turned to Pembroke and me with an expectant look on his face. "Well, do you think you can give us some material next week?" He sat down beside us, outlining the group's needs in detail. "That was a mass protest scene of mill workers you just witnessed, but now we want a skit of an intimate nature next week."

"For instance?" I asked.

"Well, write a scene showing where a worker convinces other workers in an arms plant to refuse to send supplies to Chiang Kai-shek's imperialistic counter-revolutionary regime in China. It should end with the workers shouting, 'All power to Mao and the Eighth Route Army!' " As he added further suggestions there was a hot creative gleam in his eyes. Finally he rose, saying he had to rehearse the company in a protest scene dealing with the exploited miners in Kentucky. "Of course we'll hear from you soon?" he smiled. We nodded, then excused ourselves and got away. Outside in the fresh air of the dark street, Pembroke turned to me and said: "What a waste of time! There's no money in that kind of writing, it's not commercial!"

I was silent. I had no desire to become involved in a left-wing movement and had no inclination whatsoever to contribute scripts to the Agit-Prop group, but I was glad I had made the trip here tonight—it had been educational. Pembroke suddenly said: "Hey, remember Joan who made the Pullman trip with us? She wants to see both of us, about that plan, you know."

"When?"

"Tonight. I forgot to tell you. You still interested?"

"Certainly."

We went into a phone booth in a cigar store where Pembroke called to tell her we were on our way. Walking briskly, we reached her place, the Martha Washington Hotel on East 30th and Madison Avenue in ten minutes. Seated in the plain, sedate lobby, wearing a well-cut tweed suit, Joan was waiting.

"I've been expecting your call all evening, where have you been?" We told her we had been visiting the Communist Party headquarters. "Oh, I have no interest in that," she said. "Look, I've been thinking it over. This hotel here is reasonable enough for a brief stay but far too expensive for me permanently. Let's discuss that cooperative plan we had. Where can we go and talk?"

"How about up in your room?" I asked. I reached for her hand. "Allow me to escort you to the elevator, your ladyship."

"Oh, that's out of the question. Don't you know this is strictly a woman's hotel?" She withdrew her hand.

We walked two blocks east to Lexington Avenue, to a luncheonette, and in a booth over coffee and pastry we decided to consult real estate agents to learn where large, cheap apartments could be rented.

"It won't cost much to furnish a place," Joan said. She looked very attractive sitting in the booth. "We'll buy second-hand things from the Salvation Army. And of course we'd occupy separate rooms."

I doubted this plan would ever reach fruition, but I readily agreed it was the only sensible thing to do, economically. Sitting near her, it was easy for me to think of possibilities beyond a warm friendship in the offing. The fact that she withdrew from me every so often when, in my enthusiasm for the co-op project, I managed to squeeze a bit closer in the booth only seemed to heighten the prospects for an interesting collective future together.

When we parted that night it was late. We walked her back to the Martha Washington and promised each other we'd surely see some real estate agents within a few days. It was a simply wonderful plan to save money, we all agreed. Then she went up to her room.

Later Pembroke, walking with me toward the subway, wasn't so certain the cooperative venture would work out. He mentioned the problem of getting together a "mutual financial sum," and added, "Who would do the grocery shopping?"

"And I felt you were rushing her," Pembroke said.

"Me? I don't know what you're talking about." I changed the subject. "How are the plays coming along?"

He smiled suddenly. "Swell. I've got an appointment on Monday to see Mae West's manager, who wants to look at my script."

"Great."

"How about you?"

"I looked through the phone book and sent an agent some stories the day after I got here."

"Wonderful. Well, so long, I take the uptown train."

When I reached Melvin's home, the flat was dark. Using my borrowed key, I slipped inside and found his mother had opened the sofa and made it up for me. A large brown envelope addressed to me was lying on a chair. It was from the literary agent, returning my stories with a brief note. He wasn't interested in handling my work.

A Room
with a View

I rented a room, far uptown in Manhattan, near Morning-side Heights. It was a small room in the back of the house, with a window facing some bleak rear yards. A single gas-burner rested on a shelf jutting out from the wall near my bed, in case I wanted to make coffee; and I had a small, rickety table to type on.

I was now alone, and the house was chilly during the first day of my occupancy. Through the window I could see the dull overcast sky. As I sat in my overcoat trying to get started on a new story I heard a knock on the door . . . the apologetic landlord. He stood there, a small, bald, pale man, plumber's tools in his sooty hands.

"I'm trying to get the furnace started, the heat should be up any minute." He noticed I was wearing my overcoat and became more apologetic than ever. "It never happened like this before, I got a new boiler last year, it cost me a fortune. Wait, wait, the heat will be up right away."

The house was cold all day. Toward afternoon I managed to start a story, writing half a page. It was a beginning, but nothing further would come. My mind had turned lifeless. Suddenly a deep depression gripped me. My God, why was I here? At the table my legs hardened like wood. Terrifying thoughts raced through my brain. "Listen, who asked you to become a writer? You can still quit. No one, except yourself, is interested in your future. Governments won't fall if you fail. Pale women won't wring their hands and weep. At this very moment your relatives back in Chicago are busy, their noses to the grindstone earning their living, unaware of your struggles in this small room. At this second your sister is thinking about going downtown to Marshall Field's to buy towels and sheets . . ."

Gradually my panic subsided. I felt hungry. I hadn't eaten lunch, and I went out and found a cafeteria on Broadway and 110th where I bought a bowl of soup and a roll for ten cents. With this in my belly, I returned to my room, lay on my cot in my overcoat and stared at the ceiling and waited for darkness. The room was still unheated and the autumn dusk came early, creeping across the back yards into the little room. I didn't click on the light. I just lay there, in my overcoat, in the cold house.

At about six-thirty the first peeps of steam heat jangled in the radiator pipe. The roomers who lived here began coming home from work. I could hear their footsteps on the stairs; the footfalls sounded heavy, which meant male tenants.

At seven, I went out for a sandwich and a cup of coffee, then returned and started writing. I wrote almost three pages, a good day's work. In the morning I would reread them, to see if what I had written was any good. I decided against taking the subway to see Melvin's family, as I had promised. Melvin's family were wonderful people. I would always love them for letting me stay with them for a few days, but I wanted to be alone now. They might feel hurt at my not showing up, especially Melvin, but I couldn't help that.

At nine-thirty the man in the room next to mine brought a girl to his place. Through the wall I could hear him talking. He sounded middle-aged. When the girl answered her voice was very young and inexperienced. They talked awhile and I could not make out the words until I heard her say, "Please don't. Oh, please, please don't, I never did it before . . . oh, please, please." She said that a great many times, then the room became quiet. Later I heard them leave together, and I tried to fall asleep.

As the days passed I began to work well in that room. After a week I visited Melvin's home and it was nice to know I was still welcome there. Melvin's brother Louie was now imitating Maurice Chevalier and, throwing his arms wide, sang love songs in a French accent to his mother. During these numbers, which made us roll in our chairs, the father stared balefully at his singing son until he couldn't take it any more, then carried his bottle into his room. Sadie, the Communist daughter, asked me when I was going to submit skits for the Agit-Prop group but I stalled her, saying that I was busy working on a long story and perhaps could contribute something to the group later on. Before I left, Tillie and her husband Carlo invited me to the next meeting of their I.W.W. branch to be held Friday evening and my reply was the same—I was working hard and didn't think I could make it.

But on Friday, a day during which my writing had gone badly, I decided to accept Tillie's and Carlo's invitation. I rode the subway to an address on lower Fifth Avenue near 14th Street where the I.W.W. met, and as I listened to the speakers in the small hall I knew the I.W.W. was an exhausted movement. The speeches were lifeless and most of the discussions were lifeless, too. The organization fathered by Big Bill Haywood and Joe Hill in the Northwest, which had spread throughout the country during World War I, was now bankrupt. It made me recall a recent evening at Melvin's house when his sister Sadie had screamed at Tillie and Carlo: "Your old party stinks, it had an industrial platform but no political platform like ours. Why don't you stupid people enter the twentieth century!" It had been a tumultuous family fight, with Tillie shrieking defensively, while Carlo, tense and quiet, sat in a corner, his face flushed, smoking cigarette after cigarette.

During the next three weeks I had two stories accepted, by the *Midland* and *Prairie Schooner,* both literary quarterlies in the midwest that did not pay their contributors. The editors wrote they had liked my story which had appeared in the *Dial.* Their praise and acceptance of my stories acted like a narcotic, and I set to work with fresh intensity on new pieces.

I had begun to write about my relatives. Now that I was living in New York I suddenly became obsessed with my own family and background. I recalled the conflicts, the Sunday dinners when my father had shouted that he couldn't make a living in his little grocery, and I remembered his tortured cries that had brought a silent look of intense pain to my mother's face. She sat there trying to keep back her tears while we stared down at our plates. These scenes, repeated weekly, had become almost unbearable, until two of my unmarried brothers left home to live in a hotel. This probably intensified my mother's illness. Here in my small New York room I recalled the hurried family telephone calls, the medical conferences. The memory of my mother's painful death was still fresh; and I relived the scene in Piser's Funeral Parlor on Roosevelt Road, the chapel crowded with relatives, while a bearded old rogue, the professional mourner, stood over the open coffin beating his breast, wailing loudly in Hebrew to prove he was earning his fee as he observed us coming through the door. And I remembered how on a wintry Sunday, a month after the funeral, my brothers Myer and Irving and I crowded into Irving's little Chevy coupé to ride out to the snowy cemetery at Waldheim to say *Kaddish* at the grave, only to be annoyed by the aggressive professional beggars who pulled at our sleeves and screamed for money until they ruined our visit. With murder in my heart I whirled and cursed them, while my brothers remained silent. We struggled back through the deep snow to the car and, without speaking, rode back to the wintry city.

By the end of my first month in New York, two more agents returned stories I had sent them. "No market for these," one of them wrote. "Can't place them, recommend you study the stories in the *Saturday Evening Post*," the second agent advised. Temporarily depressed over these rejections, I nevertheless continued working. I saw Melvin and his family only infrequently now. Pembroke, meanwhile, had returned to Chicago. He had actually seen Mae West's manager who had turned down the play he'd written. With his funds exhausted, and no producers interested in his Chicago gangster play either, he had wired home for transportation money and made the long trip back. That left two of us here, Joan and me.

One evening riding the subway to a free concert in the Metropolitan Museum, I saw Joan. She was with another girl and looked radiantly happy. She gave me a somewhat startled though smiling hello. I noticed she and the other girl were holding hands. She had found a suitable roommate, who, I felt, would be succeeded by another at the proper time.

Elliot E. Cohen

The weather that autumn was almost wintry. There were clear days when the air was clean and tangy, but on other days a cold rain beat down on the city. Morningside Heights is near Columbia University and on my walks to cafeterias I watched students streaming through the campus carrying their books as they went to classes; they looked carefree and happy but I did not envy them. I knew I would go back to my room after a bowl of soup or a sandwich and write until dusk fell across the back yards.

The boiler in the basement having been repaired, my small room was now steadily heated, and it was pleasant sitting at the rickety table upon which my typewriter rested. I had inserted pieces of folded-up paper under the table legs to make the table firm, but after ten minutes of typing the folded pieces of paper worked loose and the shakiness returned. I became accustomed to it, and continued with my writing.

When the boiler broke down again, this time completely, and the room turned frigid, I moved. The landlord came up to my room as I was packing, plumber's tools again in his hands, begging me to stay. "The heat will be up any minute, your room will be warm, you'll see." But the house had been cold for two days and I had already rented another room. "Please stay," he said. "I need the income, young man. I haven't paid my taxes." I continued packing my few things. "Please stay, young man. I owe on the mortgage on this house." But I shook my head and moved out.

During the next few weeks I changed my address three times. In one place the room beyond my thin wall was occupied by a bookie constantly on his private phone whose incessant quoting of odds on the races in a loud voice prevented me from working. In another place a medical student up the hall played Beethoven's symphonies on his phonograph so often and so loudly that he sent me out on long walks. In the third house a demented old lady shuffled past my door on her way to the toilet every ten minutes.

I finally found a quiet room downtown on West 12th Street near the waterfront. It was small with a hard but surprisingly comfortable bed. My fellow roomers were truck drivers engaged in hauling at the piers whom I rarely met on the stairs and whose greetings never went beyond curt nods. This rooming house was run by an ex-seaman in his mid-sixties, a short, squat man who was a dead ringer for the fine old character actor George Marion who played Anna Christie's father in the O'Neill play. Even his gravelly voice with its Scandinavian accent was like Marion's; like the O'Neill character in the play, he was also a great one with the bottle. Despite his drinking, he kept the house shipshape and warm. I holed up here for six months; and it was a good period for me, with the truckers gone all day and the house quiet and the ex-seaman with his bottle and big German shepherd in the basement.

It was a solitary, very satisfactory life. Every morning I left my room to go to a cafeteria for coffee and a roll. I soon learned I could live contentedly for weeks on end without uttering a word to anyone. At the cafeteria counters I pointed to the food I wanted, set my portions down at a table, paid my check at the cashier's desk, and left. When I purchased my morning paper I placed a coin on the newsstand and the owner picked it up.

In the evening I sometimes took long walks along the waterfront, or headed uptown to Times Square if I hungered to see people and bright lights. One night I discovered Gray's Drug Store at 43rd and Broadway; there, in the long basement, listed on a big board were the Broadway shows that weren't doing too well, the tickets offered at ridiculously low prices. I bought cheap tickets to smash hits at the end of their runs. Most of the gallery and balcony seats went for fifty cents, and so at cut-rate prices I saw the great stars of the day. I saw Richard Bennett and his daughter Joan in *Jarnegan,* Lee Tracy in *The Front Page,* the Marx Brothers in *Animal Crackers,* and plays starring Lowell Sherman, Osgood Perkins, Alice Brady, and others. It was a wonderful, solitary life, and inexpensive—I still had some of the three hundred dollars I had brought with me from Chicago.

One morning I received a letter from the editor of the *Menorah Journal,* to whom I had sent a story. He wrote that he was very pleased to accept it for publication and would I drop by his office sometime soon? It was signed Elliot E. Cohen. I had discovered the *Menorah Journal* in the magazine room of the New York Public Library. Although it was a periodical of limited circulation mainly emphasizing subjects of Jewish interest, I soon learned it was one of the best magazines in the country. I waited a few days, then walked over to the *Menorah Journal* office, which was located in a long ramshackle building on the northeast corner of Fifth Avenue and 13th Street. The big, second-floor windows commanded a fine view down Fifth.

"Hello, I wanted to meet you," Cohen extended his hand with a smile. He was a small man, dark-haired, with large, dark, gentle, sensitive eyes. As we shook hands I instantly felt this man was my friend. His manner was warm and open, but it concealed a personality which I recognized as essentially frightened and shy: yet at the same time I suspected him to be a man unyielding to compromise and a careful guardian of his own integrity. His chin was weak, but when he spoke the weakness seemed to disappear, and after a few minutes you forgot about it.

"I liked your story about the visit in the snow to the cemetery, and we're sending you a check for thirty dollars." He smiled. "A writer can always use money."

"Yes," I nodded.

I spent almost two hours in his office. He wanted to know how long I had been writing and if I had any more stories he could see. I told him I had been writing a long time and that I had many stories packed away in my room. At first my own voice sounded rather oddly far-off to my ears, probably because in my life of seclusion I hadn't talked to anyone for months. But under Cohen's friendly questioning the strangeness of my speech gradually disappeared. I found myself talking about authors, books, baseball, food, plays I had seen recently, inflated literary reputations, and the great vitality of New York I had witnessed everywhere—in the subways, in the streets, in the stores. Cohen listened with a smile.

"Do you see many people?"

There was no need to answer. He had understood. I turned at the sound of tapping at the windows. It had begun to rain outside. I saw, along Fifth Avenue, the black pavement shining under the traffic and people running into the entrances of buildings to escape the rain. I felt it was time for me to leave. I hoped I had not talked too much. I had said a great deal, perhaps too much about writing and famous authors I had no use for, but I had also praised a few good writers, too.

"Wait a few minutes, the rain will stop soon." The rain now was coming down hard and he had noticed I had no umbrella. While I waited for the rain to stop I hoped, again, I hadn't shot off my mouth. I didn't really have to worry, though. Cohen began to question me about my background in Chicago. When he learned I had worked in a foundry, a mail-order house, a loose-leaf factory and other places, he listened intently. I wondered, later, why Cohen, and other people here, were so surprised at the jobs I'd had. Back in Chicago people had not been surprised. I found myself telling him of the Polish and Lithuanian weddings of foundry workers I had gone to, of company picnics, of the fights and brawls breaking out in the big dancehalls I'd frequented on Saturday nights, and he seemed to hang onto every word. In the mail-order house, I said, I had been the only high school graduate on the big floor where bells rang every fifteen minutes calling for the picked orders to be sent down into the giant chute leading to the assembly tables six floors below where they were checked, wrapped and weighed for shipping. The kids I'd worked with had obtained their working papers at the age of fourteen. Cohen, himself, I later learned, had gone to Yale.

"You must write all this some day, Halper."

"I might."

"Don't wait. Write it all down before you begin to forget the details."

"I have a good memory."

"Yes, but everyone who is young has a good memory. Later you'll forget as you grow older. Things will blur."

"I don't think so. It's part of my life."

"Write it simply. Like the story we just bought from you."

"I'll try, when I come to it."

"Fine, good. Well, send me more stories. And come to our apartment and eat with my wife and me. What is your phone number?" He reached for pencil and paper.

"I have no phone."

"Then call me. Don't be formal. My wife is a good cook. But put it all down. What you just told me, I mean."

"I'll write it down when I come to it."

"Yes. But don't wait too long," he said.

Bohemia
in the Bronx

Elliot Cohen accepted two more stories of mine for the *Menorah Journal,* and I began to drop in at his office whenever I felt I had to talk to someone. If he was busy working on a script, or in conference with an author, I made my departure and came by another day.

It was a long winter but not as cold as Chicago winters. I continued to work well in my rooming house run by the O'Neill character and was grateful for the heat he sent up from the basement, and one day I started a novel, a novel about Chicago. I did not tell Cohen about it because I wasn't sure I had the skill to pull it off. The *Menorah Journal* office was not far from my place and when I dropped by Elliot Cohen and I always talked about a variety of subjects. The reverberations from the stock market crash were still being felt throughout the country and Cohen discussed its causes and effects many times. One day as I listened in silence he asked if I were interested in the economic determinants of the crash. When I told him I was not particularly interested, he threw back his head and laughed.

"Men are jumping out of windows."

I said that didn't concern me. I didn't own anything: no country estate, no stocks, no car, nothing. I wasn't involved. When Cohen pointed out that workmen were being laid off in factories, I said this distressed me because I had known a lot of good guys whose families needed weekly pay checks.

"I follow the news of bankruptcies and shutdowns, like everyone else. But what can I do about them? Rush to Washington? Carry a picket sign? I'm involved in my own survival." Our conversation about economics ended there, with Cohen laughing:

"You're an individualist." I let it go at that.

But mostly we ended up talking about writing and writers. Like all young writers, I was full of firm opinions. For months I had sat in my room reading books I'd borrowed from the Public Library, and now my views about them tumbled from my lips. Back in Chicago I had devoured Joyce, Hamsun, Sherwood Anderson, Hemingway, Fitzgerald, Dreiser, Sinclair Lewis. Here in New York I had discovered Sologub, Remizov, Turgenev, Pío Baroja, Mann, Lermontov, and Gogol. Gogol, especially, entranced me. I'd found myself rereading Gogol's story "Old World Landowners" five times, trying to discover the seed of his warmth, the secrets of his superb technique at portraiture as he used seemingly innocuous snippets of detail to limn the old couple in that tale. I told Cohen I'd recently discovered Goncharov's *Oblomov;* the title character, that wonderful, lazy, warmhearted, doomed man, had held me transfixed in my chair for nights until I finished the lengthy novel. When I mentioned these works to Cohen, I saw him smile warmly. He had read most of them.

"You're feasting yourself, gorging yourself. When do you find time to write?"

"I try to stick to a work schedule, like everyone else."

"How about your social life?"

"That can wait." I didn't tell him of my restless, night hungers, or the way I casually but secretly looked at pretty girls in the subway or on the street.

Time soon took care of my social needs. In March, when my funds were running low, Pembroke's letter came out of the blue, urging me to get in touch with two young Chicago artist friends of his in New York who were seeking to rent a large loft or "any cheap place with a lot of room." They were hunting for a third person, to cut living expenses, Pembroke wrote.

I immediately made it my business to meet these young Chicago artists—the checks from the *Menorah Journal* had not boosted my waning reserves much. I found the Chicago pair in a rooming house on 112th Street: Nels, a burly good natured young Swede, and Pete, a tall, gangling, red-headed Italian. Both had emigrated from Chicago's West Side, so we had a lot in common.

Lofts, we learned, were too difficult and expensive to heat. We settled on a tenement flat on East 135th Street, in the lower east Bronx, a rundown neighborhood whose buildings lay in the path of the then unbuilt Triborough Bridge. It was a "railroad" flat on the top floor, with six rooms laid out in the customary single file, overlooking a junk yard and a livery stable. Below us lived poor, large Irish families, and as we climbed the flights with our suitcases we heard cursing, children crying, and dogs barking behind the doors. Nels and Pete grinned as they carried up their unframed paintings, stretchers, and art supplies. I wasn't too happy about the noisiness of the place.

"Anyway, the rent is dirt cheap," Nels reminded me.

"And we'll do our own cooking," Pete added.

That night we slept on the floor because there were no beds, no chairs, nothing in the flat. In the morning we shopped the bleak second-hand stores along Third Avenue for used cot beds, tables, and hard chairs, which we found in plentiful supply. Our total investment, including pots, pans and dishes, came to twenty-eight dollars.

On Saturday night Nels and Pete gave a party—my first plunge into the Bohemian life. My fellow lodgers were enrolled in the National Academy art school evenings—by day they held down menial jobs in a big city hospital—and up the stairs trooped a gang of their classmates hungry for food and a good time. A half hour before the party, having located a small Italian coal dealer down the street who manufactured wine in his cellar, Pete had carried three gallons of it up the stairs. A girl guest brought two loaves of bread and salami.

It turned out to be a long and rowdy party. Hearing the noise, the dogs below began their barking and tenants stepped out in the halls to swear up the stairs at us for making such a racket but we paid little attention to them. Two girls removed their clothes and, standing on chairs, holding glasses of wine aloft, posed for quick three-minute sketches.

At midnight someone rapped on the door. In walked a big prize-fighter type with a broken nose and cauliflower ears. The girls shrieked a welcome to him, then grew quiet. He was a fellow art student, called the Galway Champ. The sudden silence, I soon learned, was due to an event that had occurred during a party held in the big fellow's flat a week ago; someone had contributed a bottle of bootleg whiskey to the evening and later, during the dancing, a male guest, not an art student, suddenly complained of nausea and before a doctor could be called this guest lay down on the floor and died. The donor of the whiskey was not disclosed, the Galway Champ was arrested when the police arrived, and he had been given his freedom only today. Now he stood, broken nose and all, glaring at the company thoughtfully.

"For Christ's sake," he shouted in a thickish, Irish brogue, "it wasn't my fault he died!"

"Of course not!" Nels said, and someone handed the Galway Champ a glass of wine, and the party roared on.

That night, the inauguration of my social career in New York, I met a little German girl, an art student, with whom I was to become involved for the next five years. I saw her staring my way; I heard her inquire about me in a whisper to Nels, and then she came over and offered me a salami sandwich. It was a meeting both of us were later to regret.

The Galway Champ sauntered over and buttonholed me. "Nels and Pete tell me you're a writer," he growled. "I was in the trouble back in the old country, I've got lots of real dramatic stories in my head. Maybe you can write them up and we'll split the money."

"What do you do besides attending art school?" I asked.

"I don't box any more. I referee fights when I can get an assignment. Otherwise I knock about at anything to make the rent. Come to my place sometime and we'll talk and I'll show you my paintings. I'm a great artist, no matter what the hell anyone says!" He looked at me defiantly. Then he drifted away.

The noisy tempo of the party increased, with couples dancing together without benefit of music and several began embracing on the floor. Three couples disappeared into the bedrooms. Later, the Galway Champ suddenly began singing "Danny Deever" in a loud, off-key voice; couples, rubbing their eyes, emerged from the bedrooms and gave him their loyal applause.

The party broke up around 3:30 A.M. and after the guests departed Nels, Pete, and I wearily picked up the paper cups, cigarette butts, pieces of salami, and bread ends that littered the rooms, and finally crawled into our cots.

You Always Have
to Meet the Family

She came up to the tenement flat the next week, during the afternoon, as I suspected she would. She knew, of course, that I was alone, that Nels and Pete were working at their jobs in the city hospital.

"Oh, aren't they here?" she said. "I brought a sketch I made yesterday and wanted their opinion of it." She opened a large envelope and displayed a pen-and-ink drawing; it was a female nude, drawn in her life class, surprisingly well executed. "If you have some coffee, I'll make a pot." She casually removed her shoes and walked about the kitchen in her stockinged feet.

We were young and alone, and of course we knew what we had to do. When, hours later, she departed, I tidied up the place.

She was a free-lance artist, accepting minor assignments from two commercial art studios and living at home. As a free lance, she was able to adjust her working schedule to suit her visits to me. We were very happy and we felt we were very fortunate to have such a comfortable arrangement with Nels and Pete gone during the day and she was gentle and I was kind and everything began well for both of us. She was very witty and intelligent, and these unsuspected qualities in her I found exciting and delightful. I looked upon her as a wonderful windfall and I blurted this fact out honestly.

"No, I've been looking and hunting for *you* all my life," she said. These were the meaningless words of love, but they fell sweetly on our ears; we meant these remarks, we were not being dishonest, and we concealed our affair very cunningly from the others by acting properly friendly and polite in their company, even flirting harmlessly before them now and then. The secrecy of this liaison, together with our play acting before friends, somehow made Hedda's visits to the flat even more exciting for both of us. Our relationship deepened. Hedda began to stare at me softly.

"I want you to come to my house soon."

"Why?"

She bit her lip. "To meet my family. To eat with us maybe."

I delayed visiting her home. I did not want to meet the parents of the girl with whom I was having an affair. I didn't feel guilty. I just didn't want to get involved with her family. I had hoped to keep this simple. But I knew that was not possible now; and I thought, enviously, of the casual relationships I had had in Chicago with girls I'd met at dancehalls. This present relationship, I knew, was different from those; it was deeper, wonderful most of the time, but did I want that? It was, in a way, emotionally upsetting, interfering with my writing; often I felt keyed up and unable to work on the days I knew she would visit me. I told myself I would have to alter this, or stop it. But how?

"I want you to come and have Sunday dinner with us," she said one day, looking at me pleadingly.

"Why?"

"Because. Just because, darling," and she reached out for my hand.

That Sunday I went to her home for dinner. She lived on the upper West Side of Manhattan, in the Nineties, and when I entered her family's apartment, its warm cooking odors reaching me as the door opened to my ring, I felt I had been blackmailed into paying this visit. Hedda met me at the door, squeezed my hand and led me down the darkened hall lined with coat hooks and clothing, to the living room where I met her parents and her fifteen-year-old brother. Her father, towering, corpulent, and bald, grasped my hand heartily and, speaking with a thick German accent, said: "You haf come here at last, Hedda has spoke so much about you!" He beamed and laughed explosively, in the *gemütlich* style, to make me feel I was one of the family at once, while his wife, a handsome woman of fifty, regarded me critically but warmly. As the son rose awkwardly from his chair to greet me, I noticed his deformed leg, due to polio. We shook hands briefly. He, too, was friendly, but later on I became aware of his darting eyes and cruel mouth.

"Well," the father boomed, "how about a little schnapps?" Moving heavily to the sideboard, he poured whiskey into four little glasses. "Hans?" he turned to his son, winking. The boy smiled knowingly, crookedly, at the offer made in jest. The little glasses were handed around. "So, prosit!" and we gulped our drinks. Hedda sat beside me. Her father's voice rolled on, humorously, roaringly at times, friendly and seemingly aimless, yet, like all remarks uttered during first meetings where a daughter's future is at stake, they had a certain hidden design.

"So you are from Chicago, the city of gangsters!" he laughed. "I don't suppose you haf shot people?"

"Oh, Papa!" Hedda smiled.

"Ho, ho, I am just inquiring because I haf to know! Do I want my daughter should go out maybe with a questionable character maybe?" He laughed again, explosively. "Hey?"

"Otto," his wife said soothingly, rising to go into the kitchen to inspect the roast, "he is not that kind of a young man." Her German accent was slight, almost imperceptible.

"So you are a writer!" He beamed at me. "Some day you will go to Hollywood and write a film and we will zee it, hey?"

"Oh, Papa!" Hedda smiled again. "He's a serious writer, he doesn't want to write trash."

"I zee, I zee!"

"Dinner is ready," his wife called, and we rose and went through a darkened hall and into the dining room. It was a big, old-fashioned apartment, with heavy furniture and weighty drapes at the windows which kept out the early afternoon sunlight. Her father, Hedda had told me, owned a tobacco shop on upper Broadway nearby and her mother assisted him in the store. Her brother went to highschool. It was a closely knit family.

During the heavy dinner both parents occasionally asked me little, probing questions concerning my family, my background. I didn't feel put out; I gave them the information they sought. When I said my mother had died last year they looked at me sympathetically and were silent for a moment; the father then sighed and nodded in the European manner, "Ach, that iss too bad." He looked down at his heaped-up plate of meat and potatoes, while the mother fiddled delicately with her fork among the red cabbage. It was all very friendly. A game was being played on both sides; I was proving to them, by my quiet manner, that my intentions concerning their daughter were honorable in every way, while they were showing me what a wonder-

ful, warm family they were. After the meal, we listened to a
radio broadcast of *Parsifal* from the Metropolitan until Hedda's
father fell asleep snoring in his big chair, while the mother, sitting upright, worked at her knitting and smiled in my direction.
The son abruptly excused himself, going to his room. The father,
his large bald head hanging forward on his chest, his great body
sagging in the chair, continued manufacturing guttural harmo-
nies through quivering lips. The mother smiled indulgently, and
kept on knitting. When at last Hedda and I rose, and Hedda
said we were going to take a walk in Central Park, she nodded
her permission.

"They both like you," Hedda said when we were outside.

"How do you know?"

"Oh, you," she smiled. "Because I know my parents."
She pressed my arm as we reached the park.

"I'll come to see you Thursday," she said happily. "I don't
feel guilty any more, after today."

A Literary Agent

Now that I lived away uptown in the Bronx, I did not drop in at the *Menorah Journal* office to see Elliot Cohen any more. Receiving my letter notifying him of my new address, he answered with a note telling me not to work too hard and to visit him whenever I was in the vicinity of his office. One day I received a letter from him inviting me to an informal *Menorah Journal* writers' dinner to be held in an Italian restaurant in the west twenties. "You don't have to answer this letter, just come." The dinner cost a dollar, one glass of wine included. It was a high price for a meal, I thought, but I decided to put in an appearance.

That evening was my baptism into the New York literary life. During the dinner I first realized Cohen possessed remarkable qualities found only in great teachers. I noted that though only a few years older than most of the guests present, he was regarded as their literary father, and I witnessed how they truly loved and respected this shy, intelligent man who, fifteen years later, was to found *Commentary* and was to publish in its pages many of the men who sat around the table that evening. Like a parent, Cohen sat at the big table and introduced me to his "family," the young contributors to the *Menorah Journal*, all unknowns at the time, like myself. I met Lionel Trilling, Clifton Fadiman, Louis Berg, Kenneth Fearing, Charles Reznikoff, Herbert Solow, William Shack, and other beginning writers. When Cohen introduced me as "the courier from Chicago," several of them, to put me at my ease, said they had read my stories.

The conversation around the table alternated between light and serious remarks. Literary reputations of big-name authors were shredded or defended. *A Farewell to Arms,* just published, was branded by some as being "important," by others, "slick, romantic." I myself had liked Hemingway's book enormously. "Gertrude Stein wears size 12 shoes," a guest quipped. It was a youthful social literary evening, with good Italian food and an Italian waiter who pocketed fifteen cents for each extra glass of red wine. Next to me sat Kenneth Fearing silently chain-smoking cigarettes down to their ends. Born in Oak Park, Illinois, a suburb of Chicago, he said at last, neighborly, "Welcome to the fold, Halper. How long you been east?"

"Five, six months."

"I've been here two years."

Lighting another cigarette, Fearing lapsed into silence. Thin and pale, taciturn and with a dry wit, he looked about the table balefully. "I hear you're one of Cohen's favorites," he muttered out of the corner of his mouth. Then he locked himself up tight for the rest of the evening.

A colorful looking character sitting across from me grinned. In his late twenties, rugged and stocky in his double-breasted suit, he was the only one at the table smoking a cigar. I shall call him Handelman. As we fell into conversation, he struck me as being a literary operator, hearty and generous of nature. He informed me he'd had one story published in the *Menorah Journal*. "I deem it an honor to appear in its pages, but

I've got my guns aimed at bigger game." He let this news sink in. "A play of mine is making the rounds of the producers." I wished him luck. "How are you making out?" he asked, puffing his cigar.

"I'm hanging on by my back teeth."

He roared, removing the cigar from his mouth. "What you need is an agent."

"I've sent my stories to six or seven of them, but they all shot them back."

He waved his cigar. "Aw, most agents are stupid, what do they know? If you can make magazines like the *Dial* and the *Menorah Journal* you don't have to worry."

I liked this kind of talk, and when he invited me to his home in Queens, I said, "How do I get to your place?" His self-assurance and vitality were contagious.

"Just take the IRT subway at Grand Central and get off at the Sunnyside stop. A twenty minute ride." He asked me where I lived and when I told him I lived on East 135th Street his eyebrows shot up. "How did you land up there? That's the crummiest part of town."

"Strictly economics," I said, and he laughed.

It was a fine writers' dinner and I enjoyed the company, but I rarely met any of them again after that evening, except Fearing whom I was to encounter later along 14th Street, and Charles Reznikoff the poet with whom I was to take long walks and would see sporadically over the years. The others at the table had been friendly; they were, I knew at once, genuine talents, but years of writing in my bedroom in Chicago followed by a lengthy hermetic spell here had left their mark on me. Except for striking up the conversation with sporty Handelman, I had sat rather quietly at the table, a listener, a watcher.

The next week I rode the subway out to Sunnyside, Queens. Entering Handelman's almost bare flat, I met his darkly attractive, gypsy-looking wife, and saw their one-year-old active son attempting to demolish one of the apartment's few chairs with a hammer until Handelman coaxed it from him.

It was a wonderful evening for me, and I felt at home at once. Here was a couple who lived from hand to mouth, whose typewriters went frequently to the pawnshops (the wife was also a writer, doing features for magazines she did not name), and we ate a big pot of beef stew which we washed down with "dago red." As we ate, Handelman told me his aims in life were simple: to become famous, make a lot of money, wear expensive clothes, own a big house under the palms, and have boxes of the finest cigars lying handy to his reach. His appetites were refreshingly direct; it was good to witness a display of such honest instincts. When he queried me about my needs, I replied that I was content for the time being to live the life of a semi-hermit as long as I continued to work well. He laughed, lighting a fresh cigar as we finished our meal.

"Hey, I've good news for you," he announced. "I think I've got an agent for you."

"Who is he? When can I meet him?"

"He's a neighbor. He lives just a block from here, and you'll meet him tonight."

That evening I met the man who was to become my literary agent, my close friend, and confidant for the next twenty years.

He lived in a small one-family house, in a row of fairly new small red-brick homes, with his wife and six-year-old son. Handelman introduced us with a broad smile, like a marriage broker confidently bringing two prospects together. "Maxim Lieber, meet a promising writer!" he said, announcing my name warmly, like an auctioneer holding up a Rembrandt.

Lieber was a small man with a tooth-brush mustache, his handshake was firm and his manner was eager and effusive,

maybe a little too friendly. During the first minute of our meeting something about him troubled me, his laugh, his sudden
camaraderie; but no other agent would have me and I was hungry for literary advice, for assistance, and starving for acceptances from editors. "Well, well, well!" he said. "It's a pleasure
to meet an unknown writer, who won't be unknown for long!"
These words didn't efface my initial lack of confidence in him;
but I didn't hold this first impression against him when I learned
the reason for his eagerness to acquire clients.

He had, until a few months ago, been the editor of Brentano's, when that firm had operated a publishing house as well
as their large, well-known book store. But like several other publishers, Brentano found they were unable to weather the Depression which had now descended upon the country, and they had
liquidated their publishing business, keeping only their book
shop. Lieber, their editor-in-chief, had been stunned by the li-
quidation; only a short time before he had purchased the small
home in Sunnyside, with the aid of a mortgage whose payments
had to be met, and now he found himself unemployed. In desperation he began making the rounds of publishing houses in
search of a new post but, because of the distressed state of the
book business, he met with no success. He continued to roam the
city in search of work, I learned later, like a madman, his savings
quickly slipping away. A high-strung man, he was gripped by a
depression and several times contemplated suicide. Then one
day he met an acquaintance on the street, Harry Hansen, a book
columnist employed by one of the city's major newspapers. After
listening to Lieber's tale, Hansen, a friendly man, said: "Max,
you know literature, you were an editor, why don't you start an
authors' agency?"

Maxim Lieber thought it over after leaving Hansen. Why
not give the suggestion a try? But where would he get the money
to rent suitable quarters, print stationery, hire a secretary? No,

it wasn't possible. He continued his futile quest for a new job until at last, out of desperation, he decided to become a literary agent. He begged desk space and telephone service from an architect friend, and sat in a far corner of this friend's office near the water cooler, trying to procure writers as clients. I learned all this later, of course.

That night he asked me, tactfully, about projects I was working on. I told him I was writing short stories and had started a novel. To my surprise he said he was acquainted with my stories, had read a few things of mine in the small literary quarterlies. He wasn't lying because he described work of mine he had read.

"I'd be very happy to represent you," he said simply. "I want to be frank with you; I'm just starting out as an agent but I feel we can work well together." Handelman, hovering over us, smoking a cigar, punched me playfully in the side.

"Go on, sign up with him. What can you lose?"

I had wanted to be allied with an established agency, but all of them had turned me down. I wavered, not knowing if I liked this man or not. Lieber looked at me expectantly, honestly. Well, what did I have to lose? We shook hands, smiled at each other; I felt relieved. I had an agent at last.

"You're the third client I've acquired, Halper. The first one is Louis Adamic, the second, Erskine Caldwell. No one would handle their work, they told me."

"I'm in the same boat," I admitted.

"Good. Good. I'm glad you told me that."

The Hunger of the Galway Champ

After having my stories returned by many agents who were disinclined to represent me, it was nice to have someone who consented to handle my work. It was nice, too, to have a place to drop into, to talk about my writing problems, even if it was only a cubby-hole near the water cooler in an office that did not belong to my agent.

I soon learned not to ask Lieber where he sent my stories. At first I made inquiries; to spare my feelings he was tactfully evasive. After a while I did not make any more inquiries. I wondered how his other clients were faring. I suspected they, too, were experiencing difficulties in selling their stories or articles. I'd learned that Adamic and his wife were living with his mother-in-law up in the Bronx, for economic reasons; while Caldwell, together with a wife and five children, had grown accustomed to a diet of potatoes on a rundown farm up in Maine. Soon Lieber said he was acquiring additional authors as clients—

Katherine Anne Porter, John Cheever, Josephine Herbst, Langston Hughes, Albert Maltz, John O'Hara, and others whose work was appearing in the small magazines. Unlike his fellow literary agents, Lieber constantly scanned the little magazines for potential authors to represent. He realized, unlike other agents, that times were changing, that the terrible depression gripping the nation was already producing a new type of writing, a different kind of author. Whenever I visited his office he spoke with vehement contempt of the big magazines and publishers, criticizing their tastes, their editorial policies, their blindness to America's true economic and social condition. "My God, they act like they never heard the words unemployment, dust bowl, foreclosure of farm mortgages by the millions! Why don't they buy work concerned with reality?" He grew flushed and shouted. Once he gripped my shoulder. "At present your stuff isn't selling. And you and I need the money. But I don't want you to compromise a goddam bit in your writing, Albert. I've said the same to Caldwell, Adamic and the others. Your time is coming." His face became more flushed than ever.

When he learned I admired the Russian writers he was pleased. "They're the greats!" He was well acquainted, also, with the good German, French and Italian writers. And as editor at Brentano's he had proudly published *The Underdogs,* the great, little-known novel of revolutionary Mexico by Mariano Azuela, and he had gotten José Orozco to illustrate the book with magnificent ink drawings. But he always came back to the Russians, to the great talents translated by Constance Garnett. Lieber's favorite story was Turgenev's "A Lear of the Steppes." "What's your favorite?" he demanded. I told him I highly admired, among others, Chekhov's "The Lady with the Dog" and Gogol's "The Overcoat." "Not bad, not bad," Lieber smiled.

It was fortunate for me that I now lived with Nels and Pete. With my funds continuing to drain away and the cold weather hanging on and only occasional acceptances of my work by editors of literary quarterlies who paid minuscule fees, it was nice to know I had a secure place where I could write, with meals included, even though frigid winds whistled through the loosely hung windows of our tenement flat. Food was ridiculously cheap in the stores and it was stupid to eat anywhere but in our draughty, oven-heated kitchen. At mealtime we saw the mice run in and out of the room like little messengers on hurried diplomatic missions, avoiding the baited traps skillfully, like seasoned politicians; and at night, in the dark, we could hear them scratching away as if seeking state secrets in the paper bags of garbage which we were too lazy to carry down the five flights outside before crawling into our cold cots.

It was an over-long winter, a terrible time. The bottom had dropped out of the country, it seemed. With the passing of each week the Depression deepened. More factories were closing down, and at night I began to see in the streets men and women pawing over the contents of restaurant garbage cans set out for the sanitation department trucks. Pride was being eaten away, and in the eyes of many people I passed in the street I saw a cornered, hunted look. The national disaster had become so huge, and the answers to its solution so elusive, that men and women slowly began to accept their fate as a new way of life, as inmates thrown into prison gradually reconcile themselves to an existence behind stone walls. My sister wrote to tell me that banks were failing in Chicago, that the life savings of depositors were being wiped out.

But despite the economic holocaust, I didn't suffer much that winter. Never having known affluence in the good times of the past, and lacking the traumatic responsibilities that went with being the head of a family during the period facing the country, I had, with relative ease, adjusted myself to this tragic era. With Nels and Pete absent during the day, which allowed me to work on my novel, and Hedda continuing her secret visits to the flat, I was too much immersed in my working and personal life to be constantly concerned about the nation's economic problems. When I saw the breadlines, the horrible signs of broken confidence on the faces of people in the subway, I was moved. When I noticed furniture on the sidewalk in my neighborhood put there by city marshals holding dispossess orders, I was angered. But I kept on writing. People were passive, not knowing what to do about their situation, while far downtown, in Union Square, the first marches were being organized adorned with crude paper signs—the banners would come later.

One cold windy evening, while currents of chilled air were soughing through the flat, Nels puffed up the flights carrying a big sack of plaster; he mixed the contents with water and that night sealed all the windows tightly, permanently.

"What'll we do in the summer, when we want fresh air?" Pete asked.

"Break the windows!"

The following evening Nels and Pete carried up the stairs a second-hand iron pot-belly stove, which they set up in the big front room which we called "the parlor." "We'll need heat," Nels said, "we're starting a cooperative sketch class, everybody contributes fifteen cents for the coal!" And on Sunday morning twenty art students arrived with sketch pads and no one contributed a cent; a plump girl stripped and became the model while the others sketched her in fifteen-minute action poses. At noon Nels, burly, sappy, good-hearted Nels, set out a long pork loin, potatoes, and coffee, and the students gorged themselves, and left. After their departure, I was silent. I wasn't too happy about the students free-loading all that food, part of whose cost I bore; but I said nothing, though I knew damn well many of those kids came from homes where there was still plenty to eat.

That night while I sat in my room reading there was a knock on the door, and the Galway Champ entered. He hadn't known the sketch class had been held, and mumbled something about "being in the neighborhood and just dropping in." We sat around the warm pot-belly stove. Nels and Pete started talking about Van Gogh and Picasso but the Galway Champ didn't join in the conversation; with his mashed boxer's face lowered broodingly, the big fellow swung his gaze about the room in an odd way. The faint aroma of the day's cooking reached his nostrils, and suddenly Nels, Pete, and I knew he was hungry. Without a word, Nels went into the kitchen and returned with a big plate of meat and potatoes. Without even a glance at us, the Galway Champ bent over the plate and started eating. At first he picked at the food hesitantly, then he began eating the meat, potatoes, and bread noisily, like an animal. We watched silently. Pete and I went into another room. The Galway Champ ate three heaping plates of food and left, without a word of thanks. Nels came into the room where Pete and I were sitting.

"The poor bastard. He hadn't eaten a thing in four days."

You don't forget a scene like that, a gift of the Depression.

An Important Connection for Melvin

One evening Melvin, whom I hadn't seen for some time, came to visit my digs, the first trip he had ever made up in the Bronx. As he entered the flat he was positively ecstatic, as though he had gotten a big raise at his job or had recently come into an inheritance. When Nels and Pete went into another room after the introductions were over, Melvin suddenly turned to me, smiling widely. "Al, I got news."

He told me he was no longer a virgin. He joyfully related the details. One evening a few weeks ago he had met the unmarried thirty-two-year-old sister of a young man working in his office. He'd called at the fellow's home on a night they had planned to attend a lecture together at Cooper Union; but his friend had forgotten the date, had gone to a movie. Contrite over her brother's forgetfulness, his friend's sister told Melvin to sit down in the parlor and she'd make a pot of coffee. She served chocolate cake with the coffee and both of them, awkward at first, starved for conversation, talked about books and music. The evening wore on, and toward ten o'clock, after each had made tentative, very self-conscious overtures, they had ended up on the sofa, then in the bedroom. "Al, she's got a face that could stop a clock, but her body is beautiful, smooth and beautiful. She was a virgin, too, just like me. At first we had a hell of a time getting connected in bed but at last it was okay, wonderful. I call her up when her brother isn't home. I've been screwing her four times a week for the past three weeks. She tells me she can't get enough of it. Al, it's wonderful, just wonderful." His face and eyes glowed as he spoke. He had to confide his marvelous good fortune to someone, and he'd made the long, long journey all the way from Brownsville, just to tell me about it.

Oh, Yaddo, Yaddo

Like most aspiring writers living in New York, I made it my business to know every small magazine being published. I often went to the large magazine room on the first floor of the 42nd Street Public Library, and, standing at the racks, I saw eager-eyed young people jotting down the names and addresses of *American Literature, Clay, American Prefaces, Blues, Frontier, Horizon, International Literature, Manuscript, The Anvil, Hound and Horn, Pagany, Modern Monthly, New Masses, New Writers, Prairie Schooner, Signature, Transition, Midland, Tanager,* and a great many others. I, too, filed away the addresses of these small but welcome literary markets.

I sold two stories to *Pagany,* a fine new literary quarterly edited by Richard Johns, and one morning I received a letter from the *American Caravan,* notifying me it had accepted a story for the forthcoming annual. I had mailed off these pieces before I'd met Lieber, so he received no commissions on them; they were negligible sums anyway. *Pagany* paid me twenty dollars for two stories; and Alfred Kreymborg, who, with Lewis Mumford and Paul Rosenfeld, edited the *American Caravan,* said I'd receive twelve dollars on publication day. "We're glad to have your contribution," Kreymborg wrote. "It's a very moving story." Though the fee was small, I was supremely happy over their taking it. To many young writers the *American Caravan* was a prime literary target; it was a thick volume bound in hard covers, and was seriously reviewed by the top critics. In the volume in which my story appeared the roster included William Faulkner, William Carlos Williams, Robert Penn Warren, Marsden Hartley, and John Gould Fletcher. It was a break for me. Lieber was happy to learn of this acceptance by the *American Caravan* and when he sent new stories of mine to the editors of the national magazines he mentioned my forthcoming appearance in the *American Caravan,* but the gentlemen who sat in the seats of power at *Harper's, Atlantic Monthly, Scribner's Magazine, Century,* and *Bookman,* along with others, were unimpressed.

When I finished writing my first novel, Lieber, who liked it, couldn't sell it. He told me more publishers had failed that winter. He reported that three of them, who had liked the book, said they would have published it if times had been better. Then, with this comment, they closed their doors forever. There was nothing else for me to do but to harden myself and think about starting another novel. Elliot Cohen asked to see the script of my novel. When I brought the carbon copy to him he said there was some good stuff in it and extracted two sections which were printed in the *Menorah Journal* as short stories. This earned me a hundred and fifty dollars, the most I had ever made by my writing—one of the extracts was lengthy and later appeared in anthologies and on college reading lists.

As the weeks passed, though my novel continued to be turned down by publishers, Lieber kept on sending it out to other firms. I admired his doggedness but my hopes for the book had about faded; though Lieber's enthusiasm for the manuscript heartened me, I began to be assailed by periods of discouragement that haunt every writer from his beginning years to the grave.

To kill time when I was unable to write, I began taking long walks during the day, through the South Bronx. There wasn't much to see except long, flat streets of tenements, people hurrying in the cold, the police station standing with its official blue lamps in front of it, and the churches on Brook Avenue with worshippers entering them on special holy days. It was all less than exhilarating; the South Bronx didn't have the color, the vigor of the lower East Side; it was a beaten area.

By April, with my novel still unsold and no further sales of my short stories in the offing, I began worrying about my ability to continue paying my share of the expenses of the flat in the Bronx. I could not expect Nels and Pete to support me financially. Watching them lugging rolls of canvas up the stairs, together with bundles of wooden stretchers and tubes of paint from the art supplies store, I knew these expensive items devoured their cash resources.

At the beginning of May, during a visit to the *Menorah Journal* office, Elliot Cohen sensed my financial predicament. The following day, without consulting me, he contacted Clifton Fadiman, who was now an editor at Simon & Schuster, and persuaded Fadiman to recommend me for a residency at Yaddo, an artists' colony in upstate New York. I knew Fadiman only slightly, having met him, casually, once, at the *Menorah Journal* dinner; the letter he sent to the colony's director evidently carried weight, for I was immediately invited to become a guest. I packed my bag, put my portable typewriter in its case, and shook hands with Nels and Pete who were happy at my good fortune. As I reached the street below, they waved at me from the front windows.

A butler met me when my train arrived at Saratoga

Springs. I was driven in a station wagon out past broad Union Avenue, which was flanked by mansions of the wealthy who opened their houses for thirty days each year for the racing season. The huge, grand trees lining Union Avenue, together with glimpses of the fine race track through the hedges, instantly made me forget the South Bronx. When I reached Yaddo, I was overwhelmed by the immense grounds, the regal splendor of the well-groomed estate of 1,400 acres in which the artists' colony was located; I had never heard of the place before.

Yaddo, to me, was an extraordinary haven. Each guest occupied a studio-room, or a room with a separate studio if these suites were available; the beds were soft, the quarters spotless, and the superb meals were served by uniformed maids in an impressive dining room. Tea was served at four in the great living room, and most of the guests took advantage of this social hour; among other things, it offered the opportunity to learn how to balance fragile tea-cups and to bite into some wonderful cake.

On my first evening, Mrs. Elizabeth Ames, the attractive, soft-voiced, always tactful director of Yaddo, introduced me to the current crop of inmates, among them Leonard Ehrlich, Winthrop Sargeant, Aaron Copland, Paul Bowles, Louis Lozowick, Pierre Loving, Percy MacKaye and his wife, Gregorio Prestopino, Lola Ridge, and Mildred Gardner. Of the remaining guests, four, I soon learned, were called, behind their backs, the Macedonian, the Armenian, the Playwright, and the Hack. During my first evening my fellow residents, most of whom had preceded me by a week or two, studied me politely and furtively, and I studied them.

It was an interesting group, none of whom I had ever met before. I was most curious about the four who had been baptized, secretly, by the others; during the next few days, I studied them discreetly.

The Macedonian was a short, wily Bulgarian, a writer

with a bony, alert face and sharp teeth who was always enthusiastic about everything. His literary output, I learned, consisted of short stories about colorful Balkan peasants, and these tales were wrought of bejeweled prose, full of vigor and endowed with the rarefied mountain air of snowy Bulgarian peaks. He swore allegiance to every guest present, predicting great futures for all. Later, back in New York, he was to denigrate anyone who became successful.

The Armenian, on the other hand, was a very shy, desperately poor painter. Tall and thin, black-haired and intense, with a soft, hesitant voice, he was extremely happy to be in a place where there was such an abundance of good food. At once over-friendly yet reticent, he was snubbed by most of the other residents. The day after my arrival, noticing the shirt I wore had a slightly frayed collar, he beckoned me self-consciously into his studio and held out two white shirts from his meager wardrobe. "They are your size, please take them. I have plenty more." When I declined the gift, telling him I was expecting a shipment of new shirts from the city within a few days, he was genuinely disappointed. He was deeply good hearted, and it was a shame the pictures along the wall showed that he had no talent. But I would never forget the warm, generous look in his eyes as he had proffered the precious gift of his shirts.

The Playwright was the guest who looked the most artistic, the most literary among us. He had a large, leonine head flowing with gray curly ringlets, piercing dark eyes, and an emphatically dramatic manner. His speech was drenched with a strong Mittel-Europa accent and he became excited when discussing his work. I learned that a play of his had been produced by an experimental company in New York a few years ago, for a run of one week. At present, he informed me, he was deep into the first act of a new play about an unhappy marriage, a drama entitled "Thank You for My Condition." Middle-aged, wildly talkative, warm-hearted, he had the fatherly habit of throwing an arm around a fellow guest's shoulders while discussing O'Neill and Pirandello. On my second day at Yaddo, he suddenly confided in me by describing his own unhappy marriage. He fixed me with his glittering, forty-eight-year-old eyes. "A writer should never marry, Halper! He should have intercourse, yes, as much as he wants, but no marriage! Marriage—children —that is the death of the artist!" Such a comradely older writer naturally drew the younger residents into his orbit; he listened to their various creative problems and became, to some, a priestly confessor. One day he turned to me, and with an odd smile said: "You are a bulldog, you don't need anyone." He added, with another odd smile: "Or maybe you are hiding something." I answered him with a smile as odd as his own.

"Maybe."

In an artists' colony, as I quickly learned, all was not sweetness and light among the guests. Each had his close friends, and almost everyone had his enemy. My enemy, I soon became aware, was the tall, tennis-playing type from the west coast secretly called the Hack by the others. Alone among us, he owned a decent wardrobe—fine slacks, expensive shoes, well-cut shirts. He quickly made it known that he disliked me. The writer's world is a small one, and each writer at Yaddo was acquainted with the work of his fellow residents. On my second evening, sitting around the huge fire-place with the others while the logs burned behind the screen, several guests told me they had read my stories in the various little magazines. I replied, playing the game honestly, by saying I had read their work, too. They didn't say I was a master and I did not counter by replying their work possessed the stamp of genius. You could tell by their voices if they respected your stuff or not. The Hack, sucking at his briar pipe, was silent for a while. "When are you going to write a zingy Chicago gangster story, Halper?"

"Tomorrow morning, at dawn," I said. His remark had hurt but I kept myself in check because I had no other answer ready to hurl at him. The next day I learned he was a contributor to pulp magazines who had gained entry here only because a critic friend of his had sponsored him with a glowing letter.

If you are working well the presence of an enemy is not important. His physical nearness is annoying but if your writing excites you, you soon acclimate yourself to his footfall in the hall, his glance, his presence at the dinner table. In the foundry where I once worked I had known men who had labored side by side with enemies. Molders had muttered to me: "I can't stand that son of a bitch at the casting pots!" And I had heard wrapping girls in the mail-order house exclaim: "I hate the very sight of that jerk on table five!"

My irritation over the Hack's remark was nothing special, I told myself. Other guests at Yaddo felt the same discomfiture with other residents. One day I noticed that a certain painter made no effort to conceal his enmity when another painter said he had finished a picture that day. "What a pity," he muttered under his breath, though still audibly. And I noted how another guest, a sculptor, once gritted his teeth noticeably when a certain composer went to play his latest composition in the music room. "What crap." A writer winced exaggeratedly when another writer reported he had written two thousand words that afternoon. These were the normal, petty animosities, I found, no doubt the result of the pressures, the uncertainties of our lives. Yet I couldn't help sometimes wishing that my enemy would drop dead. At the dinner table if I praised Sherwood Anderson, he would snidely reply: "That clumsy lout." If I damned Cabell, he'd remark that of course everyone knew Cabell was a genius.

Yet in my well-appointed studio, with pine trees outside my windows and the great lawns sloping down to the fountain and large trees of the Berkshires in the distance, I was at peace and continued working on a new novel. Each day I hammered away at my typewriter, making progress, and I didn't disclose to the others either my subject matter or the extent of my daily output.

Every night, tired from the day's writing, I looked forward to the bull sessions around the big fire-place in the living room. I felt I had truly acquired a small foothold in the world of letters as I listened to the others and began to take part in the shop talk, arguing about the merits and flaws of established writers. With the passing days I gradually felt the rough edges of my Chicago background being sanded away.

Sometimes, after the shop talk had been exhausted, I listened to the European experiences of the others as we sat before the flaming logs. Winthrop Sargeant spoke of his lean days in Vienna where he had been studying the violin and writing a novel, and I envisioned the Prater, the cheap restaurants, the small rooms he had lived in, and the whores plying their trade during the inflation. Aaron Copland, who had recently returned from a long sojourn in Paris where he had studied under Madame Boulanger, described the lively cultural scene there, relating interesting, chatty anecdotes about Ravel (whose "Bolero" had become a European sensation), and other composers. He complained how difficult it was to live on the scanty royalties here if one was an American composer. Because of the Depression, he said, he was now forced to live frugally. His only luxury, he added, was his ragged, second-hand car parked outside on the gravel lane, which an aging and thoughtful patroness had given him, forgetting that no one else here owned a car, new or used. Pierre Loving, the critic, also recently arrived from Paris along with hordes of other American expatriates forced out of France when their sources of income vanished with the hard times, spoke of the literary scene he had just left; from him we heard gossip about Hemingway, Fitzgerald, and Zelda who hated Hemingway. A fine conversationalist, Loving made the Left Bank real to us; he described the arguments in the Dôme, and he gave us the details about Robert McAlmon's recent, ample divorce settlement from his wife Bryher, which had earned him the name Robert McAlimony. One night Loving described the boxing match between Hemingway and Morley Callaghan, the young Canadian writer, during which Callaghan knocked Hemingway down while Fitzgerald, watch in hand, stood by in shock as Hemingway got up from the floor and turned the knockdown into a joke. The Hemingway fight story is common now, but it was brand new then. Listening to the speakers' voices, Lola Ridge sat near the fire-place with her great dark poet's eyes glowing in her beautiful gaunt face; she was very thin and during the day a maid carried food up to her room because Lola Ridge was ill and rarely came down, except to hear Copland play his pieces in the music room, and we all knew she was dying. Other guests told about their experiences as the nights wore on. The Macedonian, smiling wickedly, described how he had made love to a girl in the Black Sea, in three feet of water, standing up, while scores of bathers swam close by. "She was very, very cooperative!" Louis Lozowick, a small, brilliant artist in his late thirties, wearing rimless glasses, listened to the Macedonian's story quietly, after which he related some of his experiences in Berlin where he had lived. "You know George Grosz's drawings? Grosz has understated the depravity, the corruption of the Germans. It's not just the fault of the inflation there, either. They are, instinctively, the most depraved people on earth." Then he described the low cafes, the transvestite dives, the homosexual officers' clubs. "Even some of the high school girls look depraved," he said.

"What about the German working class?" someone asked. "What about the strong left-wing movement there?"

"They have a strong left-wing movement," Lozowick admitted. "And meanwhile Hitler is getting more and more financial backing from the rich."

Many nights we stayed up very late, talking, arguing, reminiscing, and, finally, staring in silence at the flames burning the big logs away, until, bone-weary, we retired to our separate rooms.

One afternoon the Playwright, his dramatic eyebrows twitching with eagerness, violated the prime rule of the colony by knocking on my studio door while I was working.

"You must excuse me, Halper, I have news. It is not world shaking news but it is about your enemy."

"What enemy?"

"Ach, don't be foolish. Everybody here knows it, we have eyes and ears."

"I wasn't sure it was that noticeable."

"My son, this is like a big family here, and in a family nothing can be hidden. Look, a man without an enemy is not a good writer, is not a man. As a playwright, I am proud to say I acquire a new enemy often, a real enemy who hates my guts. Are you interested in what I now have to say? If not, I will depart."

"I'm interested."

"Good." He sat down in a chair, another violation of the visiting rules. "Our friend the Hack," he began, "has made a tactical and fatal mistake. Guess what it is."

"He has shot himself."

"Ho, ho. No, he has *shown his manuscript to three writers here*. For their *opinions*." He waited breathlessly for me to say something. I kept silent for a while.

"So what?"

"So *what?* I was one of those who read it! He is a *worse* writer than we thought! He is writing a biography in the form of a novel about a European painter who lived fifty years ago and who cut off his ear. The cutting off of the ear is not the bad part, the whole book is atrocious, laughable. It is written like the cheap soap operas ladies listen to on the afternoon radio."

"When it's published, many women might buy it."

"Ho, ho, it will never get published. Didn't you hear me? It is an idiotic piece of trash, destined for the garbage. We thought you'd be interested. Aren't you interested, just a little?" He was looking at me closely.

"Well, only a little."

"Only a little, only a little!" He threw back his head and roared. "This man has no interest—only a little!" He rose from his chair and went out, satisfied that he had been the bearer of an important bulletin.

That night the conversation before the fire-place concerned D. H. Lawrence who had just died in Vence in the south of France. We discussed his talents, the sexual revolution he had championed. Everyone praised Lawrence's novels and short stories, but the sexual revolution he had so insistently written about seemed relatively unimportant to most of us, who led free unfettered lives. Someone mentioned Lawrence's working-class background; and suddenly we began talking about the Depression which none of us had forgotten was raging beyond the cloistered confines of Yaddo. We speculated about how much deeper it would get, how much the American people could endure. Would there be a revolution? Two Marxists present—a writer and a painter—pointed proudly to the current triumphs of the Soviet Union, citing figures of the vast numbers of tractors being built in the communist fatherland, mentioning the absence of unemployment there, the expanding Soviet culture, the "new Soviet man" arising from the proletarian masses. One of the composers snorted.

"Don't make me laugh. Look what the West has produced!"

"Yes, but capitalism has had its day!" one of the Marxists cried. "It is now relegated to the dust-bin of history!"

"If it's such a wonderful place, why doesn't the Soviet government allow its citizens to travel freely outside the country?"

"You don't understand! They need every worker to complete the task of building the socialist structure!"

"What about the massacre of the kulaks?" a sculptor asked. "Weren't they decimated, the best farmers in the country?"

"You don't understand! They were capitalists, counter-revolutionists who wanted to destroy socialism! They thought only of their own economic interests, not of the cooperative policy!"

"But what of the N.E.P., the New Economic Policy Lenin encouraged before he died?"

"You don't understand! The N.E.P. was a transitory thing, it was a studied step backward that led to two steps forward!"

"It's been said here by agricultural experts that if the kulaks had been allowed to operate before they destroyed their cattle and crops there might not now be a famine."

"There is no famine in the Soviet Union! Everyone has plenty to eat!"

This debate went on for hours, until someone suggested we take a walk. Everybody piled out of the big living room and we headed for the path skirting the estate's five connecting oval lakes. The trees, the grass, the lakes were bathed in moonlight, a background to the loud, nocturnal croaking of bull frogs. In this fantastic setting, resembling the scenery for an opera, the Depression seemed a million miles away. We forgot our crummy, leaky, city studios, our cold-water tenement flats, our rooming-house rooms back in the city. During the past three or four months we had grown soft, accustomed to Yaddo's wonderful accommodations, to the perfect quiet of our quarters, to the superbly prepared food. Suddenly someone, the Marxist painter, spoke as our shoes crunched on the gravel path around one of the beautiful, tree-fringed lakes.

"I don't think the porterhouse steak tonight was up to par," he grumbled.

"I thought it wasn't bad," his friend, the Marxist writer said, "but I felt the mousse wasn't quite—right." He turned to a composer. "Don't you agree?"

"Umm . . ."

A sculptor, long penniless in New York, chimed in. "And I thought the vichyssoise at lunch was a little—rich," he complained. We walked in silence for a few yards, our shoes continuing to make small crunching sounds.

The Hack cleared his throat, with just the correct amount of authority. "When I was in France last spring researching my novel, I ate in a little restaurant in Arles where the *coquelet au corton* was simply superb."

No one could top this, not even the Marxists, so we bowed our heads for a moment, hoping to dine one far-off day in that little restaurant in Arles. But suddenly a writer became very realistic as we continued our walk around the little lakes.

"Let's eat our heads off here, let's stuff ourselves against the coming winter's cold!" These words cleared our minds. We began shouting across the empty moonlit water.

"Hurrah for Yaddo's food!" "Three cheers for the chef!" "Fuck the cafeterias of New York!" "We'll stay and eat here forever! . . ."

We did not stay on and dine at Yaddo forever. The weeks, the summer months had flown. I drove myself hard, working toward a self-imposed deadline, and finished a brand new novel. And, all too soon, the final day rolled around when we had to depart from Yaddo's paradise. Standing in a quiet file near the

great, polished, curving staircase, the uniformed maids who had
served us stood smiling politely, discreetly, bidding us farewell
—we had been instructed not to tip them. Emerging from her
residence about a hundred yards from the mansion, Mrs. Ames,
the director, smiled graciously and thanked us for coming to
Yaddo and wished us all a good winter. George, the butler, piled
our battered, pathetic suitcases into the station wagon and we
were driven in several cars past the large red- and yellow-leaved
trees lining imperial Union Avenue, past the fine deserted race
track, past the closed houses of the rich who had departed after
the month-long racing season, and on to the little railroad station
in Saratoga Springs. We boarded the train that took us back to
New York, to our poverty, our puny struggles, our cold flats and
seamy studios and, for two or three of us, on to death. When we
reached Grand Central, we stood, a strange, silent group, holding
our suitcases. Some of us were going uptown, others downtown.
At last we shook hands, knowing we'd never form a group again,
and crowded into jammed subway trains. Many of those people
I have not seen since that day. When, an hour later, I trudged up
East 135th, the bleakest street I was ever to live on, I climbed the
five flights with a heavy heart and came into the long, cold,
empty six-room railroad flat, and saw the mouse traps in the
corners, the foggy windows, and I knew I could never live another winter in this place. I made a pot of coffee and sat down,
still in my overcoat. I thought of the wonderful place I had just
left, the good meals, the great conversations, and I remembered
my recent friends; and I recalled, too, the man who had been
my summer enemy (his lousy book was destined for a great success). In the chilly room I sat holding a cold cup of coffee,
numbed. Already the summer seemed shadowy, receding rapidly
into a mist . . .

Farewell to the Bronx

Gloom soon turned into nervousness after my return to the Bronx. I had mailed my new novel to Lieber five days before I had left Yaddo. I now felt depleted, wrung out. Was it a good book? At Yaddo, I hadn't shown the script to anyone. As the first few days passed I wondered why Lieber hadn't written to me about it. Was it that bad? I didn't tell Nels or Pete the reason for my dejection. I sat in my room in the flat, stared out the window and made no move to see Hedda or to phone Lieber. I was scared. But at last I left the flat and headed for the subway to learn the worst.

When I walked into Lieber's office, he greeted me with so much effusive warmth it was almost embarrassing. "I sent you a letter at Yaddo but it just came back today because you had left! And I couldn't reach you in the Bronx because you have no phone —I was hoping you'd either phone me or drop by!" He kept wringing my hand, grinning with delight.

"Oh, we'll sell this one! And I'll fight for a generous advance on it!"

His enthusiasm made me feel relieved and happy. "You really like it that much?"

"Listen, you went all out on it! What lyricism in those pages about Chicago, what poetry! And that character at the wrapping table; you made the poor guy almost Dostoevskian! A humorous but tragic figure—especially in that scene where his two fellow employees arrange a date for him with that slut and when he takes her to a hotel he can't perform!"

I told him that actually happened to a man in a place where I once worked.

"Of course, I know it!" He kept grinning with delight in his cubby-hole quarters near the water cooler. When I left his office, I was walking in a daze. At last, at last—I was going to have a book published, a novel.

But as the weeks passed, my hopes drained away. The manuscript was being rejected by editors. Whenever I phoned Lieber for fresh news, he was apologetic. "They all like it, but they're hesitant about buying it."

"Why?"

"They say it's—experimental. They say the material is—too new."

"But isn't that what they're always looking for? New, original work?"

Lieber answered sadly. "It's the times. Books aren't selling. And they're frightened of the subject matter, they're cowards."

"But my work isn't propaganda."

"Of course not!" His voice now became angry, directed against our common enemies, the publishers. "They don't know what the hell they want! The magazines are no better! I've got stories by Katherine Anne Porter, Erskine Caldwell and John Cheever I can't sell! Some day we'll have a long talk about politics, Albert!"

Thoroughly depressed, I hung up and walked out of the phone booth. I couldn't start a third novel; I didn't have the energy, the will to write. Stepping out of the drug store on Brook Avenue, I took a long, tiring walk. I couldn't go back to the flat because I knew Nels was entertaining a girl there this afternoon. Recently he and Pete had had their working hours cut at the hospital because the Depression had caused the hospital to inaugurate a policy of retrenchment, and now Nels spent some of his free time adding dividends to his social life. Pete did likewise, having a girl up at the flat during the day at least once a week. This new schedule of theirs meant that I, who formerly had the run of the place all day, now had to share it during certain afternoons. Last week I had had to take in two boring movies on separate days while they had visitors.

I trudged along 138th Street, killing time because I couldn't endure another movie. I thought of the rejections my novel was gathering. Reaching the Harlem River bridge, I studied the gulls and their flight patterns over the water. After almost three hours of aimless walking, I returned to the flat where I found Nels putting on his trousers; the girl was in the bathroom.

"She wasn't bad," Nels whispered, with a smile. "Maybe you want me to fix you up with her friend next week?"

Before I could reply, the girl emerged from the bathroom, a big, healthy, smiling nurse from the hospital, a kid from upstate, near Albany or somewhere. As we were introduced, I noticed she was wearing Nels' old bathrobe.

"Should I put on a pot of coffee?" she turned from me to Nels fondly.

"Sure, sure. And I think there's some cheese and rye bread left. I'm hungry."

That night as I lay in bed in the dark I decided to check out. They'd been wonderful friends—but how the hell could I do any writing here now?

A few days later, after scouting various sections of Manhattan, I came upon a small flat downtown on East 11th Street, just south of Union Square. A three-room, unheated tenement flat in the rear of the house, its rent was cheap, nineteen dollars a month. As soon as I entered the empty flat with the super, a middle-aged, talkative woman whose quarters were on the ground floor rear, I made up my mind I'd take the place. I liked the layout, the bareness, even the slanted floors. "Is it quiet here?"

"Oh, it's as still as a tomb," the woman assured me eagerly. "And it's never been unrented because it's so close to good transportation and all. He died here only last week, you know."

"Who?"

"Mr. Flynn. He was a member of the Salvation Army, on 14th Street where they have their headquarters, you know. A gentleman, sixty years or so old, you know. A nice quiet gentleman, lived here fourteen years." She nodded reminiscently, and continued: "Then on last Friday while I was mopping the halls I stepped on something soft up the hall where it's kinda dark, and when I looked down it was his face."

"What happened?"

"He'd had a heart attack, with the key to his flat in his hand. Died right before his door. The electric bulb in the hall was dead so I didn't see him while I was mopping. I stepped on something soft, and it was his face."

"I'll take it," I said, to cut her short.

She put a motherly hand on my arm. "You said you're alone, unmarried?"

"Yes."

"Tell you what, you can have his furniture, what there is left of it. A relative, his nephew from New Jersey, came here yesterday and took his bed, bureau and the carpet. But he left these things." She opened a closet door, where a small square table and two hard chairs were piled up. The little kitchen was bare, also the narrow bedroom.

"Will a dollar do?"

"Oh, I didn't mean to ask for money for such furniture." As she put my dollar into her apron pocket, I knew I'd made a friend for life.

When I returned to the Bronx and told Nels and Pete I was moving out, they were downcast, then thoughtful. They knew, of course, the reason for my checkout. "Do you really have to leave?" Pete finally muttered. In silence, they watched me gather my books together; they stood there without moving as I collapsed my fold-up cot-bed in half. They helped me carry all my stuff downstairs, and while I legged it over to Brook Avenue to get a cab, they stood guard in front of the tenement over my property. When I returned with a taxi, Nels was gnawing his underlip. I could hear the meter ticking in the cab, and I wanted to get going.

"Well, goddamit, Halper, we had some good times here, didn't we?" Nels said.

"We'll miss you," Pete put in, scowling. "You're the guy who made the coffee every morning."

"Don't forget to drop around for the Sunday sketch classes," Nels added, as he shook my hand. "Well, goddamit, Halper, good luck to you in your new place." Pete was helping me lift the cot-bed into the cab.

"Well, so long," Pete said, after the bed was inside the cab. "Watch yourself downtown and don't get the clap."

I got into the cab with all my worldly possessions, the driver shifted gears, and they waved with real feeling as we quickly drew away.

Even the Mice
Were Happy

My new digs gave me the lift I desperately needed. I felt, almost immediately, that I could accomplish a lot of work here. During my first day as a tenant I walked through the three small rooms repeatedly, sizing up the layout, growing accustomed to the sight of the old kitchen gas stove and the kitchen sink with its adjoining zinc tub for washing clothes. The flat had one drawback—no bathroom. The toilet was out in the hall, shared by the family across the way, a middle-aged couple with a retarded son of fifteen. There was no electric light in the toilet and during my visits there I carried a candle and matches; the space was the size of a telephone booth, cramped and airless. But I soon grew used to making the short trip across the hall to the "shrine." I was glad when, a few weeks later, the retarded son was sent away to an institution; he'd not been too clean.

After tramping through the rooms countless times during the first day, I stood staring out the rear windows studying the backs of loft buildings on East 10th Street. My curiosity satisfied, I went out to buy a coffee pot, a frying pan, and a few cups and plates. 14th Street, the thoroughfare I soon came to love above all other avenues, was thick with people and traffic. Along the crowded sidewalks hawkers were selling fifty-cent watches, fake "blind" beggars led by mangy dogs were chanting ballads, and "pullers" standing before the doors of stores were enticing passing women shoppers, whispering or calling, "Psst, we got some terrific bargains in underwear and cotton goods inside, come in and feel the material. . . ." It was a vigorous, colorful neighborhood. I went into Woolworth's to buy the kitchen things, then entered Hearn's basement store nearby where I purchased two chops, a can of peas, and a small cake for supper.

Hedda dropped in that evening and prepared the meal. She was excited when she saw my new quarters. As she pirouetted happily from room to room, her heels made a pleasant rapping sound against the bare floor.

"All you need is a fire-place, darling."

"Yes."

"And a terrace."

"That, too, can be arranged." Standing silently under the naked electric bulbs, we suddenly heard a slight scratching noise.

"There're mice here, too."

"Yes, I know," I said. "I'll get some traps tomorrow."

"It's so terrible to kill them, though."

"Yes."

She changed the subject. "Oh, your two rear windows face south, you'll get the sun during the day!" Suddenly she cheerfully opened a package which she quickly unwrapped; she'd kept it hidden under her coat lying on a chair. "Surprise, look!" She held a pair of bright new curtains against her body, waiting for my approval; like all New York girls, she was happiest when being an interior decorator. After I gave the curtains my approval, she stood on a chair, hung them into place, and made the flat beautiful.

Later, in bed, she turned to me and said, "I love it here. You won't get away from me. I'll follow you from place to place." It wasn't a threat, she'd said it lightly. I was silent. She laughed. "When will you give me a key to this place?"

"Why?"

"I want it."

"Why?"

"Because."

"You already have a key to my heart."

"Bull crud."

"What?"

"Bull crud." She laughed again but I knew she was serious about the key.

"I'll get an extra one made soon," I stalled.

She put her arms around me under the blanket in the dark. "I won't talk that way again."

"What way?"

"The way I spoke right after you came back from Saratoga. When I talked about marriage. You know." I was silent again. "My parents ask about you all the time. I lie to them. I say I see you infrequently, mostly by accident."

"Do they believe you?"

"I don't know. My father does." She waited for me to say something. "Please don't worry about it. I don't want to be one of those possessive ones. I'm sorry we quarreled that time."

"I am, too. I'll get an extra key made."

"You don't have to. I'll just come here and knock on your door."

"Knock three times, so I'll know it's not one of my other mistresses."

"Bull crud."

"What?"

"You heard me." She laughed and sat up in bed in the dark. "Hey, guess what."

"What?"

"I brought my tooth brush with me."

"What?" We had never spent an entire night together.

"I told my mother I was staying over with a girl friend in Brooklyn."

"What if she phones the girl friend to check on you?"

"This girl friend has no phone." She slipped back under the blanket. "Oh, darling, isn't it wonderful being together all night long?"

"Yes."

"Oh, darling, darling..."

We heard the mice in the kitchen but tonight, because there were no traps yet, they could scamper about in safety, deluding themselves into thinking they had a secure future, just as we two in bed could delude ourselves about our future together, too.

There's Always Hollywood

Union Square became my hangout. It was so near to where I lived that all I had to do upon leaving my flat was to turn the corner at Fourth Avenue, look northward, and there it was—crowded with pretzel vendors, apple sellers, orators, and shoppers. The daily activity there was endless; besides the swarms of pedestrians pushing along the sidewalks, there were weekly left-wing parades which frequently ended with clubbings by the police. On Saturday mornings I could see the mounted cops in the side streets, bunched together, resting, healthy-faced, chatting cheerfully before the afternoon's action. Usually they gathered on 15th or 16th Street, west of the square, out of sight. If the marches were peaceful, the officers had nothing to do but sit on their horses in the side streets until the speeches and the political demonstrations in the Square were over, then turn their mounts and depart. When they left, you saw the great

79

piles of horse droppings along the curbs where they had killed a whole day waiting for the action that never came.

I couldn't get started on a new novel. I still felt depleted from writing the novel Lieber had not been able to sell. I had difficulty working on short stories, too. One week as a change of pace, I wrote a lengthy satire on Hemingway, focusing on *A Farewell to Arms,* a book I had greatly admired when it had first appeared but suddenly no longer cared for. I still regarded *In Our Time* the prime collection of American short stories and *The Sun Also Rises* a masterpiece along with *The Great Gatsby* but I could not, somehow, resist the impulse to free myself forever from a total admiration of Hemingway. I titled the twenty-thousand-word satire "A Farewell to the Rising Son," and *Pagany* bought it for $180; because of its length it was the biggest fee the magazine had ever paid an author. The check came as a welcome surprise, and Richard Johns, the editor, wrote that he planned to print it in three installments. Living so close to the *Menorah Journal* office now, I walked over to tell Elliot Cohen of my good fortune.

"Hello, I was worried about you," he said. "I was discussing you with the staff yesterday, about working up a loan for you."

"I'm rich," I answered, and told him of my financial windfall from *Pagany.*

"Wonderful. But you look thin, don't wait until you hit bottom next time. We can always dig up some funds for you. What new authors have you discovered lately?"

We discussed writers and writing until his secretary appeared at the door to inform him an author was waiting to see him. Walking back to my place it was nice to know there was money available if I ever went stone broke on East 11th Street.

That night there was a loud knock on my door and in

walked Handelman very expensively dressed: a new, double-breasted English overcoat, English shoes, a Borsalino hat, and smoking a big cigar.

"Hello, you bastard," he shouted. "I got your address from Lieber." I hadn't seen him for a long time, in fact I'd about forgotten him, but here he was looking like a successful impresario, not taking his hat off as he strode through my rooms inspecting the place. Because it was cold out, I'd lit the oven of the gas stove to warm the flat. "So this is your joint, eh?" he grinned, waving his cigar. "Look, put your hat and coat on, I've got a cab waiting outside for us."

"What's the big idea?"

"Never mind, kid. I hit the jack-pot, I'll give you the details in the cab."

I reached for my hat and overcoat, turned off the oven, and we went downstairs. Settling back in the rear seat of the cab like a millionaire, Handelman looked at me with a broad smile. "Man, I hit luck at last. It's what I've been working and praying for and as soon as I hit, I thought of you. Did you see my play on Broadway?"

"What play?"

He looked pained for a moment, then grinned. "I forgot. You're a fiction writer, not a Broadway fan." I kept quiet about the tickets I bought at Gray's Drug Store, for Broadway shows. He continued. "I had a play produced, the one I told you about that time? A comedy. It's a damn good play but it lasted only a week."

"I'm sorry to hear that."

He laughed. "Don't be. Because a movie company just bought it. As a vehicle for a big star whose name I'm not at liberty right now to divulge." He waited, scanning my face, pausing to follow with the punch line. "For thirty thousand dollars."

"What?" The cab was now skimming south on Second Avenue. "You're not kidding me?"

Handelman smiled widely. He held up a finger like an actor, pausing before delivering another punch line. "Not only that, but they offered me a writing contract at a fat figure. I'm going to the coast tomorrow. The wife and kid will join me next week."

I was happy to hear his wonderful news and I told him so. I didn't mention the piece I had just sold to *Pagany,* which seemed unimportant now.

"I knew you'd be thrilled to hear about my luck, that's why I looked you up." He leaned toward the cabbie. "Turn into Essex Street, mac." The car swung east into the teeming Jewish East Side. He ordered the driver to stop at Delancey, paid him, and we began walking along the crowded streets, past the night-time push-carts, Handelman acting as my proud guide. "Here's where I used to live, Halper, and over there in that hallway when I was eight I smoked my first cigarette." He turned and pointed to another house. "And right in front of that chicken store I saw a girl lift up her dress and pee on the curb." He beamed as he led me from more sacred hallways to additional hallowed curbstones, with a running recitative of his childhood. I knew the precious memories must be flooding his mind, and I kept silent. The neighborhood hadn't changed since his childhood (the big Negro and Puerto Rican influx would not come for another twenty years), and he pointed out further landmarks of his early life as we continued along the sidewalks.

It was, I realized, Handelman's farewell to the East Side, to all his roots, before beginning the big trip to Hollywood where, in due time, he would acquire a home under the palms, with a swimming pool and all the rest of it. As we made our way along the streets he continued his monologue with increasing enthusiasm, occasionally clutching my arm as an important memory gripped him. But gradually his voice changed, his comments became fewer, and I detected a certain hesitancy, a shade of sadness in his face.

"What do you really think, Halper? Is this a good move for me?"

"Sure. It's what you've always wanted, isn't it?"

He puffed a fresh cigar vaguely. "I dunno. What about my—serious career?" He looked at me, and I knew what I had to say, what he wanted me to say.

"Listen. It's big money. After you've made your pile, what is there to hold you back from returning to New York and doing a good play or writing a good book?"

His face brightened with relief. "Right. That's what I tell myself. And my wife feels the same!" I had absolved him, and now he felt his later masterpieces could wait. In a happier mood he dragged me into a big delicatessen where he was recognized by the owner. They shook hands vigorously, over a crock of herring.

"Handelman! Where have you been all these years? And where are you going so dressed up, so prosperous looking?"

"I'm going to Hollywood!" The shop-keeper laughed, thinking it was a good joke. "No kidding," Handelman smiled. "Ask this friend of mine."

"Sure," I said.

"And I'm going to open up a bank!" the owner said.

Handelman bought ten kinds of appetizers, expensive canned goods, special cheeses, imported sausages and olives, strange, costly delicacies. The owner and his clerk filled two huge bags. When we left the store, Handelman hailed a cab and we drove north. He ordered the cabbie to stop before my tenement. I was surprised when he suddenly pushed one of the big loaded bags into my arms.

"So long, kid, eat it in good health."

"What?"

He laughed, sitting back in the cab. "Sure. What do you think I bought two full bags of this junk for?" He grinned, a rich writer giving a poor writer a handout; yet there was genuine warmth in his eyes. Then he stared up at the front of my tenement with a fleeting glance of envy. "Well, be good, kid!" He shook himself out of it, his smile returned, and he was confident again, full of the golden present and the promise of the great rewards that awaited him in the west. "So long, kid!" He shut the cab door briskly and waved back at me through the rear window as the taxi passed Webster Hall, sped by the Catholic grammar school, the darkened basement employment agencies for cooks and waiters, and sharply turned the corner. I waited until it was out of sight, then carried the heavy bag of delicatessen goodies up the stairs. Smelling the odors rising from the bag, I resolved to dine on the contents sparingly, to make them last a long, long time.

This evening, somehow, was also part of the crazy Depression.

A Proletarian
Literary Discussion

A few weeks later that same winter, when I had at last begun working again on new stories, a strange situation developed over the novel Lieber was trying to place for me. Several publishers, on their own initiative, started phoning Lieber, asking to see the manuscript for the second time.

"It's a good sign—I think I'll sell *Windy City Blues* soon," Lieber informed me happily.

"How big an advance do you think we ought to get?"

"I'll ask for a thousand dollars, but I'll settle for five hundred. Does that meet with your approval?"

"Certainly." I was living on eight dollars a week, rent and food included, and five hundred dollars would keep me going for a year. "Certainly, Max," I said.

"Oh, we'll sell it now. Otherwise, why should they want to see it again? I'll get in touch with you as soon as I get a contract."

But as the winter dragged on, Lieber was unable to close a deal. The publishers who had asked to see the novel again were unable to make up their minds. Viking Press called it back for the third time, giving it to Carl Van Doren for a final reading. Van Doren's report read: "Publish it." At the last moment, however, Harold Guinzburg and Marshall Best at Viking decided against it, and returned the script to Lieber. As the days passed, I grew tense. Why the hell didn't they take it? What did they want, Tolstoy? Wasn't it better than the tripe they published?

"It's unfair," Lieber said gloomily. "The publishing houses keep asking for new talent, for new voices, and then they accept pap—which does not sell!" His face grew flushed as his anger mounted. "If *Windy City Blues* had come to my desk while I was editor at Brentano's I'd accept it in ten minutes! Cowardly idiots!" He calmed down, and in a softer voice said: "By the way, I placed two of your stories. With small literary magazines, I'm sorry to say." He handed me a check for twenty dollars, apologetically. "Believe me, I hope to do better for you some day."

An hour later, when I returned to my flat, I saw a young fellow without an overcoat standing in the vestibule waiting for me. "Hello, your bell doesn't ring, does it?" he smiled.

"No bells in this building ring," I said.

He introduced himself, saying he was an editor who was starting a new magazine. He had the eager voice of a one-issue publisher with perhaps sixty dollars for a down payment to a printer before going bankrupt. Confidently, his words ran on in the cold vestibule.

"Come on up to my place, I'll make a pot of coffee," I said. He was the second, big-time potential magazine publisher to visit me that month.

While the kettle of water heated on the stove my

visitor informed me of his great plans to publish a magazine "with contributions from only the best proletarian writers."

"What do you mean by proletarian writers?"

"Well, you know." He searched for the correct words. "I want to print stories by writers whose deepest concern is for the workers. Like your stories, Halper."

"I write about people."

"But they're not about rich people."

"I don't know any rich people."

"No, I suppose not. But your sympathy is for the struggling masses."

"I don't know any masses. I write only about people I know, friends, enemies, my relatives. That's not the masses. I don't know that many."

"Don't you believe in proletarian writing?" He looked a little pained. He thought maybe I was kidding him.

"I don't know what proletarian writing is."

"You're joking now."

The coffee was perking. I poured him a cup. He looked at me quizzically yet still hopefully. "I'd really like to include a piece by you in my first issue. If you have a story for me, I really would be grateful if you'd let me have it. I'm sorry we can't pay for material right now. Maybe with the third or fourth issue, though." I knew there wouldn't be a second issue. The non-payment part didn't bother me. Not at this time of my life. "I won't press you for a story this minute," he continued, "but if you find you have something for me, I hope you'll send it in. There's something new stirring in American literature, you know."

"That's what I understand." I remembered my little talk with Lieber only an hour ago, about my novel, how it was stirring the publishers into not publishing it.

"I do hope you'll send me a story, if you have one for

me. Here's my address." He wrote the address on a piece of paper he got from my desk, thanked me profusely for the cup of coffee, and departed.

After he left, I stared out the window absently for five minutes. Why had I treated him in so flippant a manner? And why did I always rebel when the label "proletarian writer" was pasted on my work? It was merely a convenience for uncritical and thoughtless people to catalogue me, as well as others, wasn't it? If my work was good, what was the harm? Still, I remained wary of the label, with its cheap, easy connotations, and sensed it would have only a fleeting and dubious vogue.

Yet the Depression, somehow, was my time. Deny it or not, it was coloring my writing strongly. Though irritation and anger often gripped me as shallow and frequently dishonest pronouncements emanated from the left, theirs was the prime potent voice raised during the thirties. And I could not ignore the impact their repeated shouts and emotional appeals for change had upon me, and other young writers. The left's thrust was insistent, a campaign gaining momentum. Combatant or spectator, it was useless to tell myself I could insulate my work from its influence.

Comrade Rivera
Gets the Business

I continued to wait day after day, tensely, for news from Lieber about the fate of my new novel. Every morning I walked down to my battered mail-box in the vestibule to see if there was a letter from Lieber telling me the book had been sold. The super sensed my nervousness, and as she mopped the lower hall, she gave me a coy smile.

"Are you expecting money from the will of an uncle who died in Florida or somewhere?"

"No, only an autographed photo from Greta Garbo," I replied.

"Oh, you're joking," she chortled. "I bet maybe you're looking for a note from your sweetheart. The one I saw leaving your apartment Monday morning. Oh, don't worry, I won't tell the landlord—what he don't know won't hurt him. Greta Garbo!" She laughed, holding her sides. "Mr. Halper, you have such a sense of humor—you're so different from that Salvation Army gentleman who had your place!"

I returned to my flat and tried to work. Turning on the oven to keep warm, I crouched over my typewriter. In fifteen minutes the room became warm; for the past month I had kept the door to the bedroom securely closed so that I would not have to heat it, thereby reducing my gas bill. I had moved my bed into the living room, and if I opened the bedroom door now a cold mass of air would hit me in the face.

After lunch I put on my overcoat and went out, heading for 14th Street. Each day, like a boxer, I kept in trim by struggling against the crowds of shoppers on the sidewalks, threading my way among the hot chestnut vendors and outflanking the beggars who grabbed my sleeve asking for "A nickel for a cuppa coffee, mister!" I had come to know by sight every pretzel seller, every apple vendor, every fake blind man holding his tin cup outstretched, as well as the "pullers" and merchants standing before their retail stores. Cutting past the former Communist Party headquarters—the Party having moved to a new site on East 13th Street, surrendering their old quarters to an expanding Klein's—I passed the orators in the square screaming imprecations at the capitalists from their soap-boxes.

After my brisk midday walk, I returned to my rooms, relit the gas oven, and tried to work again. Toward five o'clock, fatigued from the day's writing, the heat still purring from the oven and making me light headed from the oxygen the gas consumed in the flat, I stretched out on the cot and watched the dusk working itself over the loft buildings of 10th Street.

At six, I made myself an omelet and a pot of coffee, and ate a five-cent candy bar for dessert. Around eight o'clock, tired of reading, tired of thinking about writing, I went outside again. 14th Street was now aglow with lights; nighttime crowds filled the sidewalks. Men were going into the Irving Place Burlesque to see the strippers, patrons were lining up before the ticket window of the Academy of Music which featured a movie and "six great vaudeville acts" for twenty-five cents, while well-dressed men and women were stepping out of taxis and into Luchow's. At this time of the evening a knot of young men, some of them quite sinister looking, began to gather near the entrance of the Tango Gardens where taxi dancers upstairs allowed the trade to writhe against them for two minutes, for ten cents a dance. Around nine, the vendors of the next morning's *Daily Worker* appeared with bundles of fresh papers, shouting down the night street: "Buy the *Daily Worker,* comrades, the only paper that prints the truth about the struggles of the laboring masses!"

I now frequently encountered young people I had met at political rallies and meetings which I had begun to attend out of curiosity. Because some of them had read my stories in the small magazines, they began to invite me to parties where I became acquainted with young left intellectuals. Because of my published work, I found I had become a figure in a literary underground. During some of my nightly walks I ran into a knot of unpublished poets and short story writers standing on a cold corner vehemently discussing "revolutionary" writing. They would call out to me, and when I joined them I would listen while they cursed the "lousy big-name boys" who got their stuff published without any difficulty; and if the evening was very cold we would all retire to the nearby Automat where, over cups of coffee, we would destroy the literary establishment of America. After literature was destroyed, the conversation always veered toward left-wing politics and I would listen to the latest Party line, to praise concerning the greatness of Stalin's leadership, which was always followed by the classic clincher: "Every proletarian artist must be a dialectical materialist!" The company of these speakers was warming; they were always sincere, vehement, youthfully impatient for the arrival of the revolution. Occasionally there was sexy and confidential gossip concerning the personal life of absent friends and foes.

Now and then, walking along 14th Street in the evening, I met Kenneth Fearing, a cigarette invariably dangling from his lip. He always greeted me casually and looked at me warily. Though he was grinding out fiction for the pulps to make the rent, his poetry, published in the small magazines, continued to be as true, as steely as ever.

"How do you keep from starving, Halper?"

"I practice Yoga. Learned it in India."

"Any time you want to earn an easy buck, let me know. I'll introduce you to a couple of Street & Smith boys, they pay a cent a word on acceptance." Then he would amble on, hands in overcoat pockets, shoulders hunched against the cold. One night he knocked on my door. "I have an extra ticket for the *New Masses* annual ball. Seeing it's just across the street in Webster Hall, I thought you might be interested." As a contributor to the *New Masses,* he had received two free tickets to the dance. "Maybe you'll meet a proletarian dream girl tonight, you never can tell." We went across the street together where a band was playing to a big crowd, and I had a good time dancing with new girls, losing Fearing in the press.

That winter I made the trip across the street many times to the big meetings and rallies in Webster Hall. As Foster, Browder, Dunne, Stachel, and other minions of the Party addressed the faithful, I listened to the thunderous applause. While political cliches dripped from the speakers' lips, I witnessed the hard hand-clapping, heard screams of delight when Wall Street, President Hoover, and Jay Lovestone, "that slimy deviationist," were dragged over the hottest of verbal coals. Benefits for Kentucky miners were big that year, and I heard genuine, moving, hill-billy music performed on the Webster Hall stage by native backwoods musicians sent up north by the strike committees, the stirring programs followed by collections among the audience. Girls canvassed the house holding collection baskets. "Please, comrades! Be generous—give, give for this great cause!"

It was always interesting, a good skillful show, even though I'd learned all the phrases by this time, all the exhortatory business that preceded, and followed, the punch lines. Webster Hall was always warmly heated, and the distance across the street from my tenement was only a few yards.

One chilly night an unpublished writer dropped by and invited me to a meeting of the John Reed Club, a Party organization of artists and writers. "Please, hear Diego Rivera, the guest speaker, tonight. He's the great Mexican comrade painter, the greatest in Mexico." I thought Orozco to be Rivera's superior but I did not bother to say so, having learned the uselessness of arguing against talent endorsed by the hierarchy.

When we arrived at the John Reed Club, a long, stove-heated loft, the place was packed with John Reed members sitting on folding chairs. There was a feeling of excitement in the hall. We found seats in the rear just in time; as other members arrived, they had to stand along the walls. When the loft was filled to bursting and the audience began growing a bit restive, Rivera appeared, a tall man, corpulent and confident, accompanied by Frieda, his darkly attractive, smiling wife who was dressed in Mexican peasant costume, neck and arms dramatically bedecked with native bracelets and jewelry.

The crowd burst into applause at their entrance, though I noticed small pockets of silence in the audience. Rivera bowed graciously, then began speaking in French, thanking the John Reed Club comrades for inviting him and his artist wife to appear here tonight. An artist I had met at Yaddo stood near the two guests and translated Rivera's remarks into English. In the long crowded hall the Mexican painter's big, oily face glowed like a moon.

"We in Mexico," he declared, "we with our heritage of struggle and successful revolution, we stretch out our hands in warm friendship to our fellow comrades of the arts in the United States. We want you to know that we, your faithful comrades, will be at your side in your own revolution!" He was interrupted by applause. "Every proletarian artist must be a dialectical materialist!" he stated with a wide, confident smile, his words being duly translated. "And I am happy to say tonight that I, Diego Rivera, am proud to be a dialectical materialist!" The applause now was louder. With his round face beaming and his stunning wife at his side glowing with pride at the sight of so many North American intellectuals gathered in this hot hall in homage to her revolutionary genius of a husband, Rivera paused for the loud applause to subside. I felt a sudden tug at my sleeve.

"He sent the John Reed Club a check for $200 this afternoon," my friend sitting beside me proudly whispered. "We certainly can use that money for rent and other expenses."

"And so," Rivera rolled on in French, "we must all join hands in the coming struggle against capitalism, against imperialism, and we shall use our art as weapons as we assault the barricades of our reactionary enemies! . . ."

At that moment, instead of the furious applause the big fellow had expected, a John Reed Club member stationed along the right wall of the long room jumped up from his chair and cried:

"Comrade Diego Rivera, you are an opportunist who sells his talent to the Rockefellers and other capitalists!"

Silence fell upon the hall. Most of the listeners were stunned. Was the speaker a crackpot? Up front, the Mexican's face was an eloquent study in shock; he was utterly bewildered.

Before the surprise of the assault wore off, a burly, authoritative figure rose from another part of the hall—big Bill Dunne, the editor of the *Daily Worker,* whose salvos against the Party's enemies I had often heard before in Webster Hall rallies. Vigorously he shook his fist toward Rivera.

"Why don't you speak in the language of the Mexican peasants and workers?" Dunne screamed. "Why do you address us in the effete language of the effete European intellectuals?" Another wave of shock rolled over the audience. Before it could adjust itself to this second blast, another comrade bounced up from his seat almost directly in front of Rivera. "You are a traitor to the revolution! You are a bootlicker to the capitalists who hire you to do their dirty work!"

Confusion gripped the hall. Rivera's wife, who apparently could not believe her ears, moved close to her husband's side, her superb face suffused with loyalty for her husband, her eyes, fiery and defiant, directed at the traducers of his political integrity. Up front, the translator's jaw hung slack; it was evident he had not been informed beforehand of the battle plan. It was evident, also, that Rivera understood English sufficiently to grasp the meaning of the charges hurled at him from the floor. My former Yaddo friend, realizing now that the attack upon Rivera had been premeditated and carefully worked out before the meeting, spluttered a few feeble words in an attempt to control the turmoil, then stammered in English: "I . . . I'm sorry . . . I find my knowledge of French inadequate to translate further. . . ." He then hurriedly lost himself in the audience. Frieda Rivera now turned to her husband's accusers and screamed in broken English:

"You wrong! You impolite peoples here tonight! Diego is great man! This is big disgrace for all revolutionary comrades! . . ."

"Your husband is a rat!" big Bill Dunne bellowed from

his seat. "He's a traitor to the struggling masses! He's sold out to the capitalist bosses! Didn't he paint that Trotskyite mural in Rockefeller Center?"

Another comrade leaped to his feet and yelled at Rivera whose face was now pale with shock and anger.

"He's silent, because he knows goddam well he's guilty! Renegade, fink!"

Finally recovering somewhat from the unexpected attack, his great body quivering like an aroused elephant, Rivera cried: "Thees charges, they unfounded! I do not do nothing wrong! Nothing! I am loyal to the revolution! . . ."

His denial was a signal for a concerted outburst of shrill catcalls and further denunciations. Those members in the hall who had sat stupefied during the initial onslaughts were now aware that this performance had come as a top directive from Party headquarters on 13th Street. The fact that they had not been informed of the planned attack upon the guest of honor before the meeting had begun had made the assault, when it came, all the more powerful and devastating. As the uproar continued, with the trapped Mexican attempting to justify his painting of the Rockefeller mural, which, he said, he had executed "in the interest of all workers," the well-rehearsed cadres in various sections of the hall hooted and screamed obscenities at their victim. The silent members of the audience sat on their hands knowing full well Diego Rivera was being read out of the Party by order of its leadership.

It was the first character assassination I had witnessed, and it was a most thorough job. Because of the obedient silence of those in the hall who did not participate in the attack, I knew that they, who had come to admire and pay homage to this talented man, now began to revile him in their thoughts. (In the years to come, Diego Rivera was to slip in and out of the Communist Party in his own devious way, making many pilgrimages to Moscow until he died, while Orozco, the truly revolutionary loner, continued creating his non-Party masterpieces, hurling his artistic thunderbolts at human meannesses and the hypocrisies of all political and religious shibboleths.)

The meeting finally broke up in disorder, with Frieda, her glorious Latin eyes still glittering with hate, following the hulking form of her husband toward the door where, his crushed overcoat tangled over his shoulder, he lurched out into the hallway.

When I reached the door of my tenement, I discovered Hedda half-hidden in the dark entrance.

"Where have you been!" she accused me. "I knocked and knocked, then I came downstairs again. I've been waiting here for hours!"

"How was I to know you'd be here tonight?"

"I want a key! Or I won't come here any more!"

My mind still filled with the drama I had just witnessed, I turned on her angrily. "Are you threatening me? I just came from a meeting where I saw an unsuspecting, gifted man assassinated! It was horrible! I never want to see another sight like that again!"

She turned instantly silent, and followed me upstairs without a word.

A month later during a New York press interview, Diego Rivera remarked that the John Reed Club never did return his $200 donation.

The Food Is Good in Summer Camps

That winter never seemed to end. With the oven going in the kitchen to keep me warm as I wrote, I waited for the spring. The news from Lieber about my novel continued to be gloomy; more publishers rejected my manuscript and others called it back for a second reading, only to turn it down again.

I began to have painful stretches when I could not work well. Some mornings I was unable to tap out more than five or six lines. To kill time I stood at one of my windows overlooking the back yard of the rooming house next door; in the courtyard a small man in a long overcoat packed sun-flower seeds and peanuts into small paper bags, which he sold in Union Square. His patience fascinated me; he portioned out the small, careful amounts into the tiny bags, gave each bag a twist to secure the contents, then placed them neatly in rows in a hand-cart which he would later wheel toward 14th Street. How much could he earn a day? Watching him push his cart along the passage that led to

11th Street, I envied him for a second and thought: "There goes a happy Gogolian character! He doesn't have to worry about stringing words into sentences! Hurrah for him!" Then I returned to my machine and tapped out a few more futile words.

Once a week I made the trip to the public bath house near First Avenue, carrying a towel and a piece of soap wrapped in a newspaper. At the bath house, I took my place on one of the long wooden benches along with a crowd of poorly dressed men, watching the clock in the waiting room to see how much longer it would be before the bathers beyond the doors would emerge, their faces shiny, from the showers. Towels could be rented here for five cents, but if you brought your own, the bath was free. As the batch of newly bathed men came from the opened doors, those on the benches grew restless, crouching like sprinters awaiting the gun.

"No one will be admitted until all the showers are cleared!" the tall attendant holding a club shouted. "So sit quiet, you're rocking the boat!"

There was grumbling from the benches, until the attendant cried: "Okay, next batch, next batch!" The stampede began as we rushed toward the showers. If you had been here before, you headed for certain booths where the water came down evenly, and if this was your first visit you found only the worst showers available, those in the cramped booths where the water squirted in all directions, drenching the clothes you'd hung on pegs. I always tried to hurry into booths 45, 17, 9 or 4, because I knew those had the good showers. The hot shower was refreshing, and I listened to the men begin singing, at first in tentative voices, then bellowing with joy as the water washed away, for a few days at least, the dirt and scum of the city. At the end of fifteen minutes the attendant would come into the big room authoritatively and start hammering against the doors of the booths with his club.

"Okay, men! Time is up! C'mon, out, out! . . ."

Then the hissing water would stop, we would get dressed, putting on clothes dampened by the steamy air of the place, and emerge through the doors, to find another batch of men sitting on the wooden benches waiting their turn. I would go back to my flat, hang my wet towel over a chair, light the oven and place the chair before the oven to allow the towel to dry. Then I would sit down to my typewriter and try to work.

The long winter finally ended. When spring arrived Union Square seemed more active than ever. A new contingent of men and boys squatted behind home-made shoe-shine kits; more apple-sellers lined the low surrounding wall of the square; the elderly Russians and Jews selling pretzels from hand-carts fought each other with increased fierceness for the best positions at the subway entrances. "Lady, I was here first!" comes the anguished cry. "I got to make a living!" "Excuse me, you can go to hell!" is the pistol-like retort. The Little Acme Theater, with its hard seats and bad ventilation, was featuring *Ten Days That Shook the World.* Greater crowds of women were now storming all the entrances to Klein's in response to the spring sales, overturning tables stacked with hand-bags and blouses while the private security police screamed: "Stop grabbing. Stop shoving! Or we'll throw all of you outside!"

With the arrival of spring I began working better. I started a new story, rewriting the opening paragraph about a dozen times and recasting the first few pages repeatedly without losing my enthusiasm for the material. The story was almost plotless, describing the characters of a large, lower-class Chicago family, and dealing with the interrelationships of its various members. I worked myself into a stupor, writing eight drafts. When at last I got the story into shape I sent it to Lieber. He was excited over it.

" 'My Brothers Who Are Honest Men' is a real breakthrough for you!" Lieber's encouragement, as usual, buoyed me up. But as the days slipped into weeks there was no news of its sale.

It was now almost summer. My money was running out again. Though I cooked and ate all my meals in the flat, washed my shirts, underwear, socks, and bedsheets—hanging them on ropes strung across the kitchen—and kept my living expenses to a minimum, I knew I would be broke by the end of May. Elliot Cohen had said that if I was in need of funds he could get up some money for me, but I was reluctant to inform him of my predicament. One afternoon, walking on 14th Street, I ran into Prestopino, an artist I had met at Yaddo. We had been rather friendly in the colony, and when he asked how I was making out, I said:

"I'm worried about the rent."

He laughed. "I was, too, until a couple of days ago. Look, I'm going up to an adult camp next week to work as a scenic designer for their dramatic group. Maybe you can get a job in a camp, too."

"I can't paint scenery."

"Can you entertain, play a musical instrument, do funny dialogues?" I shook my head. I thought he was kidding. "Or maybe you can get a job as waiter for the summer. You get tips, and the food is good."

"I never waited on table before."

"Fake it. Tell the management you've waited on table for years." He gave me the names of a half a dozen adult camps whose offices were in New York.

The next morning I began to make the rounds of camp offices. I had no luck with the first three, whose waiter quotas were filled. At the fourth office, I held my breath. Across a big polished desk I faced a businesslike, wiry little woman who owned one of the more exclusive adult camps in the Adirondacks. I lied about my waiter experience, mentioning non-existing camps in Illinois where I had worked, slurring their names quickly. "What are you, an actor?" she said shrewdly. "No, I'm a writer," I blurted. "Fine. Then you can write sketches for the acting company in your spare time, besides waiting on table. Is that understood? Do you think you can write clever sketches for the dramatic group?"

"Certainly. I can write anything." I walked out of the office with a job, also with train fare and a ten-dollar advance against tips. The season was to start that week-end, on Memorial Day.

That night I met Kenneth Fearing on 14th Street. I hadn't seen him in months. "You look thinner, Halper." He lit a fresh cigarette from his butt. "How do you get by?" It was the old routine but it didn't bother me. I noticed he looked a bit peaked himself. When I told him I was going to fatten up next week working in an adult camp he suddenly looked interested. "Who's going to occupy your flat in your absence?" I said I didn't know yet. "How about me as your tenant? I'll cook in your place, cut my expenses. I'll pay the rent." We shook hands on it, and the next day I gave him a duplicate key to the flat.

When I saw the camp I was surprised at the enormous size of it—the great number of guest houses and cabins skirting a private lake, ten fine tennis courts, a golf course, a dance hall, a theater, all sorts of other facilities to make the guests happy. Every building was freshly painted, evidence of expert management at the helm.

I met my colleagues, sixteen other waiters who were mostly college students headed for the medical, dental and legal professions and almost all of them younger than I. Before working our first meal, we were briefed by the owner; we were instructed to give careful and individualized service and to be pleasant at all times and under all circumstances. "Remember, they're paying hard-earned money to come here, and this is the Depression." Then the first meal started and, being inexperienced, I was utterly confused. I set the plates down clumsily, removed them from the wrong side, and forgot to bring bread and rolls and butter at the proper time. The dining hall was gigantic, almost the size of a football field it seemed, with five hundred hungry guests waiting for service, and the long round-trips to the big kitchen were like so many endless laps around the indoor track at Madison Square Garden. It was nightmarish, but two fellow waiters, noticing my inexperience, covered for me that first meal, helping me clear my tables and quickly teaching me how to stack my big metal tray high with plates in order to save unnecessary trips to the kitchen. Like every other waiter, I served twenty-four guests; they were all avid eaters, calling for second helpings frequently and keeping me running endlessly to the kitchen for more bread, more tartar sauce, more ice cream. At the end of working my first meal I collapsed in a chair and, looking about the empty dining hall, my spirits rose a trifle when I saw two other waiters also slumped exhausted in chairs.

It was a grueling job; but under the pressure of it I managed to become fairly adept in my duties by the end of the first week. Waiters ate in a separate room adjoining the kitchen. The food was wonderful, also plentiful, but none of us were able to put on weight; after serving large, complicated breakfasts, generous luncheons, and the big evening meal, we usually stepped on a big scale in the kitchen where we found we lost between five and seven pounds, which we somehow regained by the next day. While we worked, the perspiration poured down our faces as we jogged to and from the kitchen balancing the heavily-laden trays; for the big evening meal, the management usually had an employee standing out of sight just inside the swinging kitchen doors with two big towels with which he hastily wiped our faces as we passed him, like panting runners in a marathon race. After the evening meal was over, we sank into chairs for a five-minute respite, after which we cleared our tables, resetting them completely with clean plates and silverware for the next morning's breakfast as well as swabbing the floor with mops. Then we staggered a quarter of a mile to our quarters, a shed-like structure where our seventeen cots were jammed together in one long room, like an army barracks. We took off our damp clothes and flopped upon the beds like exhausted swimmers, cursing the management, the guests, and the surrounding mountains. Soon the strains of dance music drifted in from the casino on the lake. A flunkey from the office appeared at the doorway. "Okay, boys. Mrs. You-Know-Who wants you to get dressed pronto and dance with the female guests." "Get out, get out, you shit!" someone inevitably cried. But we soon got up, put on white shirts and white ducks and, strangely enough, suddenly felt cheerful and refreshed. Ten minutes later, in a group, we headed for the casino, all of us carrying contraceptives in our pockets. As the dance band poured bouncy music into the gaily decorated hall, the single girls in evening dresses eyed us with interest as we entered. "Here come the waiters," they murmured.

To keep the clientele amused, the dramatic company, headed by a Broadway director, put on shows four nights a week. Most of the productions were pirated from Broadway hits, played by a cast heavily Equity, whose members had been out of work when the summer call had come from the camp management. So far, I hadn't created any skits for the shows. But one night the owner stopped me in the casino. "Have you handed the director any skits yet?" she asked pointedly. "I've had a few conferences with him, I'm working on them," I lied hastily. The next day I approached the director, Harold Hecht, who later became a major Hollywood producer. He was young, about twenty-three, and studied my fatigued face sympathetically as he listened to my reasons for not wanting to write skits. "That's all right, I have plenty of material," he smiled. "I can see you're too tired to write." So I got off the hook. The other waiters were not as fortunate. One of them, a member of the N.Y.U. swimming team, gave diving exhibitions in the afternoon; another, a waiter from the Yale Law School, sang folk songs in the lounge; a waiter from Harvard Medical School, a fine tennis player, played hard-fought tennis matches with the tennis instructor before the cheering guests. Other waiters strummed guitars, sang college songs; one gave concerts in bird-calling; and sometimes waiters were ordered by the management to fill in as chorus boys in the camp's bigger musicals.

The round of cultural and athletic events in camp was unceasing. Guests ran from event to fresh event, as if to extract the last ounce of value from their stay. It being the Depression, most had made sacrifices to come here and you couldn't blame them for wanting their money's worth. Each Saturday morning we waiters watched new guests piling out of the buses that had hauled them like so much freight from the city. They arrived pale and wan from a year's work in offices or show-rooms, many of them loaded down with tennis rackets and golf clubs, the girls carrying bulging suitcases of sports clothes and evening dresses they had skimped all year to buy. As soon as they had checked in at the office, the ever-cheerful social director would mince about, introducing them to each other. By the next morning the new guests were veterans, playing tennis, paddling canoes on the lake, engaging in deep conversations, and starting romances.

It became a familiar, fascinating routine to watch. And, all too soon, the guests would leave after their brief stay of one or two weeks, climbing regretfully back into the buses which would return them to the city and their jobs. Many of the girls, their faces now tanned, would turn and wave at some of the waiters; these girls had left something they had planned on leaving back there in the woods on the pine needles, or in the bottoms of canoes, or in their cabins when roommates were not present. They turned and waved their good-byes. Days later a few waiters would receive lovely notes of gratitude from the city, letters that would be read once and tossed away. Other waiters would retrieve the notes from the bunkhouse floor, read them aloud, and the entire waiters' barracks would roar with crude delight.

One morning in the middle of the summer, I struck up a friendship with a new male guest. He greeted me as I came from the dining hall. I noticed his clothes were different from the others, less expensive, in fact slightly worn. He was short and wiry, a fast-talker, with an alert and quizzical expression; he came up to me as I was passing the camp office.

"Hello, Halper. I'm a kind of relative of the owner. I heard you were a waiter here. I read a story of yours somewhere. My name is Sender Garlin." We shook hands. "How's the job here?"

"Tough. But the food is good."

He laughed. We stood around and talked awhile. The next day I ran into him again, or maybe he was waiting for me to pass the office on my way to the waiters' quarters. We talked. He was witty and pleasant. During the next few days, when we met, I began to suspect, because of the way he purposely dropped a few key words, that my new acquaintance might possibly be a comrade. He did not hint, of course, that he was a Party member, but one morning after I'd finished serving my twenty-four guests their breakfasts, he and I sat on the dock watching girls moving about in their bathing suits, when he casually dropped a query. "You ever read the *Daily Worker?*" I told him I never purposely read the *Daily Worker* because I thought it was a dull, uninteresting paper full of dull writing and dull propaganda. He laughed. "Of course it's full of propaganda; it's an arm of a radical party with a definite program aimed at recruiting politically unsophisticated readers." He tossed a pebble into the water. "Some day, when the political scene heats up more, maybe you'll contribute a piece to the *Daily Worker*."

"I doubt it."

He laughed again. He wasn't pushing it. Under the warm sun of a summer camp casual friendships ripen easily, and the next day he told me he had just returned from an organizing trip in the midwest, attempting to form a farmers' cooperative among dairy farmers.

"They ready for the revolution?" I kidded him.

"Not yet," he smiled. "Those people living along unmarked dirt roads never heard of Karl Marx but you'd be surprised at their militant conversation when they talk about how the local banks are calling in their mortgages and how they aim to hold on to their farms come hell or high water."

"I don't doubt it."

"Some of them are starting to talk about getting an organization together, and they all own shotguns."

"I don't doubt that, either."

"I went to a couple of foreclosure auctions and when the bidding started on a farm I was amazed how they kept the bidding down to five or ten dollars for the whole farm, and then the winning bidder turned it back to the original owner."

"I call that intelligent. When do we bid on this camp? I want to destroy the waiters' barracks and put up a bold new shining structure tomorrow."

He laughed. "I'm checking out this afternoon. Maybe we'll see each other in town."

"Sure."

He left on the next bus, and the following day I missed our revolutionary conversations which had come as a relief from that of my fellow waiters whose conversation, as the summer progressed, narrowed down to simple and repetitious profanity. Their gritty expletives, I knew, were the result of their fatigue and hatred of their work. The compensations some of them had received on the pine needles in the woods or in the darkened cabins at night were not sufficient to remind them to converse like the gentlemen students they were.

Sometimes, as we waiters stood waiting for the guests to arrive in the empty dining room, I stared out the dining-hall windows at the beauty of the mountains, or at the serene lake that lay below at the bottom of the hill where the camp's eighty canoes were drawn up waiting for the guests' activity. It was pleasant, too, sometimes to pass the fine tennis courts on my way to the dining hall before breakfast, while many of the guests were still sleeping, and see Joe, the powerful middle-aged man who maintained the courts, rolling them carefully and marking the lines with his liquid chalking machine and turning to wave a hand at me while obviously enjoying his work. In the early morning the mountain birds sang in the pines and the air was sharp and clear and wonderful to inhale deeply. I almost forgot the city and my future, both of which would be waiting for me in a few weeks.

The big Labor Day weekend, marking the end of the season, had a nightmarish quality all its own. Special crowded programs were scheduled to lure guests for the next summer, and entertainment followed entertainment without letup—elimination tennis matches between guests, a golf tournament, canoe races for men and for girls, diving exhibitions, dance contests for prizes in the casino, a concert by a string quartet sent up from New York, afternoon lectures in the lodge by an "authority" also from New York (a gent who had written a book about sex and spoke to the guests about the beauties of a "fulfilled" sex life). The hectic weekend finished with a large-scale musical production featuring a genuine Broadway star, a man out of work for the summer.

At the end of the season we watched from our bunkhouse as guests struggled toward the buses that would take them back to the city. Many of them looked exhausted. The last buses pulled away. Our job was about over. We rested for a few days, with only a few guests still around, and the final stint was pleasantly easy. The acting troupe had departed, the dance orchestra had gone back to New York, the lodge was closed, the tennis courts were empty, and the huge dining hall with its handful of guests looked like a movie house doing poor business.

At last the pool of tips in the office was totaled up: each waiter received a little over three hundred dollars for the summer's work, which wasn't bad. To me, it meant six months' security. After receiving our money, we packed our suitcases. Our farewells were brief and casual, like those of workmen parting after a construction job is completed. We shook hands, without taking each others' addresses or phone numbers.

When I reached my flat I found it in good order. Kenneth Fearing had already vacated the place. There was a small note on the kitchen table. "I caught three mice while you were away enjoying the fresh air of the mountains."

Whittaker Chambers on 14th Street

It was pleasant to get back to New York, to see the crowds, to hear street noises; and after living in a bunkhouse with sixteen waiters it was also deeply satisfying to return to the solitude of my own flat. It was nice, too, to see Hedda coming up the stairs again. She looked very pretty in a new dress. Her first words were: "You're so thin! Was the work that taxing up there?"

"Not the work, the social obligations."

Her eyes searched my face, to see whether I was serious. "What social obligations? Bull crud. You can't scare me." She poked me in the ribs with a laugh. It was good to be back again.

The next morning I went out for a glimpse of Union Square. Though the mountains surrounding the adult camp had been beautiful to look at, 14th Street with its swarms of early autumn shoppers and hawkers was now far more interesting. For ten minutes I watched the pretzel vendors fighting as always for strategic positions near the subway entrances and once more I saw the bootblacks lining the wall, idling in the warm September sun, calling, "Shine, mac, shine, mac? Only five cents!" Turning away, I suddenly caught sight of Sender Garlin, the small, wiry organizer I'd talked with a few weeks ago at the summer camp; he was standing on the corner waiting for the traffic light to change and noticed me a moment after I'd noticed him.

"Hello. When did you get back from camp?"

"Yesterday afternoon."

"What are you doing in this radical stamping ground?"

"I live close by. Besides, I'm taking notes for a sociological study in depth on these pretzel vendors. I want to know if they are for or against higher import duty on foreign flour and salt."

He laughed. Instead of crossing with the traffic light, he stayed to talk awhile. He informed me, casually, that there was going to be a big demonstration in the Square Saturday afternoon. "The unemployed have been organized into councils and they're starting to apply mass pressure for relief, in case you're interested in the social scene."

"It should be an interesting demonstration," I said.

The lights changed several times but Sender Garlin continued talking as the sun slanted through a break between two buildings across the street; in the pleasant autumn light we watched the traffic. As we stood there, a man greeted Garlin with a nod and a wave of the hand, and kept on walking. Then a young girl in a hurry smiled, said a quick hello, and kept on going; she was carrying a brief-case and I noticed she and the man were heading toward 13th Street where Party headquarters were located.

"You seem to be very popular in this area," I said.

"Just coincidental meetings. It happens some days."

He had hardly said this when a young man, a hatless fellow with very light brown wavy hair and a John Barrymore profile, carrying a black battered wooden case, passed us. "Hey," Garlin called out, and the fellow turned, stopped, and came over, smiling. Garlin introduced us. "Kevin O'Malley, meet a friend." As we chatted awhile O'Malley, who spoke with a pleasant Irish accent, kept turning his head whenever a girl walked by. After a few minutes he said he had an appointment and left, carrying his flat black wooden case across Union Square. Garlin commented in an amused voice: "There goes the great romantic lover. With his wonderful prop."

"What do you mean?"

Still looking amused, Garlin smiled. "He's got a zither in that case. He finds out where there's a party and appears at it carrying that thing. He's good for four or five parties a week."

"What does he do at these gatherings? Give recitals?"

"Sort of," Garlin laughed. "He sings folk songs, mostly the sad Gaelic ones. When he places the zither on his knees and hits the strings with little soft hammers, his eyes rove romantically over the room for food, and the prettiest girl."

"How does he make out?"

"He's never gone hungry, and the legend is he's had a couple hundred girls," Garlin laughed again. "Why, I've seen him on the street after midnight with his case, going to a party he suddenly got wind of."

"He'll wear himself out one of these days."

"Yes. It's a pity because he's got a first-rate mind. He's done a lot of good things for the movement but because of his constant itch for success in the hay he's not too reliable. It's too bad."

At that moment a short, plump man in his late twenties came toward us. He greeted Garlin warmly. "What are you doing, clocking the 14th Street traffic?" he said smiling. From his bantering tone, it was obvious he and Garlin were close friends. Garlin introduced us.

"Meet Whittaker Chambers, Halper."

Chambers extended his soft hand. "You the writer? I know your work."

"I know yours, too. I read your story, 'Can You Hear Their Voices?' in the *New Masses*. It's a fine piece."

"Thanks." As he smiled at me in a friendly way, I could see the discolored stumps of his teeth. We talked awhile and I listened to the banter between Garlin and Chambers and it was pleasant being in the company of two witty men who didn't seem, at the time, to take themselves too seriously. The 14th Street traffic rumbled by. Just before they left together, Chambers turned to me:

"I've taken over the editorship of the *New Masses,* and if you have anything for us I'd like to see it."

"Sure," I said.

"So long. Nice meeting you."

"Thanks. Nice meeting you too."

I watched them cross heavily trafficked Fourth Avenue, Sender Garlin, small and wiry, Whittaker Chambers, short and plump, and Chambers threw back his head once to laugh at something his friend had said.

Two decades later I was to read in Chambers' book *Witness* that it was Sender Garlin who had served as the link that had brought him into the Communist Party. There on the corner of 14th Street and Fourth Avenue, I watched them disappear among the crowd of shoppers. I was glad I had met the talented author of "Can You Hear Their Voices?"—one of the best stories ever published in the *New Masses*—and, of course, as the two of them had crossed the street, I had no way of foretelling Chambers' tortured and unhappy future.

The Romeo of the Tenements

I spent a rather pleasant week reacclimating myself to New York. Then, while I began hoping for Lieber to relay good news to me about my novel, which was still making the rounds of the publishers, I began to feel a deep restlessness. Had all the labor I had put into that book been wasted? I sat at my desk again, trying to write a short story, but I felt stale. The truth was I had fallen upon another barren time. Seeking stimulation from new books, I began revisiting the public libraries. It didn't help much, but it was a way to kill time.

Because of the Depression, the libraries were now always crowded with people, many of whom, lacking money for the movies, had no other place to go to keep warm. Sometimes as you sat reading your book you heard the man or woman next to you suddenly mumble, then exclaim in a high voice to no one in particular: "Rent is thirty dollars, bread costs ten cents a loaf . . .

tonight I'll call President Hoover . . . I must feed the cat . . ." All this in a desperate voice. It sent chills down my back, and when it happened I always changed my seat in a hurry.

In the main lobby of the 42nd Street library you saw other Depression types; you saw young men who slipped into the phone booths, feigning calls, and quickly stuffed the slots with paper, then sat on the stone benches to wait for people to make calls. A percentage of callers always received busy signals, or the people they tried to reach were not in; after letting the phone ring a number of times you would see them jiggle the receivers for their coins to return, and peer down into the metal return cups, but they would never find them. Many callers left the booths cursing the telephone company. After a quick glance around, the character who had stuffed the return slot would slip back into the vacated booth, stick his finger up the opening, extract the paper, and pocket the coin. It was sometimes an interesting game to watch.

Then there were the female freaks who patronized the big 42nd Street library. One afternoon as I came out of the Magazine Room a girl who was not unattractive took hold of my arm and said a man had just tried to rape her in the Slavonic Room on the second floor. I was about to call a guard when I noticed her eyes. I hurried away, saying I had an important appointment. A few days later a middle-aged woman with a Hungarian accent stopped me on the third floor and began to tell me her troubles. "Mister, I got a bad son-in-law. He makes me eat one-week-old stale bread. 'Eat, it's economical!,' he says. But it sticks in my throat. Shall I call the police and put my son-in-law in jail, mister?" I told her that was a good idea and added I was late for a dental appointment.

One chilly afternoon, coming from the small Offendorfer branch library on Second Avenue, I met Kevin O'Malley, the great lover Sender Garlin had introduced me to on 14th Street. He was hatless and lightly dressed, carrying his flat, black zither case.

"Hello," I said.

"Hello, there. Live around here?" His Irish brogue reached me through the cold air.

"My place is a couple blocks from here."

"I have a little time to kill. Mind if I walk with you?"

"No." As he fell in step beside me I saw he was walking a bit oddly, as though he had bunions or painful corns. "I forgot to wear my topcoat," he said. His lips were slightly bluish, though this didn't detract from his John Barrymore looks. As we passed the Cafe Royal on the corner, a well known meeting place for Second Avenue Yiddish actors and poets and famous for its tasty kosher dishes, I caught O'Malley looking hungrily through the windows at the little groups of poets and philosophers busily eating afternoon strudel and drinking coffee. We turned into 11th Street and he stopped before my door, hesitantly.

"Got a cup of coffee for me?"

"Sure." He followed me up the flights, carrying his flat black case. I turned my key in the lock. Inside, I lit the oven for warmth, then started a pot of coffee. O'Malley put his case down and sat in one of my hard chairs with a sigh.

"You've got a nice place here."

"Yes, these rear flats can be quiet."

"It must be a good place to write in.'

"It's not bad. Comes the revolution I'll have a place with steam heat."

He smiled. "We'll all have steam heat then. Maybe." He looked around the living room while I went into the kitchen. The coffee was perking, and the good smell of the 19¢-a-lb. A&P coffee began floating through the flat. He rose to examine my books stacked on the floor. "Flaubert, Pío Baroja, Turgenev,

Chekhov, Bunin, Zola, Lermontov, Ibsen." He read the authors' names aloud. "They're all foreigners, I see."

"The Americans and others are in that pile to the left."

"Oh yes, over here." Bending over the volumes, he handled them like a book lover. "Joyce is really the modern master, isn't he? *A Portrait* is a jewel, perfect."

"I like his *Dubliners*."

"Yes, that book of his stories is very fine. I've reread them many times." He thumbed my copy of *Dubliners*. "Only an Irishman can appreciate Joyce."

"Well," I said.

He took the cup of coffee and the cheese sandwich I offered him and smiled. "I didn't mean any offense. But you take a writer like Ring Lardner. Can any one but an American get the true essence of his work?"

"Perhaps not. But Lardner writes slang, wonderful slang, almost a dialect sometimes, while Joyce is a purist who writes classic English."

"I'll half-agree with you there. Got another sandwich? And a little more coffee?" I made another sandwich and poured a second cup of coffee. "Turgenev in one of his books is something like Joyce, isn't he? His Basarov, like Stephen Dedalus, I mean." I could not help but catch the yearning in his voice. "Basarov—he's ageless. Every generation has its Basarov, its nihilist." After he finished his second sandwich and cup of coffee he began pacing the room. Again I noticed his odd way of walking.

"What's wrong with your feet? Tight shoes?"

He smiled crookedly, in an unpleasant way. "It's not my feet, if you really want to know." He took off his shirt to show the deep welts all across his back. He hiked up his trouser legs to expose the bruises on his shins and calves.

"My God. Where did you get those souvenirs?"

"Exercising my rights as an American citizen." He put on his shirt and rebuttoned it. "Three days ago I helped organize a march of the Unemployed Council up in the Bronx. I was walking with the leaders as we headed for Fordham Road when the squad cars came."

"What squad cars?"

"The police cars. They arrived in force and broke up our demonstration, no holds barred. They took four of us who were at the head of the march to the police station where they booked us for creating a public disturbance. When the cops questioned me and heard my Irish accent they looked at each other and laughed."

"Why?"

"Don't ask me, ask them. They led me, alone, to a big room down in the basement of the precinct station where they beat me, all over my body. They were laughing all the time. 'Why are you a commoonist? We thought only Jews and niggers were reds. So you're a commoonist, hey?' They laughed and hit me again. All of them were Irish cops. 'Do you come from Mayo now? Or maybe from County Cork?' They hit me again. They roared with laughter as they kept striking me. They detained me in a cell overnight, then released me."

I was silent for a while. "That's some story."

"I still can't walk properly because if I move my feet normally my calf muscles hurt like hell. I guess I'll be better in a few days." His eyes were grim. "Got another sandwich?"

I made another sandwich and a fresh pot of coffee in the kitchen. He continued talking from the other room.

"The reason I took part in the march was because I wanted to get back into the Party."

"I didn't know you were out of it. You and Garlin seemed very friendly."

"I'd been out of the Party six months. They gave me this

assignment to help organize and lead the march to test my reliability. I'm back in now." Taking the fresh sandwich and coffee I offered him, he looked over the low roofs of 10th Street where the autumn dusk was slowly working its way. "You're lucky you're a writer. It's difficult to explain."

"What is?"

"Well, I mean the hold the Party has on you once you've been active in it two or three years. You feel that despite some of its flaws it's a worthwhile movement and there're a lot of decent people in it who are making sacrifices in an effort to effect some much needed change in our social structure, and if you check out you miss it like hell after a month or two—you yearn for the Party activity, the close friendships you formed, the cell meetings, the discussions, the assignments. It's difficult to me to explain it to you, Halper."

"Why do you say that?"

"You'll never be a Communist." He frowned. "All I have to do is to look about this room at your typewriter, your pile of manuscripts over there. You don't need the Party. I do."

After a while he picked up his wooden case, walked delicately to the door in his oddly crippled manner, and left. He had forgotten to mention one additional reason for his return to the Party—the warm, democratic girls in the movement who admired his musical talents.

After this first visit to my flat O'Malley began to drop in occasionally, but if he saw I was working he never stayed longer than a few minutes. He always carried his instrument with him. He had a genuine love for good literature and it was pleasant to discuss authors and writing with him, as well as politics and the ever fluctuating Party line. "The line has to fluctuate, Halper, because conditions change."

"Truth doesn't fluctuate."

He smiled wryly. "Truth. There's a poetic truth, and a

political truth. The Party line has to be flexible, to take advantage of political opportunities when they arise. You surely can understand that."

In the colder weather that came on that winter, he continued to go hatless, wearing only a short thin jacket, and people along 14th Street stared at him as he carried his long black case up the sidewalk. During a few nights he and I sat over coffee in the crowded Automat with some of his friends, and I listened, unimpressed, to the usual political arguments swirling around us. It was warm and pleasant in the cafeteria and the tall manager frequently came by frowning at us because we only bought cups of coffee instead of something more expensive, but we ignored him. In the Automat O'Malley seemed to know a great many people, and whenever he saw a new pretty girl comrade he would hastily excuse himself for a minute, go over to talk to her, then return to his seat.

As the really cold weather set in, I saw less of him. I hoped he had found a warm and friendly place to park himself and his black case for the winter. I did not see him for a long time. Someone told me he had dropped out of the Party again. Then one day I saw him on Fourth Avenue, but he crossed the street and avoided me. Later I heard he had become a Trotskyite.

As time went by, every so often I caught rare glimpses of O'Malley in various parts of the city. He looked older, thinner, more worn and shabby. He was still carrying his black wooden case, probably to some rendezvous where he hoped to make a new conquest. A girl I met told me he had quit the Trotskyites and was no longer interested in any political movement. Where he lived, how he fed himself, no one seemed to know.

Mencken

Elliot Cohen came to see me one noon, his first visit to my flat. It was Monday, the day I washed my shirts, socks, and bedsheets, and I was about to sit down to my typewriter, after finishing my wash, when I heard a tap on the door. There stood Elliot Cohen in the hall, smiling quizzically. As I ushered him into my place, he was unprepared for the washing that hung on the lines in the kitchen and the wet sheet that met his face. He laughed as I led him into the living room. He was wearing his overcoat and, though I had the oven going, he did not remove it; the oven warmed only part of the flat. He went to a rear window to get a view of the buildings across the yards. Then he sat down on my cot, still in his overcoat, smiling.

"You've got a palace here, really." He noticed the pile of books on the floor, the volumes I had purchased at the second-hand stores on Fourth Avenue. "A place to work, good books, what else does one need?" He placed a palm tentatively against the bare floor. "Only thing is, your floor is cold."

"I never walk around in my bare feet," I said.

"A wise decision." He still looked amused as he checked

out my digs, his warm glance taking in every detail. "Why haven't you dropped up to the *Menorah Journal* office all this time? And Sylvia was asking about you last night. 'How's Albert getting along this winter?' she said. So I came over here. How're your funds holding out?"

"Oh, I'm getting by."

"Really? You're not broke?"

"No." I was one month overdue on my rent and the real estate agent had recently sent me a warning note, threatening to dispossess me if I didn't send him the rent. I knew Cohen would advance me the money, and I cursed myself for answering his query automatically. It wasn't pride. I didn't know what the hell it was, maybe just stupid hard-guy Chicago stuff that had made me turn down his generous offer. Or maybe it was living alone, eating alone, wanting to make it without outside help. Suddenly Cohen stood up, his quizzical smile returning.

"Come on. I'll buy you a lunch."

I put on my coat and locked the door and we went downstairs. It was a cold bright day, invigorating weather, and the El thundered overhead on Third Avenue. Cohen took me to a small Italian restaurant near Sixth Avenue where we ate a good meal and talked about writing and politics but mostly about politics. The *Menorah Journal,* which had never made ends meet, relied on subsidies for its existence, and Cohen informed me that lately, because of the worsening of the Depression, the subsidies had fallen off sharply. During lunch I became aware that Cohen, who had always been a liberal, was quickly becoming a radical. His conversation, today, was very left; he said major changes would have to be made on the economic front if the present democratic processes of the country were to survive.

"I hear the voice of the *New Masses,*" I said jokingly.

"I read the *New Masses.* I read the *Daily Worker,* too— it's a terrible sheet but I read it once in a while." He ordered a second cup of coffee and kept on talking. I sensed he had reached a crisis in his life, like many intellectuals had that winter, some of them joining the Party. "How do you feel about all this?" he suddenly asked.

"About what?"

"About the times, about getting involved?"

"I want to be a writer."

"Don't you want to be involved?"

"I want to be involved in my writing."

"Yes, I know. But is that enough, haven't you thought about being involved politically? You of all people, with your background? Haven't you thought about it?"

He was speaking now like all the others. But how could I feel annoyed facing this wonderfully good and intelligent man across the table? What could I say to him, this editor who had accepted my stories, who had encouraged me? I had learned, in the two years I'd lived in New York, to put on the humorous act to avoid hurting people I truly liked.

"Tell you what, Elliot. I admire one living writer greatly, James Joyce. I'll write to him, and if he says to get involved, I'll get involved."

Cohen laughed, his lecture to me finished. He became relaxed more over his second cup of coffee. He told me, before the meal was over, of the difficulties he was encountering with Henry Hurwitz, his superior, the publisher of the *Menorah Journal*. Hurwitz was a small, dandified, pompous older man whom I had once met in the *Menorah* office. "He wants me to soften up some of the articles and fiction." Cohen stared across the restaurant gloomily. "I hope some day, if these times ever get better, to start a new magazine of my own. I think about it constantly. With the *Dial* gone now, and with the exception of Mencken's *American Mercury,* the magazine field is pretty barren."

"The *Menorah Journal* isn't barren."

"We have too limited a horizon and circulation."

"It's still a fine magazine."

"Yes, I like to think so." He stirred his coffee slowly. "But if you soften the material, you ruin everything." Again his eyes roved about the restaurant moodily. "To really have my own magazine some day, to control editorial policy, that is my hope." His voice trailed away, with his unhappy glance still off somewhere, as if focused on some vague future.

When I returned to my place I found a special delivery letter in my mail box. It had arrived while I had been dining with Elliot Cohen. The letter was from Lieber. When I opened the envelope in the vestibule it was all I could do to suppress a sob of happiness. Lieber had sold a story. It was "My Brothers Who Are Honest Men," the story I had rewritten eight times— and H. L. Mencken had accepted it for the *American Mercury.* My eyes were glued to Lieber's note informing me of my first major sale to a national magazine. "I first tried the other magazines that pay better, but they all turned it down. Mencken took it immediately. He says he wants to see more of your work, and he plans to run your picture and an autobiographical note in the back pages. Have you a photo of yourself? Check is enclosed." The check was for $135.

I went upstairs with Lieber's letter, entered my flat and sat, numbly, in a chair with the letter in my hand, staring at the wall for a long time. At last, at last. I was on my way, and I knew it. Sitting there in a cold room, I felt the deepest happiness I had ever known. Mencken had bought a story of mine. In the quiet of the flat I could feel the blood pounding through my veins. I didn't work that afternoon. I sat around the flat, or stood near the rear windows gazing at the back yards, or walked the bare floors, savoring my happiness. I remembered that at Yaddo one of the writers had remarked that he knew a successful, popular author who had told him he would give a thousand dollars to be published in the *American Mercury*. Was that true? And I recalled the rumors I'd heard at Yaddo to the effect that William Faulkner's "That Evening Sun" and F. Scott Fitzgerald's "Crazy Sunday" had been rejected by all the magazines before Mencken had accepted and published them in the *American Mercury*. Later I found these rumors were based on fact.

I stayed in the flat all afternoon. Toward five o'clock I shaved, put on a clean shirt, and headed for 14th Street. Finally, I found a photographer located on the second floor next to the Tango Gardens. It was a beat-up studio that catered to truck drivers who needed identification snapshots for motor vehicle licenses. To lend the place the authentic air of a studio, the walls were graced with old flyblown photos of Italian weddings and Polish family reunions. A small, unshaven man with a cough came out of a rear room and, before I had spoken a word, asked if I wanted the three-for-fifty-cent snapshots.

"I want a bigger size," I told him. "I'll go as high as a dollar for a single good one." Immediately impressed, he began to fuss with lights and dimmers. At last the flash went off.

"That looked good. It'll be a fifty-cent deposit, mister."

"When will it be ready?"

"Tomorrow morning."

When I came outside and hit 14th Street, with all its color and pulsing life despite the Depression, I felt exalted. I walked a few blocks in a euphoric state, before I caught myself up. What had I accomplished? I had sold a single story. One story.

I walked on, a bit calmer. Suddenly the world seemed exceedingly quiet. Yet when a truck rumbled by and two frightened pigeons fluttered past, I heard the triumphant rush overhead of a thousand war planes.

Spring
Is Always
a Good Time

A young painter's first one-man show, a writer's initial sale of a story to a major magazine—these early events give a thrust to a career, a life.

By the end of the week I had written and sent off to Lieber a new manuscript about the past summer I had spent in the adult camp in the mountains. Instead of my usual fiction, it was a piece of personalized journalism, and I held my breath. Mencken accepted it at once and wrote Lieber from Baltimore: "It's a worthy article, but tell Halper to send me some stories." When I received Lieber's second check, I went out and bought some shirts, a pair of good shoes, and a new suit; I also stopped doing my own laundry. Lieber was beginning to sell stories and novels of his other clients, but he seemed particularly jubilant over these two sales to Mencken. "We'll give him one or two more stories of yours, Albert, then I'll try to place your pieces in other magazines to widen your market and to boost your fees." I was all for his strategy.

I sat in my flat with the oven going, in a state of excitement, trying to plan future work. In my note-book I had notes for additional stories, stories that had been simmering inside me for years. Which ones should I write first? I debated with myself for several days, sitting and mulling over possible choices. Suddenly, looking out the window at the roofs across the yard, I recalled the shop talk I'd heard among older writers out at Yaddo. "It's fine to get short stories into good magazines," they had said, "but there's nothing like a book to put you over."

The recollection of those conversations shook me. Tense and undecided about my next move, I went out to walk along 14th Street, trying to come to a decision. Shoppers, as usual, were surging around Klein's while heavy traffic pounded past Fourth Avenue and the corner bank. The pretzel vendors, the orators shouting on boxes, the hot chestnut sellers with their little fires burning in their little carts, the blind beggars begging for dimes were out in full force, but I paid no attention to them. I passed the apple sellers and bootblacks kneeling in the cold waiting for business, debating in my mind whether to continue writing short stories or to begin the long pull of work involved in a new novel. Be reasonable, be reasonable, I implored myself. You've already got two rejected novels gathering dust in Lieber's office. My God, how much punishment can you take? I walked the streets for over an hour, unable to make up my mind, then returned to the flat where I lay on my cot staring at the ceiling, feeling a headache coming on.

Suddenly I rose from my bed and went to my typewriter, one half of my brain excited, the other half cold as ice. I sat down and wrote Lieber a letter, informing him I wanted to write a novel about young people against the background of 14th Street and Union Square. I said my plan was to make the book lyrical, jazzy, almost like a revue—but with a cohesive, collective story line to cement the whole thing together. The entire outline had jelled within me in less than a minute. I composed a résumé of the novel carefully because I knew he would have to have a concise presentation with which to interest an editor. I typed out the two-page résumé, mailed it, and waited.

In three days Lieber sent me a letter. Viking Press was interested—the same publisher that had rejected my second novel, then had recalled it twice, only to turn it down in the end.

Within a week Lieber had gotten me a contract. Because of the depressed state of the book business, the advance offered by the publisher was small, only $200. Lieber advised me to accept it, and I signed the contract. Standing in his new office on Fifth Avenue and 45th Street, Lieber hovered over me smilingly as I fixed my signature to the contract. "Things are starting to get better for my authors, Albert!" He added that "someone is even interested in dramatizing Caldwell's *Tobacco Road,* even though its sales were only 1,200 copies. You boys will soon be eating chicken instead of beans!"

I spent four weeks carefully outlining the book and scribbling many notes about the main and secondary characters, one half of my brain still excited, the other half still as cold as ice. Then one morning I started typing.

It wasn't a difficult book to write. I let myself go but at the same time always kept myself under control—like a jockey holding the reins firmly on a horse running in the Preakness. At times the book went so fast I had to brake myself for fear I might be out-pacing myself and thus have nothing left for the home-stretch. I lay in bed each night thinking about the next day's writing and hardly slept, but when I got up in the morning I was not tired.

In five weeks I had completed a first draft of one hundred thousand words. It was exhilarating. Except for a single visit from Hedda, I had seen no one and rarely gone outdoors, except to buy groceries. I felt I was running a wonderful, high fever.

After completing the first draft, I waited for the initial excitement to drain away. I lay about the flat enjoying the first pleasant symptoms of exhaustion. It was a gloriously idle, introspective time. It was spring. I didn't know if the book was good or bad, but I felt, somehow, I had accomplished what I had set out to do.

To keep myself occupied during this period, I saw a lot of movies but found myself restless in the darkened theaters and, unable to keep my attention on the action against the screens, I got up and left. Walking along 14th Street, I bought a half a dozen shirts I didn't need. One morning, still feeling I was not ready to look at the draft, I sat down and began a short story. I finished it in two days and mailed it to Lieber. He sent it to Mencken who bought it. A few days later the first story Mencken had accepted was published and when I saw it in print, in the double columns of the *American Mercury,* I felt very happy. Readers and several writers I had met during my summer at Yaddo sent me letters about it; and Lieber told me editors of magazines who had rejected my work in the past were now asking him if I had any stories for them to see.

I sat in my room, twenty-six years old, calm, the exhilaration now gone. I wasn't excited any more. Why was that? What had happened to me? Though I knew to the outside world I hadn't accomplished anything that was in the least spectacular, what I finally succeeded in doing was very important to *me.* And the fact that several members of my family were extremely unhappy about the material I had worked into my stories didn't worry me. "Why do you always write about us?" my oldest brother had complained in a recent letter. "Do you hate us? My

God, can't you pick better subjects?" And my sister wrote: "Listen, Albert, Pa feels just terrible about that last story of yours in the *American Mercury*. Of course you didn't mention our name or anything like that, but do you have to write only about your relatives' *flaws?* We're only human." What was there for me to reply? *They were my material.* I had fictionalized them, enlarged them, foreshortened them, until their personalities on paper, to me, had become more real than they were in actual life. Was I disloyal to them, as my brother and sister had so strongly hinted in their letters? I wanted to answer: "Since leaving Chicago, trying to become a writer, I've revolutionized my life! And it's your tough luck you have now a writer in the family!" But how could they accept this? How could they understand that writing had become my life, and that a writer pursues his special material like a hunter tracking down an animal, his only prayer being that his marksmanship will be accurate?

As for myself, family or no family, I only hoped I had the stamina to last the course, for I felt the immediate years ahead would be a dangerous era, one laced with every kind of political and literary opportunism. Booby-traps had already appeared— slogans and battle-cries from the left adjuring writers to repeat that "The future lies with dialectical materialism!," that "Art is a weapon!" And added to these, new banner-like phrases rolled from the great eastern citadel, that Mecca of Meccas of the faithful followers, where the order had come down to defend the holy words of the Visage himself, the Boss-man with the smiling pipe and the mustache.

Friends
and Ex-Friends

It took me five months to complete the final draft of the novel—a relatively short time in which to write a full-length book. When I finished the script I still didn't know if I had succeeded or failed with my material. I took the novel up to Lieber, and waited.

He was enthusiastic about it. When I came to his office he was grinning from ear to ear. "You pulled it off! And that ending in the snowstorm with Jason walking away in the square, it's like a Chaplin movie—the fade-out is sad, funny—great!"

"You think Best and Guinzburg will like it?"

He laughed. "Don't look so worried. It's good. If Viking rejects it, another house will grab it."

I left somewhat relieved over Lieber's opinion but still worried about the novel's future. I remembered my two unpublished book-length manuscripts in Lieber's files. Was this one any better?

A few days later Lieber sent me a telegram: "Book sold." He could have used up the full ten-word Western Union allotment but, being the actor he sometimes was, he knew the impact of the two-word message would give me the bigger wallop.

I didn't tell Hedda about *Union Square's* acceptance for a week. I felt happy about it but the sale of my first story to Mencken had, somehow, been more special to me.

When I told Hedda about the book's acceptance, she was overjoyed. She said she wanted something to celebrate and remember the event with. She suggested I buy her a ring, so we went into a pawn shop on Sixth Avenue and there, under the lights, an elderly clerk helped us pick out a ring with a small blue stone for six dollars. Then we ate in Il Faro's Restaurant on 14th Street, and went back to my place.

The book was scheduled for fall, a long wait. During the interval I wrote several short stories to take my mind off the novel's publication date. Lieber placed one of my new stories with *Harper's,* and he sold another one to Mencken. He also had acceptances from the *New Republic* and the *North American Review;* and then, because one of the editors at *Harper's,* George Leighton, pressed Lieber for more of my work, I wrote another story which *Harper's* accepted. Mencken was now paying me $150 a story, and *Harper's,* $200. "Oh, we're really rolling now," Lieber wrote me, sending along the checks.

During the late summer the publication date of my novel was suddenly postponed until the following spring. A book club, the Literary Guild, had taken it for its March selection.

Because I had not yet received any royalties yet on *Union Square,* I lived in the tenement until fall, until cold winds started to blow over the back yards toward my windows. Then, on impulse, I moved uptown to a new place on 125th Street, between Fifth and Lenox Avenue, into a two-room, steam-heated apartment over Soling Brothers Clothing Store, in Harlem. I rented the place because Pete, one of my former fellow lodgers, was living with a girl on that block, a wonderful girl who liked to cook, and they were always inviting me to meals, and one day while going to their place I had seen the for-rent sign over Soling Brothers' store. Because the apartment had steam heat and a private bathroom, I took it.

It was Harlem in the Depression, not all-Negro along 125th yet, and you still saw several white faces. During the long days the white shop-keepers stood gloomily inside their doorways, as if waiting for impending bankruptcies; I seldom saw a customer enter their stores. At night, while a chill wind blew along the sidewalk, white prostitutes worked my block and black ones, too—the white women middle-aged and past their prime, the colored ones younger and more attractive. As they approached, I shook my head, and when they learned I lived above the clothing store and was not a potential client, they stopped soliciting me.

I lived above the clothing store all that fall and winter, enjoying the steam heat and going often to Pete's flat down the block where his girl cooked her good meals. Frequently in the evenings I went to the Apollo Theater or the Harlem Opera House where, after buying a ticket for twenty-five cents, I saw the comedy team of Butterbeans and Susie, or Chick Webb's Band, or Lucky Millinder's Band, all great acts.

Nothing unusual happened to me in Harlem, until one day around noon, while I was working, there was a knock on my door. When I opened it I saw a young writer I knew, a talented contributor to small experimental and left-wing magazines; I shall call him Hugo Bookbinder. His face was covered with perspiration and he smiled queerly as he stepped quickly into my place and shut the door.

"I'm glad I found you in. Halper, I'm in a terrible jam. My God, I just laid a prostitute five minutes ago and I'm afraid

I'll catch a dose." The crooked smile took on a pleading quality. "Know anything that'll help me?"

Behind his foolish smile I saw intense worry—because he was married, he was afraid he might infect his wife. I suddenly remembered a conversation I'd overheard between mail clerks on the night shift of the Chicago Post Office.

"Urinate right away," I ordered, pointing to the bathroom.

He obeyed me instantly but when he emerged from the bathroom he still looked worried. "God, I know it was a stupid thing for me to do. But when this tan woman approached me and said it would cost only a dollar, I acted on impulse and went up to her room. You think this one trip to your bathroom will safeguard me?"

"Tell you what. Go to Liggett's at the corner, get a prophylactic and come back here and use it. That way, you should be okay."

He smiled again, oddly, foolishly. "Let me have a buck. I'm broke."

After I gave him the money he hurried to Liggett's, returned, went into the bathroom where he followed the directions on the packet and in a few minutes emerged looking relieved, if somewhat contrite. "Yes, it sure was a stupid thing to do. But Anne's in the hospital about to have a baby and I haven't had a piece in two months. So while I was in this neighborhood working for the boss at my lousy collection job, this woman solicited me, and in a weak moment. . . ." He laughed nervously, and before he left he touched me for another dollar. At the door he tried to grin: "Man, you saved my life, or at least my urinary tract."

This was the sole dramatic incident of my six-months stay on 125th. The area no longer interested me, and I told myself I'd get out in another month when my rent was up.

The day my book was published I got out of bed nervously. I dressed, went to a cafeteria for breakfast, and returned with all the newspapers. There were black headlines on the front pages which, in my excitement, I ignored. I turned at once to the book review section.

My novel got big coverage in all the papers, receiving the prime spots and in some papers running to full columns. The reviews were enthusiastic. Most of the critics had gone the limit in praising the book, two of them stating something to the effect of, "At last we have the first really good proletarian novel. . . ." Reading the reviews pleased me but I gritted my teeth over that cardboard word. I phoned Lieber, who was greatly pleased at the novel's reception. "But did your novel have to come out on a day like this?" he exclaimed. Then I learned the headlines I had ignored had announced a national bank holiday. Having taken the oath of office only two days ago, President Roosevelt, to avert a panic, as his first official act had closed all the banks. Lieber, and Viking Press, were understandably aghast; people wouldn't have money to buy copies of my book. After a week, however, when the banks reopened, my novel started to sell well.

I began to receive fan letters from friends, from strangers. I revisited my old hang-outs along 14th Street, where I listened to warm, congratulatory comments over coffee in the Automat. "Halper, you really caught this area in your book." "It's not only realistic and honest, it's humorous." And a comrade whispered hurriedly to me, "I'm glad you gave it to the phonies in the movement—they had it coming to them for a long time!"

Then, a week later, the review of my book came out in the *New Masses,* and suddenly everything was changed. Michael Gold, the current head guru of left-wing writers, the author of an over-praised, sloppy, sentimental collection of short stories dealing with the East Side, declared in the *New Masses* that my novel was a gold brick, an utter bourgeois sham. His furious, scathing review screamed from the page stating that writers like Sinclair Lewis, Upton Sinclair, Carl Van Doren, Horace Gregory, Lewis Gannett and others who had praised the book were "reactionary liberals" who were totally ignorant of the fermenting revolutionary stream flowing through America.

Viking was not displeased by comrade Gold's blast—they felt the review would actually help the book's sales. Lieber's reaction to the *New Masses* attack was almost traumatic. When I paid him a visit in his office he appeared pained and his manner was strangely evasive.

"Maybe you shouldn't have been so severe with those young people in that party scene in your book. The scene where you poked fun at those poets and hangers-on."

"But Max, it was a funny scene based on the truth. I myself attended such a party."

He looked troubled. "I know, I know. But do you have to give our enemies such ammunition?"

"But you liked that scene, and others, too, that Gold panned in his review."

He gnawed his lip. "I can have second thoughts about it, can't I? The Party doesn't like a lot of other stuff in your book."

"Look, Max, some of the characters might be caricatures, but most of them are based on real people. Besides, I'm not a Party member."

This last statement troubled him deeply. "Whatever you may think about the Party, you ought to be in their corner. They're trying to make a better America." It was his blind side again, which I knew so well now. There was nothing for me to do but to attempt to turn this dour moment into comedy.

"I'll send an explanatory note to Stalin, Max." But this time he waved my attempt aside.

"Don't make a joke of it, Albert." He looked oddly saddened. "Whatever faults the Party has, it's deeply involved in bettering the lives of the masses." I made another go at comedy, the only tack for me to follow with an agent and friend who had worked so hard on my behalf.

"Max, you think my book will bring down the structure of the Party?"

He smiled at last. "Never mind, never mind." As I left his office he seemed to be in a somewhat better mood.

That evening I had occasion to visit an acquaintance downtown, a teacher in the public school system who was trying desperately to write in his spare time and who had, for weeks, begged me to look at some of his work. When I came out of the subway at 14th Street and began walking east, I met some young people I knew who suddenly turned their heads to avoid recognizing me. These were mostly the same people who had rushed up to me recently in the Automat, before Gold's review came out, and had so warmly congratulated me. At Third Avenue I met Hugo Bookbinder.

"Bastard, counter-revolutionary!" he muttered as he passed me quickly, without stopping.

When I reached the apartment of the young writer I had come to see, his wife stood at the top of the stairs and in a friendly voice said: "I'm sorry, Albert, but Fred is sick and wants to postpone seeing you until another time. But thanks."

"Sure." I understood. I rode the subway back uptown to 125th. "Ah, forget them! To hell with 'em all!" I told myself. Yet I had been hurt.

The Bookish
Establishment

The adverse reaction from the *New Masses,* the Party's
official cultural organ, didn't haunt me for long. In fact, in two
days I had fully recovered from the blast. Unlike poor Kevin
O'Malley, who had said he needed the Party to fulfill himself,
I felt no attachment to it whatsoever. I was sympathetic to some
of its aims, as were many non-Party intellectuals, but these broad
aims, I knew, were not the exclusive property of any political
organization—anyone could be in favor of them—and conse-
quently I didn't feel any sense of loyalty to the Party line.

One day I walked into Lieber's office and was surprised
to see a new secretary. She was New England Yankee, a tall,
attractive girl whom I shall call Nellie Hampton. Lieber introduced us. She extended her hand. Her face was warm and open.
With an amused smile, she said, "I liked your *Union Square,*
but I think you can do better."

Lieber turned, frowning. "What?" Then he exploded in

laughter. "Albert, of course she's kidding." But I wasn't sure. When I left his office his new secretary's face stuck with me. She was a beauty, and had the kind of mocking sense of humor I liked in a woman.

In the lobby of Lieber's building I ran into Louis Adamic who was on his way up to see Lieber. I'd met Adamic some time ago in our agent's office and we had become rather close friends; our political views at the time were almost identical.

"I saw Gold's review," he laughed. "You rat, you deviationist!" He clapped me warmly on the back.

Adamic was an interesting and complicated man, with genuine literary ability and great personal dignity. Tall and lanky, Adamic somewhat resembled Henry Fonda, even moving with an awkward grace similar to the movie star's. Because he was five years older than I, he sometimes talked to me in a fatherly manner. When he became excited he stammered badly and his chin quivered so much that I turned my head away. But other times he could be relaxed and smiling and his speech was perfectly normal. He had a hearty explosive laugh and loved to listen to jokes, though he himself was an inept story teller who always ruined the punch line. During the first stage of our friendship, he had told me a lot about himself.

Born in Yugoslavia, he had emigrated to the United States when he was fourteen. He had come alone, without his family, making contact with one or two distant relatives here. Somehow he had managed to learn English quickly by holding down a succession of odd jobs. At eighteen, he had enlisted in the army during World War I and saw service in France. Upon discharge, he began wandering across the country, landing in California where, after more assorted odd jobs, he opened a bookstore in San Francisco. He started writing about labor, drawing upon his experiences and observations. After selling his first articles to magazines, he wrote an autobiographical work, *Laughing in the*

Jungle, which he followed by *Dynamite*, a history of violence in the American labor movement, both books published prior to our first meeting.

Adamic's wife Stella was a very attractive girl from the Bronx, and they lived with her widowed mother on Jerome Avenue near 168th Street. I began to be invited there to eat Stella's mother's very good cooking. Stella had a wonderful smile, she loved Louis very much, and she studied modern dancing seriously in hopes of becoming a member of a recognized dance group. At that time Martha Graham, Doris Humphrey, and Mary Wigman were beginning to establish their large, underground reputations. Louis was totally uninterested in Stella's aspirations and one night I became aware of a cruel side of his character when he denigrated Stella's talent in my presence. "Fool, why do you want to become a dancer?" he shot out at her. "It's just a damn waste of your time!" Stella cowered in her chair. But these spats were infrequent, and overall I felt it was a very good marriage.

Now he clapped me on the shoulder again in the lobby of Lieber's office building. "I tell you it's really an honor, a decoration of merit to be panned by the *New Masses!*" he shouted, accompanying his shout with his explosive laugh. "They roasted both of my books, too!" He let fly another explosive laugh, after which he changed the subject. "Look, stop turning me down. I'm your friend, I want to help you make your debut."

I knew what he meant. In New York the author of a successful book is sometimes sought after at gatherings, and invitations had come to me in the mail, or through my publisher. Louis had been urging me strongly to start mixing with people in the book world. "It doesn't pay to be a hermit, some of them can do you a lot of good." He did not mean it strictly opportunistically but just as sensible advice. He himself had become friendly with many people in the literary life of New York.

A few days later, after Louis Adamic's fresh prodding, I began attending several cocktail and dinner parties of the bookish establishment; and it was through him that I met a small, influential coterie made up of intellectuals whose political orientation, or stance, fell shakily between liberalism and the radical left. The members of this group, men and women both, were highly educated, extremely witty and clever, and older than I. Their conversation glittered with a political sophistication that was at once pleasantly shocking and novel to me—a kind of jet-set conversation of the thirties. At cocktail parties their favorite game was to score political bulls'-eyes all evening long, utilizing their knowledge of the current economic scene and private gossip from allegedly secret sources. Some of their quips were delightful, others vicious.

The cleverest and the wickedest of these people was Ben Stolberg. A small, plump man in his early forties who lived from hand to mouth—no one knew how he managed to pay the rent on his apartment or how he continued to eat in good restaurants —Ben Stolberg had the round, smooth face of a gourmet, the watchful eyes of a womanizer, and the dagger-like tongue of a true court gossip. Once, at a literary gathering, when Carl Van Doren, the tall, elegantly turned-out critic and biographer and a man active on many literary fronts, went to the bedroom for his overcoat and left graciously after thanking the hostess for the evening, Ben Stolberg waited a dramatic moment, then said in a soft, silken voice: "There goes the floor-walker of American literature." Carl Van Doren at the time was almost an Olympian figure, and many guests sucked in their breath at the daring of the remark. Then the laughter exploded—and to most people who were there that evening Carl Van Doren's stature was wrecked forever.

On another evening Stolberg destroyed an important writer's reputation while dining in Luchow's with literary friends.

I wasn't present at the destruction, but Louis Adamic told me about it. A gigantic writer who had an equally gigantic fame during the thirties entered the restaurant with a woman. Sitting down at a table, he began waving his arms, calling for drinks and food, lots of food. Luchow's, famed for the generous portions it served its patrons, obliged, and the writer was soon draining glasses and dramatically devouring the courses the waiter set before him. When he paid the check and departed with his partner, Ben Stolberg waited a long, silent moment, then turned to the others at his table and began batting his short arms about and grunting.

"Please—I don't want food and booze, I want to drain oceans, eat continents, gulp railroads, lay a million broads. I'm just a southern mountain boy with a big appetite!" The friends at Stolberg's table roared, and from that evening on no one present, as well as others who subsequently heard about Ben Stolberg's performance, could ever quite take Thomas Wolfe seriously again.

Stolberg had other notable performances to his credit. His take-offs on John L. Lewis and General Hugh Johnson, chief of the National Recovery Act, had become classics among his coterie. Stolberg genuinely admired John L. Lewis but he could not refrain from cruelly imitating the facial expression and rather pompous voice of the country's most important labor leader. It was a merciless sport, played to perfection by a master, but occasionally it left a bad taste in the mouth. Besides his party performances, Stolberg was an astute and talented writer in the fields of labor and economics. When given assignments by editors, he wrote penetrating articles which were carefully read by labor leaders and government officials. Even his enemies on the left read his writings assiduously, for it was widely rumored he possessed pipelines to important Washington sources. Later, Stolberg landed a lucrative job with a major garment workers union, but to the time of his death from a heart attack he remained a parlor performer par excellence.

I soon stopped going to these cocktail parties and gatherings. The people I met at them were charming, the drinks were always good, but I felt many of the members of this crowd, whatever their celebrity, had feet of clay. When I told Louis Adamic about my feelings, he laughed.

"Of course, you're right. But they're the best we have, and most times they're fun."

"He's in
the Underground..."

Because of the rather good sale of *Union Square* in the book stores, Viking Press decided to publish a collection of my short stories. I was very pleased when Lieber informed me that Best and Guinzburg had agreed to bring out the book; most of the stories dealt with my family and I considered them to constitute my best effort so far.

I was working hard on new stories and had about forgotten the hostility of my former friends down on 14th Street over the publication of *Union Square*. Suddenly one day everything seemed to change for me along the unfriendly left. It was as though a sunny, moist wind had started blowing up from Miami. Certain people once more began to smile and greet me warmly whenever I ran into them downtown. If anything, their greetings were now more effusive than before.

"How are you, Halper?" "You look great." "Say, there's going to be a party tonight at . . ."

The reason for this sudden change was simple.

After an absence of three years, I had returned to Chicago for a brief visit with my family. My sister had married a young doctor who, in order to supplement his fees during the lean times, had taken a post with the Chicago Health Department, as a public school doctor. One morning in their apartment my brother-in-law John said: "Want to kill a few hours by going with me on my inspection rounds?" We got into his car and I accompanied him into the grammar schools on the impoverished West Side where I was born. As soon as we entered a school the corridor bells rang and the kids lined up in the classrooms, showing their outstretched palms, sticking out their tongues for the doctor to inspect, and standing patiently while he peered down their throats and into their ears. Most of the children looked undernourished; they stood in their worn, ragged clothes, big-eyed and silent as my brother-in-law looked them over thoroughly and patted their heads. The rest of the morning was heart-breaking. After our visits to the schools we went into homes where the children were absent from classes because of illness, and here John gave toxoid injections and handed out pills. Before we entered the first house, he warned me: "Don't touch the furniture or place your hat on a chair. You might take home bugs." We left a trail of feverish, screaming children who had received injections; more than once, at John's command, I had to hold a child by force until he could get the needle in properly. The mothers stood by tense and silent, watching as their terrified children shrieked. In one house I couldn't get a strong grip on a young boy who wriggled out of my grasp again and again, screaming and spitting at me. He was burning up with fever and his mother yelled at him to behave. "It's for your own good— I'll give you a nickel, a nickel!" I finally pinned him down on the floor while John slid in the needle.

When I returned to New York, I wrote a piece about it

entitled "A Morning with the Doc." Lieber couldn't sell it any-where. His secretary, Nellie Hampton, told me with a smile when I entered the office, "I knew you could do better than *Union Square*."

"Why do you say that?" I knew she was taunting me in her bantering way, but she had begun to irritate me lately. What kind of a girl was she anyway?

"Never mind," she smiled. "It's a good piece."

"Yes," Lieber broke in, "but we just can't sell it. No magazine will touch it. One editor told me it's a propaganda pitch against the system." His secretary laughed but his old anger had returned and he glared at her. "He wrote it as pure factual journalism, not a line of propaganda in it!"

The next day, without consulting me, Lieber sent the ar-ticle to the *New Masses,* who accepted it immediately. When it was published, the old warmth seemed to return to the hearts of my downtown acquaintances; my appearance in the sacred pages of the *New Masses* had, in their opinion, brought me back into the fold.

Lieber was especially glad my piece was published in the *New Masses*. During the past year, despite its Party stand, it had become an influential magazine with an ever-widening reader-ship among liberals, radicals, and students. Its pages had begun to feature work of non-Communist authors, writers like Sherwood Anderson, Edmund Wilson, Thomas Mann, John Dos Passos, and Malcolm Cowley. One day, out of the blue, Hemingway mailed into the *New Masses* office an unsolicited manuscript con-cerning the plight of distressed World War I veterans who were living under abominable conditions in Key West; a moving piece of writing, it far surpassed the articles on fishing and big game sport he was sending to *Esquire* at the time. With the appearance of such prestigious authors in the *New Masses,* there soon arose a new literary snobbism of the left; many writers were now very anxious to contribute to its pages. Other magazines, to be sure, were now beginning to publish, tentatively, occasional pieces concerning mass unemployment and the current social crisis gripping the nation. But only in the columns of the *New Masses* did a writer seem to find the burgeoning, avid audience of awakened American readers.

A week after my article appeared in the *New Masses* the doorbell of my new apartment on Lexington and 90th Street rang, and a delegation of Post Office workers from Grand Central tramped into my place and informed me of the plight of the underpaid postal workers who tossed mail in the big, dusty, unventilated mailing room.

"We got your address from the *New Masses,* and we're from the union. We know you worked in the Post Office. Please write a story about us."

They stayed all evening, and I sent out for coffee, and we swapped stories of Post Office life, and in the end I took notes and wrote a piece, and the *New Masses* published it.

This second entry of mine in the *New Masses* advanced my name further in the hierarchy of writers now identified, by certain critics, with the left. For me, it was just a piece of reportage, but to many vocal *New Masses* Party readers it became an added argument for the slogan: "Art is a weapon!"

The day after my Post Office piece in the *New Masses* appeared, I was sitting in a big cafeteria on Fourth Avenue and 28th Street, a place patronized by cab drivers, office workers, and shipping clerks. It was noon and as I sipped my coffee I overheard my name being mentioned. I turned my head slowly and saw a young man and a girl talking earnestly at the next table; the girl held a copy of the *New Masses* and sticking out of the pocket of the young man was a copy of the *Daily Worker.*

"I know Halper belongs, he's in the underground," the girl was saying to her companion. "That's why he never speaks at the rallies or the meetings."

"Did you hear it from an unimpeachable source?"

"Certainly, certainly I did . . ."

Nellie

Because *Union Square* had sold well, I suddenly found myself an anomaly—in the depths of the Depression I was moderately affluent. It was a peculiar situation for a young writer in the thirties to be in. I bought more new clothes, found myself strolling along Fifth Avenue looking at shop windows, and began haunting art galleries to view the work of painters I liked. Like many writers, I was strongly drawn to painting. Back in Chicago I had sometimes spent long wintry Sunday afternoons in the Art Institute on Michigan Avenue, torn between the wonderful collections of the Italian primitives and the French impressionists. But during the past three years of my stay in New York I had been so involved in the struggle to become a writer that I had visited the Metropolitan Museum only twice. Now my interest in painting seemed to surface again. I wasn't wealthy enough to purchase works of established artists whose paintings really excited me, so I bought nothing. It was pleasant, however, to walk into Rehn's, the Downtown Gallery, Rosenberg's and Knoedler's, to see the work of talented modern Americans of stature and then to view the works of the great European artists.

On days when I wasn't working, I sometimes dropped into the studios of two painters I knew, Gregorio Prestopino and Louis Guglielmi, who lived in leaky, unheated studios in a loft building on 23rd Street near Sixth Avenue. If they weren't working we talked an afternoon away, sitting around Presto's or Gug's pot-belly stoves, arguing about art, politics, and the Depression. The ever present familiar odors of canvas and paint reminded me of the fall and winter I had lived with Nels and Pete in the Bronx. Often the question of money dominated Prestopino's and Guglielmi's conversation; they were constantly worried about the problems of eating and paying the rent. Later, both obtained jobs on the Federal Art Project, the stipend being about ninety dollars a month, which gave them some measure of security.

I could have purchased fine paintings from either artist at ridiculously low prices but, in my stupidity, I never did, though I admired their work. Guglielmi, who labored slowly and painstakingly, offered me a gem of an oil for one hundred dollars, that had taken him months to complete; it was an East Side street scene, depicting a group of Italians solemnly carrying huge religious candles in a church parade. I regretted my indecision later, but my modest affluence had followed years of penury, and I hung back.

One day my visits to the galleries and to my two friends stopped abruptly. I started work on a new novel, and as I got my teeth into the material painting ceased to interest me. I filled over a hundred pages with notes and tentative outlines, recalling and reliving four years of my life spent in a Chicago electrotype foundry; and at night as I lay in bed entire scenes and pages of dialogue flashed across my mind, keeping me from sleeping. It was the usual time of frenzy every novelist goes through before the actual period of writing begins.

Now that I had a phone, Lieber called me at least once a week to inquire about the progress of the novel and to prod me into working harder. He hadn't seen a line of it, and I laughed at him. "It's about a boy who works in the stockyards and eats his mother, then kills his father. Very Freudian."

"Don't laugh, don't laugh. Many writers get soft after their first novel is published, then sit on their asses and dream for the next ten years."

"I never sit on my ass, Max. I sit on a cushion when I work."

"Never mind, never mind," he lectured, but he always hung up with a chortle.

In my comfortable one-room apartment on upper Lexington Avenue I looked at the bare walls, at my library stacked in uneven piles on the floor and wondered how many pages the new book would run. I hungered to cram all the characters I'd known in that foundry into colorful solid scenes; I recalled the arguments between the molders, and the company's annual rowdy picnics held on the prairie west of Chicago, and the mysterious breakdown of that new labor-saving machine that had sent the place into an uproar. I remembered, too, the suicide in the company toilet, and I recalled the morning one of the finishers confided to me that he was lonely and yearned to rent a room in the apartment of some wealthy widow. "Please put a want-ad in the paper for me. No objections to any children, y' understand." I wanted to control this material, and the only way to find out if I was capable of doing so was to begin the first chapter, then write the second, then start the third.

Looking for a release from the tension of writing, I sometimes dropped into Lieber's office to talk a bit, though never about my work. Lieber's conversation always circled about politics and labor—the growth of the new C.I.O., unionization efforts, the bloody riots before the gates of Detroit's auto plants, and the foul-up of the N.R.A. program in Washington. Occasionally Lieber's new secretary, Nellie Hampton, would join the discussion. With a slow smile on her lips, she would look at Lieber, then at me and say, "It will all come out in the wash." Comments like these would nettle Lieber.

"Yes, yes. One profound remark deserves another."

It was hard to remain angry with his secretary however. She was extremely competent, all the clients liked her, and besides she had given up a position as assistant editor in a major publishing house to learn the literary agency business and she was working the first year in Lieber's office without salary. Wearing her simple but expensive Lord & Taylor dresses she sat with an amused calm behind her desk, and ran the office efficiently, reading scripts and sending letters of encouragement to writers. If she didn't like a new story she would write: "This is a dud. You can do better than that." Lieber's irritations were short-lived because he knew he had a good thing going with this girl in his office.

Returning from my agent one afternoon, I found Pete, my old roommate, pacing the sidewalk before my building. His face was haggard as he followed me up to my apartment; the girl he was living with on 125th Street was pregnant.

"My God, my God," he repeated over and over, in agony. "All of a sudden after two years, after two years, she said in the middle of the night she couldn't stand the feel of rubber! So like a fool I gave in to her, and the next month, bang, she missed." He lit a cigarette nervously. "You're the only guy I know who's got money, or I wouldn't be here asking for it."

"How soon do you need the money?"

"Tomorrow. We have the appointment with the doctor all set up. He wants cash."

"I'll have it for you," I promised. "Call for it here."

He thanked me voluably and left. That spring there seemed to be a sudden rash of pregnancies. During the next month two more friends borrowed seventy-five dollars from me "to take her to the doctor."

One evening my doorbell rang and Hedda came up the stairs looking pale and nervous. She hadn't phoned beforehand.

"What's the matter?" I asked.

She sat down in a chair, staring at me imploringly. "Darling, I'm in so much damn trouble."

I knew at once what she meant. We were soon to become involved in the same experience.

"How late is it?"

"Two months." She looked at me silently, appealingly, sitting with her knees oddly pressed together. Then she began talking rapidly of marriage, of a future together, and she promised she'd never stand in the way of my writing or my career. Still stunned, I did not reply at once. Her words were those of a girl deeply in love offering a man everything he did not need at this time. "Don't you care for me, darling? After all these years?"

Of course I cared for her. But how could I tell her I wasn't ready, for anybody? I had seen too many promising young writers and painters get married, have children, after which I had witnessed their silence, their creative deaths because of the responsibilities that went with marriage and a family. I wanted to explain to her why I had to keep my life simple, to live alone, to work alone, but I remained silent before the sight of her taut suffering figure. Yes, mine was a selfish life perhaps, but it suited me fine during these years. Yes, yes! Look, show me a writer or painter worth his salt who was not selfish and ruthless! Show me! These thoughts raced through my head. Hedda cringed as she watched my face. I tried, unsuccessfully, not to raise my voice.

"How did it happen? How? When?" I felt trapped. I was sweating.

"I don't know—I swear I don't know!" She actually

wrung her hands, like women in grade B movies. We stared at each other helplessly for a long time. We were trapped in one of those "accidents," our silence seemed to signify.

The next afternoon I took Hedda to a doctor in the east eighties, in Yorkville. I got his phone number from Pete and had made the appointment. After I paid the doctor his fee his nurse told me in a soft voice to see a movie or to take a long walk for two hours. I went to Central Park and tramped around the big reservoir several times until my legs grew tired, then headed back to the east eighties. When I rang the bell the nurse stuck her surprised face out the door.

"You're too early."

"But you said two hours." I glanced at my watch.

She hesitated. "All right, you can come inside. Your wife is resting."

A few minutes later I entered the small room where Hedda was lying, her eyes closed. The smell of a hospital rose from her and I was frightened. With her eyes still closed, she reached out and clutched my hand.

"Oh, I'm so glad you're here! I love you . . . we won't fight any more. . . ."

The nurse whispered, "Your wife will be all right," and withdrew.

A half hour later I took Hedda to my place in a taxi. She was brave throughout the night and only bit her lips now and then when she asked for a glass of water. "It won't make any difference to us, will it, darling?"

I shook my head. "Of course not." But to myself I said: "This has got to stop, I can't spoil this girl's life. This has got to finish." The next morning I sent her home in a taxi.

Despite this, I somehow managed to continue working on my new novel. I was now deeply into it, had written several hundred pages and did not stop to reread what I had finished but kept on hammering out the scenes. Insistent, Lieber phoned me twice a week. "Can't I get a look at it? Viking is anxious to know something about it." I tried to avoid showing him the unfinished manuscript but as his phone calls continued at last I gave in.

"I'll type up a quick second draft of the first seventy-five pages, but I warn you it still needs polishing."

"Of course, of course. Don't you think I know? Seventy-five pages is fine, if you can't grab the reader in seventy-five you'll never hold him, right?"

A week later I went to his office with the first section of the manuscript. Returning to my apartment, I felt a letdown and was unable to work for two days. I waited for his opinion. I hadn't wanted to show him those pages, but he had bullied me into it. On the third day he phoned me. His voice was guarded even though he said he liked what he had read. "But you have so many characters, Albert. A hundred or more. I hope you have a great ending for it, to pull it off."

"I'm sorry I showed those pages to you, Max."

"No, no, they're good. Really. Come down to the office and we'll go over it."

When I reached his office the next day he had the manuscript spread out on his table. He was friendly and said he had taken the liberty to pencil in suggestions for changes and cuts.

"You're not being very tactful, Max," Miss Hampton called out from her desk in the outer office. "He hasn't finished the book."

Instead of shouting at his secretary, Lieber reddened a bit. "Maybe she's right. But I've known you so long, Albert, I took the liberty anyway." We sat down and discussed what I had written and some of his suggestions were valid and some were terrible, especially his penciled suggestions that I put some comments in the mouths of my characters about labor. During the last year I had begun to watch him on this because I knew his hardening political beliefs had begun to interfere with his literary judgment. When we rose from the table he said somewhat encouragingly, "Your opening needs a little cutting but it grabs the reader." He didn't say anything about the rest of the pages and I had begun to walk out with the envelope under my arm when he added: "Miss Hampton took your script home last night and read it. She told me she liked it. Talk to her about it. I have to go to lunch with an editor now but stay here for fifteen minutes and listen to what she has to say. Miss Hampton, I'll be back in a couple of hours." Grabbing up his expensive Cavanaugh hat from a chair, he departed.

"I'll be right with you, Mr. Halper," she called from the other office, "as soon as I finish this short note to a starving third-rate writer."

I sat alone in Lieber's office and waited. Nellie Hampton was still an enigma to me. What, I wondered, was behind that calm, amused smile. During our first encounters she hadn't struck me as being very acute in a literary way; yet in the office she had made several penetrating and unexpectedly intelligent statements about writing and politics which had surprised me a little. A month ago, before I had hit my working stride on my new novel, I had begun dropping into Lieber's office more often, always casually, keeping my hat on, not staying too long. Then I had begun visiting the office when I knew Lieber would most likely be out to lunch. I wasn't fooling myself. This girl, this very original, opinionated girl, intrigued me. I noticed other male clients beginning to put in an appearance frequently to inquire how their last story was doing. Lieber's office sometimes almost resembled a small social club.

"I'll be goddamned if I'm going to serve tea here," I once heard Nellie say ferociously, with an accompanying laugh. "What are you jerks looking for, a mother?" And the three or four writers who had been present, myself included, had laughed oddly, embarrassedly. Once I saw a client reach for a second piece of chocolate out of a box of candy on her desk. "Don't be a selfish prick," she told him. He drew back at once, not knowing how to take this comment, not knowing how to reconcile her personality with the shock of her words. Leaving the office that afternoon with three of the writers, I heard them discussing her earnestly.

"She's wonderful but tough." "Knows all the answers." "I feel she's essentially kind underneath it all." "Yeah? You should have heard her give out the four-letter words a few days ago to a client who started to get fresh. Brother!" "Well, no one will ever get to first base with her, I guess . . ."

I heard her chair scrape now in the outer office. Her pleasant voice reached me. "You can bring your script in here now, Mr. Halper. Maybe we can talk about it."

I carried the pages into her outer office and sat in a chair near her desk. We began to go over the first few pages. She flipped them rather rapidly, shaking her head over many of Lieber's penciled suggestions. "Oh dear," she said worriedly, "I hope Max isn't starting to become a literary shit."

"Why do you say that?"

"Well, look at this note he made on page ten," she pointed. "You know, where you wrote your introductory description of the office boy, about his head, to save the cost of future hair-cuts, that was shaved to the skull and looked a little too big on his skinny neck and resembled a big, gray, old-fashioned frosted gas lamp. What the hell's wrong with that? It's good writing. And here Max penciled, 'Too realistic.' " She threw back her head and laughed. "Sometimes his criticism can be way off, can't it?"

"Well, maybe. But he's still about the best agent around," I said, not wanting to be disloyal.

"Of course he is. The rest are god-awful." She flipped a

few more pages, again rather rapidly. "Of course you know this needs some polishing, Mr. Halper."

"I told that to Max."

She bent over another page and laughed. "This is good. About one of the owners' entrance, the first time the reader meets him, at the very moment there's a big crisis in the shop. It's a dramatic scene. You ought to be a playwright. And the colorful way you describe his *ears*."

"I'm glad you like a few things in the script." I was starting to feel a little better now, after Lieber's criticism. "I don't want to follow *Union Square* with a poor book."

"Oh, you won't. I think you've got hold of something good."

I began to put the pages into a large envelope. "Thanks for your good criticism, Miss Hampton."

"Oh, you're welcome. It needs polishing but it's all there. Don't look so discouraged, Mr. Halper."

"I'm not discouraged. Just a little tired." I tried to smile as I left.

A few days later Lieber phoned me. "I've changed my mind about your new book, Albert. It's got some good things in it. Miss Hampton really likes it. It needs polishing, a lot of it maybe. She's offered to work with you on it when you get further on with it, editing it. It will have to be after hours and you two can use my office. What do you think about it?"

"I'll think it over." I wasn't too happy when I hung up; I smelled their worry about my script.

I didn't phone her for over a month. Lieber had stopped calling me. I was working hard and my telephone remained silent. When, after a great deal of effort, I finally finished a complete first draft which ran to over five hundred pages, I phoned her.

"I thought you'd never call, Mr. Halper. What took you

so long? Max and I thought you had committed suicide or something. Of course I'd like to see what you've done."

"When would you have time?" I had worked so hard on the draft and I had lived without seeing anyone during this period that her clear, buoyant voice over the phone suddenly made me feel confused and a little unsure of myself.

"Well, how about this evening? I'll be here."

That evening around five-thirty I rode the subway to Grand Central and walked through the home-bound crowds of office workers and commuters, carrying my manuscript. She was alone in Lieber's office, going over a client's short story. She looked up from her work cheerfully. "Hello. You're not dead after all, though you do look beat." She opened the big envelope I laid on her desk and without saying anything began reading the first fifty pages—the early chapters she had seen some time ago. I watched in silence as she penciled notes lightly in the margins, and I waited for her reaction.

"It's a hell of a lot better, really. You've cut and you've also done some good rewriting. I'd like to take the whole script home and read it and make notes on it and then we can discuss it. Is that okay with you?"

"Sure."

"Don't look so discouraged, Mr. Halper. I said that to you before."

"I'm not discouraged. Just a little tired." Again I tried to smile as I left.

We met two or three times a week after office hours, to work on the book. At first our conferences were painful to me because she had made suggestions for major changes. I didn't mind the minor ones but the big ones hurt. In my mind I began to question her judgment because *Union Square* had been accepted virtually intact. But this was a different kind of book, jammed with characters from start to finish, and she kept saying:

"You've simply got to keep the main story moving constantly, without letup. It's that kind of a book." After these gloomy sessions I sat alone in my apartment and finally figured out the big changes myself, which were different from her suggested ones. When I typed them up she said they were fine. "In fact they're better than mine, Mr. Halper."

I began to look forward to these evenings in the office with her. The book was getting tighter, better. In my apartment I kept polishing and cutting conscientiously and submitting the new pages for further criticism. My strength was being drained away and in its place I began to feel that marvelous fatigue I had experienced while finishing my last book.

All during this time, throughout our conferences and meetings, my feelings about Lieber's secretary were simple yet somehow complicated. Seated next to her, with the pages spread out on her desk, I was often conscious of the smell of her skin, the faint fragrance of her hair as I watched her indicating possible cuts or revisions. Like other of Lieber's clients I sometimes felt a hunger for her but I always checked myself, knowing she never dated any of the writers and feeling she was impregnable. In my fatigued condition that was all right with me.

Our final evening in the office lasted longer than usual. A charwoman came in to mop and dust and give us sidelong glances as she banged the waste-baskets, then withdrew. We had had only a sandwich and coffee around six-thirty and at eleven we were still working. We had come to the last page of the manuscript-but somehow it was awkward, lacking the ultimate feel and rhythm I wanted. Finally, with an effort, by cutting and revising, we attained what I was striving for.

"Well, Mr. Halper, I think we made it. Goddammit, I feel weak as a kitten from all this goddam work."

I said I was truly grateful for all the time she had given my manuscript, and I didn't know how to thank her adequately.

"If you ever open up your own agency I'll quit Lieber," I said this half-kiddingly, though I think I almost meant it.

She laughed. "Don't give me any of that crap. Or I'll throw it right back at you." She suddenly caught herself. "Oh, I'm sorry. I'm supposed to be a lady, aren't I?"

I smiled through my exhaustion. "You're not fooling me."

She reddened. "You mean to say you've seen through my act, after all this time?"

"Sure."

She looked embarrassed but half pleased. "I don't know how to take that, Mr. Halper."

"Oh, you're still a tough person. To all the clients of this office."

"Including you?"

"Sure."

She reddened again. "About your book. I really think it's cut to the bone, and I think Viking will like it. Now don't thank me any more."

I helped her with her coat, then we turned out the office lights, closed the door and walked to the elevator in the deserted corridor. The silent building had a pleasant feeling, with its rows of darkened offices and covered typewriters seen dimly through glass partitions. I pressed the elevator buzzer and we stood waiting. At last the watchman came up in the car, with a rounds-clock looped around his neck with a leather strap.

"It's raining hard," he said. "You got your rubbers?"

We hesitated in the doorway of the lobby. An empty Fifth Avenue was black with pouring rain. "Didn't I tell you?" said the watchman, who locked the doors of the building behind us.

"Can I buy you a meal, or a drink?" I asked. I held my manuscript under my arm.

"It's so late. I think I'll grab a taxi and head for home."

"I just thought I'd ask. And I want to thank you again for your work, for I *must* thank you twice."

She hesitated. "All right, about the meal. But let's go Dutch."

I laughed. "You're still a tough one. But okay."

We walked in the rain to a bar and grill on Third Avenue which was almost empty at this time of the night. We each ordered veal scallopini, and as the waiter was leaving the table I told him to bring us a bottle of red wine. The food turned out not bad, the wine better. I looked across the table at her empty plate.

"Christ, that was good. I ate like a horse tonight." She took her mirror from her purse and held her lip-stick to her lips. "Are you married, Mr. Halper?"

"Not yet."

"You have a semi-married look about the eyes sometimes."

"I always look half-married when I'm tired. You should see me when I'm not tired. I look like a traveling salesman who scores in every town." I knew I shouldn't have said that.

For the third time that evening she reddened. She snapped her purse shut. "Here, let's see that check. I'm paying half, remember?"

I left a tip at the table and we shared the bill at the cashier's desk. Outside it was chilly and still raining. The wind blew down Third Avenue, the rain dripped from the El overhead. I raised an arm and yelled for a taxi, but all the passing cabs were taken on this lousy night. I kept trying to get a cab, but with no success.

"What part of town do you live in, Mr. Halper?"

"Lexington, near Ninetieth Street."

She told me where she lived—a dozen blocks north.

"You can drop me off on your way home."

"Okay, fine." I kept signaling to taxis, but still no luck.

"It's hopeless. Look, are you game to walk? My place isn't that far."

"Sure. Why not? After I see you to your place, I can get a subway at Sixty-eighth and Lex." We started hiking in the rain; "What a lousy night."

"I think it's divine, Mr. Halper. With all that good wop food inside me, I think it's heaven. Excuse the denigration of the Italian people, because they're my favorite underprivileged minority."

"Sure," I laughed.

"You're Jewish, aren't you, Mr. Halper?"

"My parents are." I laughed again. "What are you?"

"New England scum. My great-grandfather made his pile crookedly, in mortgages. He laundered his money with a bit of church charity. My God, what divine wet rain."

We sloshed up Third Avenue, block after block. "Only one more street to go. Lord, my feet are soaking wet. How're yours, Mr. Halper?"

"Soaked. But that wine will keep the flu away."

At her street, we turned left; it was a street lined with small, expensive looking brownstones, off Park Avenue.

"You live in one of these?"

"Oh, not me. I live in one that's cut up into small apartments. This is it, the next building. Care to come up for a cup of hot coffee?"

Holding my script, I felt beat. I looked up the deserted street, at the rain slanting past an arc lamp. My socks were wet in my shoes.

"You look frozen. I'll give you a pair of dry ski socks. You can leave right after you drink your coffee." With a smile she put a hand on my arm. "Come on, don't be a twirp. Do what mother says." She pulled my coat sleeve hard, and I followed her into the building, half amused, half irritated.

Her small apartment was modestly but expensively furnished, with dully shined mahogany period pieces; there was a Persian rug on the floor.

"I'll start the coffee in a second. Take your shoes and socks off. The ski socks may be a trifle small but they'll stretch." She went into the bedroom and returned with a pair of white woollen socks which she tossed to me across the room. "Squirm into those, Buck, they're from my rah-rah collitch days. I'll put the coffee on now, after which I'll chase you home."

The socks felt tight but warm. I leaned back in a soft chair. My wet jacket hung in the hall. I felt tired but relaxed. I knew I wouldn't tell any of Lieber's clients I'd been in Nellie Hampton's apartment tonight; that would be bragging. She set two cups of steaming coffee on a small table, which she put between us.

"Aren't you glad now that I asked you up for a cup of hot coffee, Buck?"

I smiled. "The name is Al."

"Oh, it's like that, huh? Then you'll have to stop calling me Miss Hampton. It's Nellie. Al."

"Okay, Nellie. This is good coffee."

"It has to be. I just took the stuff out of a fresh jar of instant." She took one of my cigarettes. "I think I have some fruit cake left. An aunt sent it to me from Asheville." She went into her tiny kitchen and came back with two small slices of fruit cake on two small plates. "To hell with calories tonight. Al."

I picked up the cake with my fingers. "Right. Nellie. Right." We ate. It was good cake. She licked her fingers.

"Can I ask a question? Where are you from originally?"

"Chicago."

"Oh. That's why you're not a smart New Yorker."

"How do you know? Have you been watching me?"

"More or less. You work in a literary agency, you watch the clients. It's fun watching, isn't it?"

"Yes."

"Do you watch me?"

"Often."

"Want another piece of cake?"

"No."

"I don't, either. But it tasted good, didn't it? Can I borrow another one of your cigarettes? I left mine back in the restaurant. Thanks. What do they say about me at the office? The male clients. I'm not interested in the lady writers."

"They like you."

"That all?"

"They think you're tough."

She smoked her cigarette thoughtfully. "They do, huh?"

I set my coffee cup down. She was still an enigma. "I can't figure you out, being a secretary. Why don't you start your own agency? You'd be wonderful at it. A smart girl like you could be very successful. I'm not flattering you."

She set her own coffee cup down. "I want to get married."

"That shouldn't be a problem, for you. When is it happening?"

"Don't rush me. I'll let you know." She swung a crossed leg up and back. "I was only fooling. I'll never marry. All of my schoolmates are divorced. Why should I share their misery?"

"I feel the same way. My favorite cousin, a swell girl, is divorced. With two young children."

"Well, we have something in common now. I knew if we talked long enough we'd have something in common. Mutual identification, as the Madison Ave boys say."

I laughed. She went into the kitchen and returned with a bottle of bourbon and two glasses. "Just one small drink apiece and then I'll chase you home."

After we had two drinks apiece, we sat in silence.

"I bet you think I'm trying to seduce you," she said.

"No."

"Why not?"

"I couldn't get to first base with you. Your iron rep in the office. I've got a word for you." The drinks had made me frank.

"What is it?"

"Formidable."

Her face changed, the facial muscles altering against her will, especially around the mouth and eyes.

"Let's not drink any more tonight, Al."

"Okay."

She pointed at my shoes near the fire-place. "They're still soaked. Want to spend the night on the sofa? I've got extra blankets. I'll make breakfast."

"No."

"No what?"

My heart was pounding. I took a chance, what did I have to lose? "I want to spend the night with you."

Had I shocked her? She seemed to be holding her breath a moment. "That's what I wanted you to say. Sit there and I'll go and fix the bed."

A minute later, in a strange small voice, she called out. "Okay. Put out the light and come in."

I entered the bedroom, feeling around in the dark, and shed my clothes on the floor. I bumped against the bed, then got in beside her, under the quilt. I had an erection. We pressed against each other, skin to skin, kissing, exploring with our hands.

"Oh, Al. Oh, darling. Oh, my darling. Oh, oh, oh, Al."

She repeated my name over and over.

She wasn't tough at all. She was like a school girl. Totally inexperienced. It shocked me. All that tough talk, that gutter language had been a fraud. I tried but I could not enter her. I tried various positions, with no success, while she, though willing enough, was unable to assist me and grew tense and rigid. "Oh my God, darling, I'm not a freak, am I?"

"Of course not. We'll be all right. There's no hurry." We were both perspiring. We rested a few minutes, then I tried again, a little more forcibly. Yet I was gentle; and finally my patience, which involved an almost brotherly guidance, was rewarded by victory, accompanied by a sudden gush of gratitude.

"Oh, Al. Oh my darling. My own darling. I can't tell you how happy I am. I'll never let you go now. Never, never."

I wondered if I should bring her down a bit from her wild emotion. "Wait until I tell the other writers."

"Oh, you wouldn't."

"No." She knew I was kidding. I felt the sheet under us. "Are you bleeding?"

"No. Not much, really. I don't care."

Later we lay back in the dark, fingers entwined, in silence. Then she chuckled. "I had my eye on you for a long, long time."

"You did?"

"You never knew it. Nobody knew it."

"You certainly fooled me."

"Yes."

In the morning she gaily made breakfast. My shoes had dried in the night. I used her dull razor and cut my cheek. I left her apartment before nine so she could get to work on time.

Our affair, our secret affair, was to last almost six years. It had begun at the right time for me because I had just broken off with Hedda.

No one ever found out about us in Lieber's office. We were always careful. It was Miss Hampton and Mr. Halper to each other when I entered the agency. We met two or three nights a week. It was wonderfully different in her apartment. I wondered why Lieber's other male clients never caught on. Several of them remarked, "Say, she looks terrific these days, doesn't she? Must be skiing weekends, or ice-skating, or something." They never suspected. I told Nellie about their comments; she laughed and hugged me.

"Oh, we're actors. Goddam wonderful actors."

Meanwhile *The Foundry,* my new novel, had been accepted by Viking. Lieber informed me Marshall Best was excited about it.

"They'd better like it," Nellie told me. "You did a solid job." She never mentioned her own contribution.

One night in her apartment she said, "I hope you don't get tangled up politically with Max."

"What do you mean?"

"Well, you know. He's gone a little screwy on politics, you know."

"I'm sympathetic to some of the things he advocates."

"Of course. So am I. More than sympathetic. In fact, he's managed to involve me in a way, playing on my sense of guilt due to my background and all."

I laughed. "He wants to involve everyone. You're not a member, are you? I never ask that question, but I'll ask it of you. Are you?"

"No. I'm just a frightened fellow traveler. Mixed up."

"Well, it's a mixed-up decade."

She started to mention names, names of people who phoned Lieber at the office, but I was amused by her sudden seriousness and stopped her. "Don't tell me any secrets. I might tell the F.B.I."

She stared at me. "I'm not joking. Certain phones are being tapped. And the Party has started to buy and hide extra printing presses."

I laughed at her. "And I hear I'm in the underground."
She changed the subject, and I forgot the names she'd mentioned. That night it was good to be together, as it always was.

As the weeks went by, while waiting for the galleys of my
new book from my publisher, I thought I sensed a change in
her attitude toward me. She didn't mention marriage but I began
to read her thoughts.

"Don't you think we could make a go of it, darling?"

I sparred for time. "You told me all your schoolmates
were divorced."

"I was just talking. Only half of them are."

"Doesn't that scare you?"

"Not with you it wouldn't."

"How do you know?"

"I know."

I stared down at my drink. She put her hand on mine.
"I'm not pressuring you, Al. You don't even have to think it
over. Forget I mentioned it."

"It'll only come up again some day soon."

"Let's wait and see, huh?"

Alone in my apartment I sometimes wondered why I was
hesitant about marrying her. We were both twenty-nine. I felt
I loved her. But something in our relationship held me back. I
knew what it was but did not want to admit it to myself. She was
too maternal toward me. She was, in her own way, a strong,
dominating woman. I didn't mind the maternalism too much;
most of the time I liked it. But I sensed she would run our marriage. She would continue to love me, no doubt deeply and un-
selfishly, but she would also run me. Did I want that? Definitely
not. Yet she was so wonderful in so many ways that when I was
with her I sometimes felt myself giving in to the idea of
marriage. Only when I left her and was back in my apartment
did my strong doubts begin. I went through hell, wavering,

thinking one way and then another. And meantime I kept seeing her, enjoying her company, making love to her.

One evening she said: "Are you afraid to take a chance because I'm a shiksa? I'll turn Jewish, if you want me to. Is that it?"

"No."

"Are you afraid of my money?"

"No."

"I'll give it away to my nieces and nephews if that's what's holding you back."

"That's not it."

She bit her lip, her face perplexed. "What is it, darling?"

"I don't know." I wanted to be honest, but I couldn't bring myself to tell her.

Our affair dragged on. We didn't fight but our relationship had altered. In bed it was still the same, maybe better than ever. She had been an able student of sex, eager to learn. But outside the bedroom, despite deep feeling for each other, we were aware of the change in our emotions.

One night we had a bitter quarrel, over nothing really. We broke off. I walked out. At Lieber's office our formality became genuine. It took a lot of acting, but we managed to speak to each other normally about literary and business matters. Then one night she phoned.

"Don't leave me, darling. My God, don't leave me."

I didn't know what to say. Our breakup had been a rending experience for me, yet at the same time a big relief. I felt I had gotten out of a deep trap. But her voice on the phone tore at me. She was a wonderful woman, and the old pull came back, as strong as ever.

"Do you want me to drop over?"

"Please. Take a cab. Please."

So our affair resumed. It was now more wonderful than

ever, with both of us feeling happier than we had ever felt before. In a few weeks, however, we were back where we had started from. We were both afraid to terminate it because we still felt deeply involved with each other; we hesitated to make the break, knowing this time it might be final.

She said one night, gaily, "One of these days I'm going to shoot you. Then it'll be all over."

"Go ahead."

"Oh, I wouldn't. But it's a thought I've been thinking." She laughed suddenly. "Look, it started to rain outside. Like that first night. Look."

I came over to the window, and we watched it pouring outside. Pouring down hard.

Of London,
and Edward
and Constance Garnett

In the thirties many writers went to Moscow, at least those who could afford the trip. For $191.25, you could manage a round-trip tour to the Soviet Union, which included passage, hotels, meals, interpreters, visa service, etc., and return via Poland, Austria, Switzerland, and France. This was before the jet age, and you went by boat.

Some writers went to Moscow for instructions, some went out of curiosity, while others went because they had seen Paris and now wanted to walk through Red Square and meet the true, authentic proletariat. It was the trip to make. A writer I knew returned from the grand tour and told me solemnly, "The great thrill of my whole life was when I stepped into the mausoleum in Red Square and saw Lenin lying there. I felt a hush inside me

—I was three feet from the man who had started the world revolution." He gave me an exalted look. "Your work has sold well. You simply must go there." He continued to look at me that way.

"If it can be arranged," I said.

"Oh, you must!" he cried.

It was eventually arranged, in a roundabout way. The truth was, I yearned for a leave of absence from Nellie, from the intermittent abrasiveness that surfaced from time to time in our affair. I was tense, too, about the imminent publication of my new novel. Would it be received well? Would it sell?

One day I confided in Adamic, telling him my private life was in a tangle. I did not of course mention Nellie. "Get out of the country for a while," he laughed. "Listen, apply for a Guggenheim. Live in Spain, or France." Following his advice, I applied for and was awarded a Guggenheim Fellowship which stipulated a year's stay abroad, but instead of going to Spain or France I chose England. Because I was nervous and eager to get out of the country, I left a week before *The Foundry* was published, for which Adamic called me a fool. He had learned that Sinclair Lewis, who had liked *Union Square,* had written a laudatory review of my new book which was to appear on the front page of the Sunday *New York Herald-Tribune* book section. "Fool, listen, wait till his big review comes out!" Adamic shouted. But I had already bought my steamship ticket, and I sailed.

I arrived in London on the day my book appeared in America. Lieber cabled: "Lewis gives rave review. Book selling." The novel received a good press, except from the left. A reviewer in the *New Masses* criticized the novel harshly, declaring the author did not understand the true revolutionary fervor of the American workers. Lieber sent me the *New Masses* clipping with an apologetic note; he had liked the polished manuscript very much and was hurt by the *New Masses'* review. I wrote him it

was my book and not to worry about it. Nellie sent a letter:
"Those dumb left shits. I could shoot them, darling. Really!"

A few weeks later I received a friendly letter from a func-
tionary in Moscow informing me the state publishing house liked
my "foundry novel" and was publishing it in the Russian language. The Soviet Union did not recognize American copyrights
and so would not give me money for publishing my work. But
there would be rubles waiting for me in Moscow, where I would
be warmly welcomed.

All this was very flattering, but I preferred to remain in
London. I found it a wonderful city with extremely likable
people. I lived in a small flat in Hampstead, near the heath, and
one of my frequent walks followed the number 24 bus route
that took me through Camden Town and eventually into Totten-
ham Court Road. If I felt I wanted to walk farther, I branched
off into Holborn, or toward Elephant and Castle. That year
Britain was also in the grip of the Depression, and young girls
from the factory towns of the north had come down to London,
many to become prostitutes and send some of their earnings
home. I used to see them in groups standing near the pubs at
closing time, waiting for clients. As the men emerged in the
cold weather wearing mufflers instead of overcoats, and walking
hurriedly in the chill air without stopping, the girls would begin
calling shrilly after them. "Hello, dearie! Wot's your rush?"

Viking had written several English authors on their list
about me, and two or three of them were gracious enough to get
in touch with me. Through them I met some interesting people.
A few months later, when *Union Square* and *The Foundry* were
published in England, I met still more people. Enjoying this
spurt of social life, I completely forgot about the scheduled publication of *The Foundry* in the Soviet Union.

Americans were still scarce in London in the thirties, and
at parties people seemed to be intrigued by my Chicago accent.

I had brought a copy of Ring Lardner's stories with me and I showed the volume to a young writer, John Davenport, who was enthusiastic about it; he immediately tried to interest publishers in Lardner, but the English firms had never heard of him and none of them believed Americans really talked that way. Lardner had just died, and Davenport and I failed to interest any publisher in his work.

I sat in pubs with newly made literary friends who asked me questions about the American literary scene, especially the scene on the left. In England, I learned, the younger writers were just getting into the proletarian swing, and the first few novels about English working-class life had only recently appeared; if anything, they were even poorer than their American counterparts. But due to the impact the current Depression was having upon English life, these books were seriously reviewed in the press.

One day I received a note from the critic, Edward Garnett, who wrote that Harold Guinzburg of Viking had requested that he get in touch with me. Would I care to lunch with him? He suggested a restaurant in Chelsea and gave instructions how to get there.

A few days later I met Edward Garnett in a small restaurant patronized by Russian refugees. He was sitting near the wall, a tall, hulking, white-haired man in his sixties and, upon seeing a young man wearing American clothes, he motioned to me as I entered. He introduced himself in a warm, courtly fashion, saying we would have a good bottle of Burgundy for lunch. We ordered borscht and a meat dish, and as we dined I could hear the Russian language spoken all about me. London had thousands of Russian refugees.

It was a pleasant meal. Because Garnett was hard of hearing, I frequently had to raise my voice. He hadn't read my books so we didn't have to waste time talking about my work.

While we bent over our food he asked me casual but penetrating questions about current American writers. He took in my comments with noncommittal nods. I was soon aware of his opinions about Hemingway, Faulkner, Anderson, Dreiser, Sinclair Lewis, and some of the younger American authors; he thought them good writers but some of them much overpraised. At the end of the meal, he lit a cigarette. When I remarked that his cigarette had a distinctive aroma he smiled. "It's full of non-tobacco, because of my asthma. Some day when you have the courage I'll let you smoke one."

He paid the check, and out in the street he invited me to his rooms a few blocks away. He told me his wife, Constance, lived in the country. His flat consisted of two or three cosy rooms, lined with bookshelves; his desk was piled with manuscripts. As chief reader for the publishing firm of Jonathan Cape, he wielded power in the London literary world, for Cape was one of the best publishers. We sat and chatted for about two hours, about writers and writing, and when I noticed him getting tired I left.

I saw Garnett often after that. Every week or two he sent me a note—he never phoned—asking me to dine with him at the small Russian restaurant. I looked forward to these meetings, and the short walk through Chelsea after lunch to his rooms was always pleasant. On some occasions, after we reached his flat, he would speak about literary figures he had known in the past.

He mentioned D. H. Lawrence, Conrad, W. D. Hudson, Galsworthy, Frank Harris and other writers he had known. I listened in silence, intently, as he reminisced about those well-known figures. A few weeks later, when I happened to open a copy of *Sons and Lovers* in Foyle's Bookstore, I noted Lawrence had dedicated the novel to Edward Garnett, a bit of information Garnett had never bothered to tell me.

These visits to his flat after our luncheons were not only a source of deep pleasure for me but, I felt, served as a kind of release for the aging Garnett. Perhaps I intrigued him because I was an American, or maybe he was friendly when he learned of my admiration of Gogol, Turgenev, Goncharov, and the other Russian greats, writers he himself, as he told me, respected above all others. During some of my visits he was silent, and I just sat there wondering if he wanted me to leave. He always saw me to the door, in his warm, courtly manner, and never spoke about future meetings. Then I would receive another note from him after a week or two.

His stories about Stephen Crane fascinated me. It was he, Garnett, and Conrad who had rented Brede Place in Sussex for the ailing and debt-ridden American writer who had come to England with his wife. Garnett greatly admired Crane's best work, especially "The Open Boat" and "The Bride Comes to Yellow Sky." But Crane's later output, his sketches and stories of the London scene, was, Garnett thought, disappointing stuff for a man of only twenty-nine. "Perhaps the quality of this writing suffered because of his final illness," he said. He described in detail the last meeting he and Conrad had with the luckless, dying young author who had come to England after covering the European Near East wars.

"Brede's Place, which Conrad and I had gotten for Crane, was a damp stone monster of a house. We advised him not to rent it when we saw he was ill but even though the roof leaked Crane seemed stubbornly to like it and moved into it with his wife, an attractive young woman he had met somewhere in Florida, I believe. That house, those gloomy quarters, were horrible, and his wife was no housekeeper; the place was like a gypsy camp with pieces of sandwiches lying about. When Conrad and I came into the cold damp place on our final visit—even

coal fires never seemed to warm the wet stone walls—Conrad
and I saw Crane lying there exhausted on a rumpled bed. He
stared up at us with his big, beautiful, burning, dark eyes—I
shall never forget his eloquent, accusing stare that damned us
for getting him into this terrible house—and he didn't say a
word. Conrad and I didn't stay long, though we offered to be of
assistance. His wife saw us to the door in silence. The next day
she took him to a health spa in the Black Forest, where he soon
died. He was a very talented man, very talented. He liked to ride
horses, even when he was ill. A pity he lived so hard and fast,
isn't it?''

Once Garnett asked me what I thought of Galsworthy
who had just died. I could never read Galsworthy, but I told him
Galsworthy was immensely popular in America and had a fine
reputation there. He nodded, non-committally; but during my
next visit he said Galsworthy's reputation had sunk appreciably
and he doubted if it would ever revive much. I gathered he and
Galsworthy had been very close friends; he greatly admired
Galsworthy as a man and he saw Galsworthy's widow frequently.
But he was not fooled about his friend's true literary worth.

"Galsworthy never had children. He was very much in
love with his wife, and he was afraid he might lose her in child-
birth.''

I sensed Conrad had been Edward Garnett's favorite. "He
was very sensitive, a gentleman. He was an artist, a true artist in
the best sense of the word. He worked indefatigably, he polished
every paragraph to perfection. As you know, writing did not
come easily to him because English was not his mother tongue,
but his determination to thoroughly master and create his work in
the English language was the most overwhelming thing I've
known in my life.'' Once he pointed casually to a bureau drawer.
"It's full of Conrad's letters to me, his theories, his doubts, his

complaints; I haven't bothered to sort them yet but one day I shall."

During one luncheon Garnett said abruptly: "If you're free this Sunday we'd like to have you come out to Oxted. I've spoken of you to my wife and of your admiration for Russian writers. Oxted is about twenty miles out of London, it isn't far."

On Sunday morning I took the train to Oxted. When I got off at the small village a hired car met me and drove me to the Garnett house some distance from the station. When I arrived, Constance Garnett, whose translations of Chekhov, Turgenev, Gogol, Tolstoy, and Dostoevsky I had read and admired for years, was standing in the doorway—a slight, tiny, vibrant woman. She greeted me warmly, peering at me through her thick glasses, while Edward Garnett stood in the doorway, tall, thoughtful, and silent.

We talked for hours. Suddenly Constance Garnett rose to prepare lunch. As his wife moved about, Edward Garnett pointed to the big, solid wooden table upon which Constance Garnett was setting plates; he got up and thumped it, turning to me. "See this table? It's much older than I. My wife and I bought it at a secondhand shop in the East End right after we married. The proprietor was an old harridan of a woman who pounded it with her fist and told us, 'You can build a house on it!' And she was right. We still have it."

"Yes," Constance Garnett added with a smile. "Not only have we eaten many meals on it but I've corrected thousands of pages of proofs on it, too." We had lunch and kept on talking about writers and writing. Constance Garnett asked me whether I had read *The Golovlyov Family* by Nicolai Shchedrin. When I replied I hadn't, she urged me to read it. Turgenev was their favorite of all the Russian writers, and Garnett remarked: "His creation of Basarov at that particular time was a stroke of intui-

tive genius; even though he alienated a lot of liberal people at the
time, he had written a monumental character, a character that
will attract future generations of young people, I daresay."

"But Tolstoy is the giant," Constance Garnett said, and
her husband nodded in agreement. Neither thought much of
current Russian writing.

"You can't expect good work under their present setup,"
Garnett grumbled.

When I informed them I had a novel of mine about to be
published in the Soviet Union, and that I had been invited there
to collect some rubles, they became immediately interested. A
second invitation from Moscow had reached me only two days
before.

"Oh, you must go there," Constance Garnett told me.
"You must really go there and have a look at Russia." She turned
to her husband. "Tell him about our good friend Prince Mirsky."

Garnett cleared his throat. "Mirsky had a good job
teaching in a university here, he was being published and he
knew everybody here. Then one day someone at the Soviet em-
bassy in London urged him to go back to Russia. Several people
told him not to go."

"Did he take their advice?" I asked.

"Not at all. He heard the call of the fatherland, I guess.
He went back, and later wrote some caustic stuff about the
English who had given him a good home for years." Garnett
stared off into space for a moment. "It won't help him, they'll
get him eventually, I suppose." His prophecy came to pass, for
Mirsky was liquidated during the purges.

"Yes, you must go there," Constance Garnett urged me.

"Yes," agreed her husband. He chuckled. "You're an
American, they can't harm you."

"Bosh," Constance Garnett said. "You must go there and
see Russia." Before I left them, she gave me an autographed

copy of her translation of Turgenev's *A Month in the Country*, and her husband pressed into my hand a slim volume, *Papa's War,* a collection of his anti-war satires written during World War I. "You must go there," Constance Garnett repeated.

"Yes, I think I will," I said.

Moscow,
Oh, Moscow

I arrived by train in Moscow. It was well into April. The big railroad station was gloomy and cold—snow had been visible outside the city—and as soon as our railroad cars rolled to a halt in the terminal big, broad-shouldered women with shawls over their heads began uncoupling the cars and oiling the engine. At first they looked like silent, professional football players going into plays after a signal had been called. But crawling patiently around the cars they more resembled Asiatics, working silently, stubbornly. This Asiatic aspect of Russian life was my first impression of the Soviet Union.

Along with a group of tourists from Yugoslavia and Australia who had traveled second-class, "hard-seat" all the way from the west and through Warsaw, I rode the special bus toward the hotel and stared out the window at the city about which I had read so much in Chekhov and Tolstoy. The dreary streets flowed by me in a gray panorama of low houses—it was before the era of the high-rise apartment structures. I was not disappointed as the bus rolled through bleak neighborhoods; I had not expected shining, architectural masterpieces. Though books and articles by pro-Soviet writers in America had been published insisting there were no slums in the Soviet fatherland, the area we were now in more than rivaled the West Side slums of Chicago.

The bus came to a stop before the New Moscow Hotel, an unpretentious looking old building six or seven stories high located on the Moscow River with an unobstructed view of St. Basil's Cathedral and the nearby Kremlin. The driver piled our luggage in the lobby and left. We stood about in a group with our interpreter until we all signed the register and handed over our passports. Then the interpreter began her cheery monologue about the pleasures that awaited us.

"Where did you learn how to speak English?" I asked the woman, a stout, amiable hausfrau type in her forties whose strong Bronx Jewish accent astonished me.

"From American tourists I have learned my English," she replied proudly. "Tomorrow I will be the guide for this group. We will visit factory, children's nursery, art museum, and family court. You will see socialist society at work." She smiled warmly. "It will be very interesting for you." Before we went to our rooms, we were given books of chits for our meals.

That night I ate a poorly prepared dinner in the restaurant on the hotel's top floor and listened to a six-piece Soviet jazz band play "Sweet Sue" and other standards. The musicians wore tuxedos: they put forth their best efforts, but their music was of the caliber of a high school band playing a senior prom in Moline, Illinois. Down in the lobby we had been informed by our friendly interpreter that tipping was an outdated capitalist custom, but when I tipped my waiter, who hovered above me expectantly, he accepted the tip skillfully with the technique of an old hand. This didn't bother me, either; he was a pleasant aging man in a shiny worn waiter's outfit, the type one saw in Second Avenue restaurants in New York.

The next morning our group climbed into a special bus and toured all the places promised to us by our guide. Our visits were pleasantly brief and generally uninteresting. None of the tourists asked embarrassing questions. In the factory I had noticed oily rags close to the crackling copper brushes of humming generators. I saw women wearing long shawls and smoking cigarettes while bending over machines which lacked appropriate metal guards. Tools were lying on the oily floor, directly in the path of workers who moved about the machines. I wondered about the accident rate in this model factory. But I was not critical; this was not my country and I did not feel it my place to impart what knowledge I had about proper safety measures and factory maintenance procedures to the interpreter or to anyone else.

When I got up the next morning I wondered how I could avoid going on the day's tour. I speculated about how I might get in touch with the state publishing house. A maid knocked on the door and in halting English told me there was someone waiting for me in the lobby. I went downstairs, and met two smiling Americans who had been living in Moscow for three years: a former editor of the *New Masses* and his wife, Walt and Rose Carmon. Though I hadn't known them in New York, we were on a first-name basis almost immediately. Walt was now the editor of the English edition of *International Literature* printed in Moscow, while his wife Rose kept house and assisted him occasionally in his editing duties.

"Why didn't you call us when you got in yesterday?" Walt said. "Your book was published here two months ago and sold out quickly." He added that it had good reviews in Moscow.

We talked for an hour in the lobby, until Walt said he had to return to his office.

"I'll take over," Rose told me, smiling. She was a short, sturdy woman in her forties, pleasant looking and very likable. She and her husband were reliable, utterly dedicated types, veteran Party members who had lived through good times and bad. They voiced no cliches to prove their radical background, and one felt that wherever the Party sent them, they went without demurring.

Rose spoke to the hotel manager in Russian and extricated me from the tourist group at once. Then she took me to the state publishing house where I listened to her speaking in her surprising Russian (she came from Ohio). An editor bent his head attentively, then smiled and went to a cashier, and returned to hand me two thousand rubles in crisp new bills. Rose then guided me to another department where she spoke to someone who made it possible for me to pay my living expenses in Moscow with the rubles instead of the English pounds I had brought with me from London.

That night I dined with Walt and Rose Carmon in their cramped apartment. They were still hungry for news about New York. They knew I had been living in London for about ten months, and though I did not know the latest New York gossip they continued to pump me for what additional news I was able to give them. I learned Walt knew Lieber.

The next morning Sergei Dinamov, the head of the all-powerful Russian Association of Proletarian Writers (R.A.P.P.), visited me in the hotel accompanied by an interpreter. A small, sharp-eyed man, he was immediately friendly and uttered a few welcoming words in halting English, then turned to the woman who was his interpreter and between the three of us we carried on a stilted but friendly conversation about American writing.

Dinamov said: "I like Dreiser, Caldwell, Steinbeck, Farrell. They understand the social issues. Do you know our writers? What Russian writers do you know today?"

I said I had read Boris Pilnyak's *The Naked Year,* a very original work, and added that in London I had picked up a copy of *Red Cavalry* by Isaac Babel. "Now I am an avid Babel enthusiast, he's wonderful." This delighted Dinamov.

"Babel is a great writer, a true talent." Dinamov cleared his throat. "Who do you think has written the best American novel of the Depression?" He smiled. "Besides yourself."

I thought a long moment. "John O'Hara. He did it with *Appointment in Samarra,* a study in depth of a small town in Pennsylvania—a wonderful narrative as well as a fine social document." Dinamov made a note of it; he had never heard of O'Hara. Dinamov smiled often as the interview progressed, and I was fascinated by his front steel teeth. He was a warm, perceptive little man, but it was difficult to say anything really meaningful through the plodding interpreter, so we continued to smile at each other. When our meeting ended he pressed my hand, looking at me kindly, and I felt I had made a friend.

That evening Rose called for me at the hotel and we went to the apartment of Sergei Tretyakov who, as Rose whispered to me, was a bitter rival of Sergei Dinamov. "Don't tell him you met Dinamov today, Albert." Tretyakov, a tall, bald man, was the leader of the Left Front (L.E.F.S.), another literary organization. A poet and dramatist, he had lived and taught school in China, and one of his plays, *Roar China,* had been produced in the twenties by the Theater Guild in New York. Tretyakov's wife, a pretty woman, was serving snacks and coffee when Rose and I entered the apartment. There was another guest present, sitting quietly in a chair—Bertolt Brecht, the German dramatist, who had escaped from the Nazis and was now living in Moscow. Since he knew no English and I had no German, we merely smiled and bowed to each other when we were introduced.

My meeting with Tretyakov did not go as well as my session with Dinamov. Tretyakov's command of the English language was better than Dinamov's and he began to speak to me at length about the writer's "mission." At first our conversation was friendly but perhaps because Tretyakov had been a pedagogue for years in China he began to lecture me. I soon found myself disliking him. "We writers of the Soviet Union, we *exist* to further the revolution. It is more than a cause, it is a destiny for us! . . ." He was, I felt, a sincere, honest man, but there was nothing for me to do but keep silent and give him one of my inscrutable, noncommittal Chicago stares.

As for Brecht, knowing no English, he sat there with the half-smile of a Buddha, sipping his coffee and now and then reaching for a piece of Soviet chocolate on a plate. He and I continued to exchange polite smiles every so often, but all evening we did not say a word to each other. Occasionally Tretyakov turned and uttered something to Brecht in German, to which Brecht answered briefly or nodded.

When Rose and I rose to leave, Tretyakov saw us to the door and became suddenly very friendly. The lecture was over and we were buddies, it seemed. He shook my hand warmly. "Come again," he pressed my hand. "Come soon." Out on the street Rose chuckled.

"He's not as bad as some of them, Albert. Give most of them a chance and they go into a six-hour speech on dialectics. You should sit through some of these literary meetings like Walt and I do." She rolled her eyes, and groaned.

On those days when Rose was too busy to take me to places of interest, I left the hotel and roamed through Moscow for hours on my own. It was a strange, interesting city. I visited the town house where Tolstoy had lived. I saw the wild beggar boys scouting the avenues in packs. I stopped at the many book stalls and leafed through cheaply priced illustrated editions of the Russian classics, sorry that I did not understand the language. I tramped through areas of the city which were not listed in the tours. In the cold late spring I could not help but notice the poor clothing of the people, and their unsmiling patient expressions. I felt, somehow, I had been here before. I saw hundreds of women who looked like my mother. Because they saw I was a foreigner, pedestrians stared at me—quickly but thoroughly. In their tennis sneakers and thin clothing, they noticed the good, stout walking shoes I had purchased in London, also the fine British overcoat I wore. I did not blame those who stared at me with hostility; but the majority looked my way with eyes of friendship. Once I turned and stopped in my tracks, hearing magnificent choral singing, which came from fifty singing soldiers with towels under their arms marching in step to the public baths.

One day a girl stopped me on Gorky Street. She spoke in perfect English. "Are you an American?" She said she was a Canadian working in a Soviet bureau and living permanently in Moscow. She was quite pretty and friendly, and after we talked a while on the cold street I said I had some extra meal chits and would she like to have dinner at the hotel with me? "Oh, I'd love to. Then we can talk a bit more."

She came to the lobby of my hotel that evening. We ate in the restaurant on the top floor and listened to the Moline-Illinois-type high school jazz band as my waiter hovered over us. Her name was Helen, she had lived in Moscow for two and a half years, and she was cheerfully talkative. Wearing a well-cut black dress, she looked very attractive. When I complimented her on her new, Soviet-made dress, she smiled.

"This is from Canada, the last good dress I have. I don't wear it often."

It was a very pleasant dinner. Helen spoke to the waiter in Russian, and he smiled and brought us dishes not on the menu or specified on the printed chits.

After the meal, we walked outside and wandered about Red Square and around the Kremlin. The well-lit streets were deserted and without automobiles. When I asked Helen if she planned to visit Canada soon, she avoided the question.

"Are you going to the May Day celebration tomorrow?" she asked.

"I'm among the half dozen in my tourist group who have been invited." I had thought people from the entire Moscow environs always swarmed freely into the great square for the annual May Day fete, like Americans crowding ten deep along Fifth Avenue to watch a Fourth of July parade, but I had learned viewers were handpicked and carefully screened here.

"Oh, you'll enjoy the celebration," Helen said. "It's festive, very exciting."

"I still have some extra meal chits. Care to dine with me again tomorrow night?"

She hesitated a moment, then smiled. "Yes, all right."

Next day the May Day parade was spectacular. The huge square was crammed. Tourists had been warned not to bring their cameras, but at the hotel when I saw some of them slipping small cameras into their pockets I put my own small camera into my overcoat pocket.

The military part of the parade was like all military parades in all countries—tanks, big guns on carriages, soldiers marching stolidly in unison, flags. During this review the tourists did not bring out their cameras, and the secret service men, who could easily be spotted because their eyes were darting constantly at everyone in the huge crowd, made no move. Only when the display of military hardware was over, and exciting contingents of peasants in colorful dress from far-flung parts of the Soviet

Union came into view did the cameras appear. Beautiful Mongolian girls with long, streaming, black hair danced by, singing; Cossack riders rode past the mausoleum at breakneck speed executing acrobatics on their mounts; Ukrainian gymnasts performed; Uzbek girls marched by carrying banners. The great square became a mass of moving color. The secret service men shouted at us to put away our cameras, moving toward our group menacingly. A tourist standing next to me quickly appealed to our interpreter. "Tell them the military part of the parade is over, where is the danger if we take snapshots now?" Our interpreter spoke in a rapid undertone to the men who had advanced toward us, and at last, after arguing with the woman, they frowned and moved grudgingly away. "But you must put away your cameras now," our interpreter told us, and we obeyed.

That evening when I dined again with Helen in the hotel restaurant she was rather subdued. She asked if I had enjoyed the celebration in Red Square, which I said I had. Again we listened to the jazz music that came with the meal, and the dreariness of the restaurant bore down upon us. Toward the end of the dinner when I inquired again, merely to make conversation, if she planned to visit Canada to see her family soon, she was silent. I changed the subject and told her I was leaving Moscow tomorrow. Then she said:

"I can't ever go back to Canada."

"Why not?"

She bit her lip. "I gave up my Canadian citizenship and this is my home now."

I must have looked at her in horror. Why had she done such a foolish thing? Walt and Rose Carmon had lived here for three years, longer than she had, and had not given up their American citizenship. Suddenly the truth struck me. This young pretty girl who had arrived in the Soviet Union as a tourist had been naively swept up in the excitement of her visit. And during her escorted trips to the model factories and collectives, moving among the wonderful Russian people she must have met, she had impulsively decided to remain and work for the revolutionary future of the world. Her whole story was stamped upon the face sitting across the table. Quickly, I tried to suppress my horror. I felt sickened. With the forfeiture of her Canadian citizenship she had given up all rights to travel outside Russia. She was permanently trapped, a clerical worker in a Soviet bureau, seven thousand miles from her family in Toronto.

After dinner we again strolled along the deserted nighttime Moscow streets, in silence now. What was there to say? At last, after a long walk, I took her down into one of the beautiful subway stations and stood on the platform beside her waiting for a train that would take her to her room.

As an approaching train shone its lights in the distance of the tunnel, she suddenly turned to me. "Do me a favor—please send me one of your books," she said. "Please send it to me." The train rolled in, and she pressed my hand quickly. "Please, I want to hear from you."

I stood there until the train roared off with her into the tunnel.

When I returned to America, I sent her a copy of *The Foundry*. It never reached her. Three months later I received a plain post-card with a simple message inquiring why the book had not been sent. "I'm still waiting, Albert." She did not sign her name.

I sent a second copy, but I never heard from her again.

The Long,
Long Journey
of Louis Adamic

When I returned to the United States, Lieber greeted me with a bit of very good news. He had sold the movie rights to *The Foundry* to Metro-Goldwyn-Mayer for fifteen thousand dollars a few days before my arrival. As he handed me the check for the sale, minus his commission, I was overwhelmed.

"But you wrote to me many months ago in London saying all the film companies had turned it down."

Lieber grinned. "They did, even Metro. But when Dashiell Hammett read your book he forced Metro to reconsider their decision and pressured them into buying it. *The Thin Man* and his other movies are making a fortune for them, and when he told Metro he wanted to work on the scenario of your novel they gave in and bought it." I did not know Hammett, had never met him.

Lieber and I went out to lunch, where he was eager to know what I thought about the Soviet Union. I answered in two words. "It's bleak." He gave me a look of pain. "I liked the people there, Max, but Moscow is a gray, poverty-stricken town —like Akron, only worse."

"Didn't you go out into the countryside?"

"No," I said, "I didn't." I explained that I had seen the rich farm lands of Illinois and Iowa—they had bored me—and what would I gain by looking at the struggling collectives in Russia? And I murmured something about what I had heard in London about the Russian countryside, the famine, the kulak rebellions. Again Lieber looked uncomfortable, until I said, "I saw the wonderful May Day celebration, Max. I stood near Stalin, and I waved, and Stalin waved back and shouted, 'How is 14th Street?' " Lieber grinned weakly; my humor was not very successful today.

That evening I had dinner with Nellie. She had lost a little weight and looked more attractive than ever. Her greeting was warm and my return to America seemed to have excited her, but I felt she was holding something back from me.

She no longer worked in Lieber's office. I sensed she and Lieber had quarreled. It was only later that I heard from some other clients of Lieber's, who told me she had quit because after she'd worked for him *gratis* for a year Lieber had failed to make her a junior partner in his agency, thereby violating the terms of their agreement. That evening she refused to talk about her break with Lieber. She had been hurt, I felt, but she was not bitter.

"I learned a lot working with him, and I met you there."

She had recently started her own agency, a small one, and it was becoming a success. "I didn't write you about it because you were traveling all over Europe. Of course I'd never represent you as an agent," she told me. "And I'm not out to take away any of his clients, either. Let's not talk about it any more."

Later, when we had satisfied our hunger for each other in bed in her apartment, she said to me in the dark: "Darling, I have a confession to make."

"Go ahead. What is it?"

"Well, I was true blue to you all the time I knew you must have been screwing those girls in England, but I weakened a few times, I admit. Three or four men were after me; I guess they smelled I was no longer a virgin. And I was willing to go the limit with a guy."

"What held you back?"

"He was a nice guy but he was impotent with me. We tried a few times but he couldn't make it. He's an editor; you don't know him."

"Why are you telling me this?"

"I don't know. I'm just dumb honest, I guess. He called me up today but I said I couldn't see him. I felt so sorry for him."

"Are you going to see him again?"

"No. But I want you to know that if I meet the right guy I'm going to marry him." She burst into tears. "I missed you, I missed you."

We made love again and she seemed to be all right, but I knew she had meant what she had said.

The next morning my phone rang in the hotel where I was staying temporarily. It was the editor of *Soviet Russia Today,* a writer who was one of Lieber's clients and is today an editor in a second-rate publishing house, who asked me to do an up-beat piece on my trip to Russia. He himself had never visited the Soviet Union, but he wanted me to write an article on the happy lot of the workers there. I declined.

A few days later the *New Masses* asked me to go on an

extended lecture tour under the auspices of their new lecture bureau. Their circulation was rising more rapidly than ever, copies of their latest issue now rested beside the *New Yorker* on the coffee tables of the intellectuals of the country; and college students as well as Party members and fellow travelers read each number avidly. It was a strange request from the *New Masses.* Its people had reviewed *Union Square* savagely, had panned my book of short stories, and had sharply criticized *The Foundry,* and now they wanted me to go on a lecture tour for them. I declined.

Upon my return to America I found the left-wing movement had grown immensely during my absence. There was a new, aggressive excitement in the air. In the demonstrations and well-organized marches, middle-class college students were now taking part in large numbers, shouting slogans about jobs for the unemployed and demanding recognition of unions. They screamed obscenities at the police as they churned in Union Square, their yelling frequently ending with, "Down with the Cossacks! . . ."

The scene had, indeed, altered during my stay in Europe. The hot breath of radical culture was everywhere in the air. Modern dance groups now gave concerts emphasizing "social messages." In New York a Federal Theater subsidized by the government and with a branch in Harlem had come into being with enthusiastic followings. As for the commercial theater, the first plays of the newcomer Clifford Odets had received major recognition on Broadway during my absence, and he had become the mainstay of the Group Theater. Meanwhile, F. Scott Fitzgerald's fine novel, *Tender Is the Night,* published during this period, was utterly ignored, buried under a heavy output of "revolutionary" writing.

Louis Adamic and I discussed the changing scene. Like many of Lieber's clients, his literary and financial fortunes had altered for the better recently; his articles now appeared in well-paying magazines and his latest book, *The Native's Return,* a book-club choice, was on the best-seller list. We were heartily in favor of the upsurging left-wing cultural boom, which had followed a long era of ivory tower lethargy, but we were critical of some of the bombast, the lowering of literary standards, and the self-appointed messiahs who had wormed themselves into major literary-political positions.

I was now living in a small modern apartment on 34th Street near Lexington Avenue and I knew Adamic, who was swiftly becoming affluent, longed to depart with his wife Stella from his mother-in-law's flat in the Bronx. One day while visiting me he glanced about my flat and said, "I think I'll leave the Bronx next week. I like this neighborhood around 34th Street." I told him I had seen several for-rent signs in the vicinity, and we went outside and within a half-hour he had rented an apartment across the street from mine. From then on I saw Louis and Stella often. Perhaps too often.

The Louis Adamic story, tragic and fascinating, unfolded before my eyes like a drama; and the front-row seat I occupied gave me the opportunity to witness all three of its acts. During my years in New York I had observed that when luck touched some writers they remained unchanged, while others underwent a definite and sometimes radical change. Adamic was among the latter. With an assured financial income now, Adamic's living habits and personality began to alter; at first the gradual changes I noticed seemed natural enough. Money and a growing reputation quickly gave him confidence; he rarely stammered any more, only when he was especially excited. His explosive laugh boomed with more heartiness than ever, and a beautiful smile of security often lit up his Slavic face. When Stella did not feel like cooking in the apartment, which was frequently, they began to eat at Lindy's and other good restaurants.

Adamic began to meet "important" people, foundation heads, top labor leaders, wealthy hostesses with radical leanings. He dined often with the president of the United Fruit Company, a man named Samuel Zemurray, an immigrant from Eastern Europe who had come to America as a boy and had amassed great wealth in the banana republics of Central and South America. This man liked to eat in places where gypsy music was being played and, overwhelmed by nostalgia, wept and used to fling money generously at the musicians, Adamic told me. "Why don't you get out and meet people?" Adamic prodded me repeatedly. "You live like a hermit. These people are interesting, I learn things from them." I had no ready answer.

He was attracted to strong, successful men, leader types. The left regarded the president of the United Fruit Company as an enemy, but Adamic said the United Fruit Company had built schools, roads, and hospitals for the indigent peasants. "The corrupt generals and governments down there don't give the poor workers a damn thing, but the United Fruit Company has spent millions, millions to improve the lives of the natives."

He began to travel frequently to Washington, where he met officials in labor and government circles, from whom he gathered useful facts which he worked into his articles. For a whole year he kept telling me of his great admiration for John L. Lewis, the head of the United Mine Workers Union. Then, he later told me about the greatness of Walter Reuther, and spoke of Lewis with less enthusiasm. He met and spoke with President Roosevelt and Eleanor Roosevelt and members of the cabinet, who had become interested in his articles and books about immigrants. One felt he had traveled a long way from his little village in Slovenia. It was pleasing to see the thrill he felt at making these people's acquaintance. Louis told me foundations wanted to give him money to explore the immigrant subject further because, as President Roosevelt had proclaimed: "We are a nation of immigrants." He accepted foundation money and, though the immigrant theme absorbed him, somehow he always seemed to return to his search for a strong man, a leader who would solve the great problems.

One afternoon he rang my bell to tell me excitedly that he had just met the greatest educational genius in America. He sat in my apartment for two hours extolling John Andrew Rice, who had just founded Black Mountain College near Asheville, North Carolina. John Rice, he said, had been a professor down at Rollins College, Florida, where he was fired because of the progressive educational innovations he was attempting to establish there. Immediately other instructors, rallying around Rice, handed in their resignations and together with Rice started Black Mountain College on a shoestring. A great talker, a magnetic personality, Rice attracted other teachers from different parts of the country, and soon his faculty included Josef Albers, Walter Gropius, John Cage, Ben Shahn, Alfred Kazin, Buckminster Fuller, Marcel Breuer, Merce Cunningham, Robert Motherwell, and other brilliant men who taught classes for the most modest of stipends.

"You just have to meet Rice," Adamic said. "Stella is making dinner tonight and he'll be with us. Come over and meet him."

That evening I crossed 34th Street and met the founder of Black Mountain College. A small, plump man, John Rice was sitting in a soft chair, and when I entered Adamic's apartment and we shook hands I liked him immediately. We sat down to a good dinner with wine. Adamic and Rice discussed the future of American education, and I listened. Rice had a puckish sense of humor, chuckled often, was soft spoken and highly articulate, especially about his profession. I watched him as he tactfully and smilingly corrected some of Adamic's wild assertions about educational values and goals. It was a very pleasant evening. As I was about to leave, Adamic told me he was leaving in the morning with Rice to see and inspect the college.

Upon his return from Asheville a week later, Adamic was wildly enthusiastic about Black Mountain College. "A radical and tremendous idea is taking place down there, I tell you. Black Mountain is a co-op in the best sense of the word. The faculty owns the college, there are no outside trustees, and the students share in running everything—in arranging the curriculum, in the maintenance of the place. The college operates its own farm and the kids work on it, together with the teachers. The whole educational idea of the place is based on a close teacher-student communal relationship, with everybody sharing responsibility and contributing ideas. I met some wonderful kids there. I tell you, it's a major revolutionary educational concept. This might be my mission, to help revamp American education from the bottom up and thereby revolutionize America." Adamic described how the students had installed plumbing, had cleared the grounds, and had repaired a group of abandoned houses on the property, after which they had assisted Walter Gropius in erecting the Study Building, which consisted of small, individual rooms for each student. Underneath the overhang of the Study Building, Adamic reported, Jean Charlot, the Mexican painter, had executed a mural. "Albert, you ought to go there and see how exciting it all is!" As he spoke, his face was aglow with a proselytizing fervor.

Within a few days of his return, he wrote a long article glorifying Black Mountain College. Lieber placed it with *Harper's* magazine, and when the piece was published it drew more readers' letters than any *Harper's* article had in years. Because of Adamic's piece, *Life* sent a reporter and photographer down to Asheville and within a few weeks ran a generous picture-and-text spread about the school.

Soon students from as far away as Texas and California began heading for Asheville to enroll in Black Mountain College. Many of them were highly talented. Among their number were Arthur Penn, James Leo Herlihy, Charles Olsen, Robert Rauschenberg, Kenneth Noland, Robert Creeley, and Richard Lippold. Those who couldn't afford to pay tuition were given full scholarships.

Adamic made further trips to Black Mountain, and after each visit he rang my bell to tell me again that John Rice was a genius who eventually would change the educational structure of America. His high emotional pitch on Black Mountain could not last forever. Soon Louis' eagerness to find the answer to the great problems led him in search of new idols, new leaders. His quest carried him into the big foundations, into organizations with "new visions," into meetings with groups whose platforms were based on peace-among-nations and the food production of the world.

Adamic's search ended with his great enthusiasm for Tito. As a Slovenian keenly aware of the suffering in his native country under the ruthless occupation of the Nazis, Louis had followed the activities of the underground movement there very closely. He had been elated and filled with understandable pride when he learned that partisan bands had blown up German troop trains, blasted Nazi supply dumps, and assassinated Hitler's officers in hit-and-run forays. Suddenly Tito became not only the hope of Yugoslavia but the savior of Europe, the world. Adamic turned very nationalistic. "I tell you the Yugoslav people are the greatest on earth!" he told me. "In them Hitler has met his match!" Soon he became deeply involved with Yugoslavian societies in the United States, spoke at their meetings in Detroit, Cleveland, Chicago, helped to raise funds for the Yugoslav underground. He took it upon himself to become Tito's spokesman in America.

When during the war Winston Churchill arrived in the United States to discuss the complex military and political situation in the Balkans with President Roosevelt, he said he wanted to meet Louis Adamic, whose articles he had read in England. Perhaps he believed that Louis could contribute some ideas concerning the ticklish and confused Balkan situation. At the time the Yugoslav partisans were splintering into various quarreling factions and there was virtually a deadly civil war in progress between these splinters, even while under the German occupation. Adamic was summoned to Washington, where he and Stella dined at the White House with President Roosevelt, Mrs. Roosevelt, and Churchill. Listening to what Louis had to say about Tito and his rivals, Churchill nodded, sipped his brandy, smoked his cigar, and occasionally put a question to Louis.

It was a fantastic meeting for Louis—the high point of his life. Upon his return to New York, he briefed me about this epochal meeting with the British prime minister.

Later, Louis wrote a book about that memorable evening, *Dinner at the White House.* It was really a heavily padded article, with extraordinarily egotistical overtones, and was not received very well. The war had ended as Louis' book was published, the public had lost interest in Tito who had ruthlessly assumed absolute power in Yugoslavia, and the book's sales were small. To add to Louis' unhappiness, he received a legal notice one day informing him that Churchill, through his lawyers, was suing him over statements in *Dinner at the White House,* which he, Churchill, claimed he had never uttered that evening. Adamic became distressed.

I played a small part in his drama's final denouement. A few years before World War II, I had purchased a small summer house in Hunterdon County, in hilly northern New Jersey. When Louis and Stella came to visit me, Louis was so delighted with the countryside that he said he'd like to own a place nearby. I introduced him to the real-estate agent with whom I had arranged my own purchase, and that very weekend Louis acquired a fine, hill-top stone farmhouse with acreage and a large stone barn. He and Stella gave up their apartment on 34th Street and settled permanently in the country; soon they began to entertain weekend guests, and this added a new facet to Louis' life—the role of a country gentleman.

But later, owing to the legal embroilment he found himself engaged in with Churchill, Louis was forced to spend large sums of money on lawyers' fees to defend himself in court. It was a painful and costly undertaking. The trial dragged on, with Louis pumping more of his funds into legal fees, until he finally lost the case. When he was forced to make a generous financial settlement with Churchill's lawyers, he found himself practically bankrupt. With his last book a failure and his Tito market wiped out, he suffered a rapid loss of self-confidence. Like many emotional people under the stress of a major reversal, he went to pieces. When I saw him one day, he looked beaten, haggard, puffy. I had long since sold my place in the country, but he continued to cling to his, living out there in reduced circumstances. The change in his personality was startling. Later I heard from mutual friends that he began to have violent quarrels with Stella. Always neat, impeccably dressed, he now went around for days without shaving or changing his clothes, blaming his wife for his misfortunes. These quarrels mushroomed into fiery domestic scenes. At last, unable to endure his depressions and outbursts, Stella left him and went to California, where she found a job as a typist.

In the end, seeing no one, broken, living alone on his New Jersey farm, Louis shot himself.

Stella came back from California for the funeral.

William March's Parties Were Always Good Ones

Though Nellie was no longer working in Lieber's office and so did not come in contact with him, we continued to keep our relationship a secret. When I saw her I did not inquire about the fortunes of her clients, and she never pumped me about Lieber's writers and their activities. This arrangement was a sound one for both of us, because her own clients' burdens were all she cared to worry about; and as for me, I had enough writing problems of my own without needing to hear about the agonies of other writers.

Our affair, being secret, continued to have the special private quality it had from its beginning. This subterranean aspect lent it at times a passion, a note of dangerous urgency, that had become oddly half fatalistic, half bitter-sweet. I phoned Nellie almost nightly, and it was good to hear her cheerful voice after I'd had a lonely day at my typewriter. Sometimes when my hard days stretched into weeks Nellie, to cheer me up, laughingly urged me to go to Africa, to Bermuda, to Chile, to do something to shake myself out of my impasse. "Anyway, for Christ sake, get a new apartment and I'll put up new curtains for you!" she said.

But I continued to live on 34th Street for three more years. It was a good neighborhood, lively but not too noisy, until one day a vegetarian and his wife, both no longer young, moved into the empty apartment with a terrace directly below me and my pleasant little flat with its small kitchen, fireplace, and modern bathroom was no longer quiet and conducive to work.

This vegetarian couple ran a retail shop down the street for other food faddists. In their shop window they displayed fifty different kinds of bottled honeys, nuts, raisins, herbs, dried breakfast foods, and a large assortment of magazines devoted to the beautiful benefits to be derived from a meatless life. I had not known there were so many publications in America dealing with the fine points of carrot juice, prunes, and nuts. A glance at the products and the periodicals in this window always made me want to rush to one of the good restaurants in the neighborhood for a steak dinner.

At the approach of warm weather, these childless, aging vegetarians began to dine outdoors on their terrace below my apartment. Soon they began to entertain vegetarian friends for lunches and dinners, while their clerk took care of their shop up the block. Peering down from my windows I saw colorful repasts of carrots, celery, glasses of beet juice, and wheaten crackers artistically arranged on a snowy tablecloth. As my neighbors and their guests dined, their emphatic voices rose to my apartment, and all during the lengthy, sociable meals I was treated to detailed and scientific discussions on the merits of pepsin for the inner lining of the stomach, the surge of energy available from tablespoons of honey, and positive statements on longevity for followers of a non-meat diet.

My nightly phone calls to Nellie soon degenerated into acid recapitulations of the conversations I had listened to under my windows interspersed with thorough attacks on all vegetarians.

"Move to Paris, Madrid, or Brooklyn!" Nellie laughed. "Or how about Coney Island?"

Luckily my lease was drawing to a close. I moved out a month later.

I found a quiet apartment on East 30th Street, off Fifth Avenue. Located in a beautiful converted old brownstone, its rear windows overlooked the well-tended gardens of the Little Church Around the Corner, on 29th Street, which was a small oasis among tall buildings. It was only a few blocks from department stores and the frantic garment district. The only sound that reached me at my desk now was the low, distant hum of city traffic and the occasional pealing of the church bells, on Saturdays, announcing weddings, mostly between people from the theatrical world. Nellie came over to inspect my new place, bringing fresh curtains. "It's great, I love it, when do I move in? Hey, don't look scared." She laughed, though I hadn't looked frightened, and she hung the new curtains.

I sometimes liked to walk from my flat north up Fifth Avenue through noontime pedestrian and motor traffic past the fine shops. I frequently dropped into Lieber's office at 45th. The dramatized version of Caldwell's *Tobacco Road* had now been running for years on Broadway, with many companies playing it on the road, and Lieber and Caldwell were both receiving generous weekly royalty statements. His increased reputation as an agent now forced Lieber to turn many writers away, except the most talented ones. Like most other agents, he of course lost several good writers because of their restlessness or dissatisfaction over contracts, among them such writers as O'Hara, Cheever, and Farrell. In the meanwhile he acquired Carson McCullers, Nathanael West, Maxim Gorky, Dreiser, and other name writers. At times, despite his lucrative roster of writers, Lieber didn't look too happy. His first marriage had ended in divorce; soon he would marry his current secretary, his fourth since Nellie had quit, a pretty, dark-haired girl. But this marriage, too, quickly began to go on the rocks. He never mentioned Nellie's name, and of course I never told him I was seeing her. Once when I visited him in his office just before his second divorce, he stared at me with a tortured expression.

"I've gone through hell lately, I can't sleep!" He waved his arms. "Listen, you're single, you want her? You can have her!" But a few minutes later, when he had calmed down, he was speaking enthusiastically about a new manuscript one of his clients had sent him. He was having lunch with a publisher, and he said he was going to ask for a huge advance.

But though he mingled with top editors, ate in the best restaurants, and wore well-cut tweeds, Lieber continued to talk about the downtrodden and the unemployed. In restaurants I had seen him send a steak back to the kitchen because it had not been broiled exactly to his instructions, shouting at the distressed waiters, then turn to me and begin talking about the striking auto workers in Detroit. In the space of a minute, he could be warmhearted and understanding, then turn irascible and domineering. He now owned a large farm in Bucks County, Pennsylvania, and when he invited me there for weekends he was the perfect host, cooking gourmet meals with an apron around his waist and setting out the best Scotch. I knew he was anxious to get married again, to try his luck for the third time, but two disasters had made him cautious. "Albert, being single is hell, isn't it?" he said. I kept silent about Nellie. My thoughts wandered back to my own past. Hedda had gotten married, had children now, and other girls I'd known had also found husbands. No matter how great the loves had been, I thought, how torrid the nights, how tortured the quarrels, the girls always found someone else to marry.

Sometimes I met William March in Lieber's office. Lieber admired March's talent, and they joked and laughed together, but I always sensed they did not especially like each other. When March arrived in Lieber's office, his lips curved into a gracious Mississippi smile, yet it was a subtle smile, faintly ironic and mysterious. March was always well dressed, and with his hat off you noticed how very carefully he combed his very wavy brown hair. His early novels did not sell well, but he had a fine reputation among writers and a small, loyal public.

March was a partner in a prosperous Gulf steamship company and wrote his books during his spare time. When I was in London, March had been in charge of the European business for his company's steamship freight trade. He made frequent visits to Hamburg and Berlin. When he returned to London, where his office was located, he used to tell me of his experiences with Nazi shipping officials. He was shrewd and clever in his dealings with them, and nothing gave him more pleasure than to best Hitler's minions on a freight contract. When he wasn't giving an account of his transactions, he spoke of the depravity of the Germans. Some of the Nazi officials had taken him to parties which he described to me; and in his soft, well-modulated voice, March detailed the perversions he had witnessed. The details of so-called abnormal behavior are always fascinating for a while; but soon, if these details are repeated enough, one feels the narrator is perhaps obtaining too much pleasure from telling them, and this is what I felt about March.

London's literary world, like New York's, is a small one, and during my stay there I began to meet March at small, informal literary gatherings I occasionally attended. With his soft, southern drawl and impeccable manners, he soon became popular at these parties. He was a wonderfully skillful storyteller, and it was difficult to know when he was telling a straight story or pulling your leg. He gave parties in his flat on Baker Street, and told everyone the apartment had been occupied by Conan Doyle when Doyle wrote his Sherlock Holmes tales. During one evening he told his British guests, in his southern drawl, that he and William Faulkner had been childhood friends and had gone to school together.

March had been in the Marine Corps during World War I, had seen active service in France, and was fond of telling his combat experiences. He said he had been gassed, and had been blind for a year in hospital, after which he had recovered his sight. When asked how it felt to go suddenly blind, he replied that blindness was a bland, cool world. Everywhere he went he was always original, amusing, and popular.

He returned to America after his firm had sold its shipping interests at a great profit to a syndicate. He looked me up and I began seeing him again in New York. He told me his share of the firm's shipping sale had made him a wealthy man. He rented a large apartment on Central Park West, then moved to an even larger apartment in Gramercy Square. He hired an art expert to assist him in acquiring a fine collection of modern French impressionist paintings, which he hung on his walls, and proceeded to throw big parties. At these gatherings his smiling, well-trained Filipino butler circulated among the guests always ready with fresh drinks that had been prepared and chilled beforehand, without ice. These drinks were potent and at many of his parties March watched with his subtle smile as some of his guests passed out. During one party I attended, an ex-strong man who had gone into the publishing business, printing pamphlets describing how you, too, could be muscular and healthy if you followed the printed directions of his setting-up exercises, became the hero of the evening. This big sturdy man, no longer young and now running to fat, after downing six or seven drinks, proceeded to demonstrate his prowess, executing knee-bends, push-ups, and other physical feats. His demonstration, which came when most of the guests had consumed a great deal of alcohol, was greeted with great delight, and soon men and women were shedding jackets, shoes, and other articles of clothing, seeking to emulate his performance. Many guests, after one or two push-ups, lay prostrate on the floor. Viewing the figures adorning his rug, a kindly look on his southern gentleman's face, March turned and ordered his Filipino servant to prepare large batches of bacon and eggs for the moment when his guests regained consciousness. "And have three or four big pots of coffee ready," he added.

Despite his partying, March was a steady writer. His reputation grew and with the publication of *The Bad Seed* he enjoyed, for the first time, the satisfaction of a best-seller. He had parted from Lieber by this time, and was now represented by another agency, the Harold Ober office. As always with Lieber, when he lost a good writer he was bitter. "And after all I did for him!" he told me after he had lost March. It was a rather normal agent's reaction; you represented an unknown, or little known, writer and when that writer began to sell and left you, you naturally became bitter. Once when a client, a writer who had been raised in Hell's Kitchen on Manhattan's West Side, abandoned Lieber for another agent, Lieber turned to me and shouted: "What can you expect from him? He's not a writer, he's just a gangster!" He sent the man a nasty letter. A few months later, however, when his anger had cooled somewhat, he met this writer at a cocktail party where he greeted him warmly.

As for March, he seemed happier with his new agent. *The Bad Seed* was dramatized by Maxwell Anderson and enjoyed a huge success on Broadway, after which it was sold to Hollywood. One day, not having seen March for some time, I had a phone call from him during which he told me he was giving up his New York apartment and was moving to New Orleans.

"After all, I'm a Southerner," he said pleasantly, "and New Orleans is more civilized, more relaxed than New York."

When he died there, in the French Quarter, I was shocked. He wasn't old, just sixty.

Turmoil in Spain, and in Yorkville

The great trauma of the thirties for many of the country's intellectuals was not the Depression but the tragedy of the Spanish Civil War. To watch a noble cause turn into something ignoble, to watch from afar the fragmentation of a democratic people with too many leaders operating behind a facade of slogans concealing internecine strife, while a fascist foe marched from victory to victory, was an excruciating experience. It was endured only with the greatest emotional pain by onlookers who, three thousand miles from the Spanish earth, read about the Spanish war and envisioned a nightmare in which Hitler's and Mussolini's bombing squadrons blasted Teruel and Madrid.

Some American intellectuals went over to fight Franco and died there. Several came back to tell of the people's endurance and sacrifices and to raise money for the Loyalists. A few returned to tell bitter stories of the small but deadly civil wars raging within the larger civil war; but they found only tiny audi-

ences. No one, it seemed, wanted to hear unpopular versions of
the struggle going on in Spain. It was more thrilling to listen,
enraptured, to tales of heroism, uncomplicated acts of bravery, of
self-sacrifice performed by simple people pouring out their life-
blood for a victory which would eventually be theirs.

For the duration of the Spanish agony, New York was a
city of stirring mass meetings, rallies, and fund raisings. Committees were regularly formed to exhort the government in Washington to send arms to the Loyalists. Almost every writer, artist,
and professor in the country signed endless petitions.

I happened to be at a fund-raising gathering held in a
large Central Park West apartment at which the guest of honor
was a representative of the Loyalist government sent to America
to rally support for his people. The man spoke faulty English but
his ungrammatical sentences somehow ennobled him and made
his address to us all the more powerful.

"My good friends," he began, "my government is not
beggar. We have gold, we have money. But I am sorry to say
each way we turn for support we get nowhere, no one is help us.
My friends, I was with delegation to London last month. We say
to important government people there, 'Give us planes, give us
tanks, we have gold, we no want these things for nothing.' The
English they listen, they very polite to us. When we return to
Spain our people ask us, 'Did you succeed in mission, will they
give us arms?' 'No,' we say, 'we have failed.' 'How is that?' our
people ask. 'How can you tell?' 'We know,' we answer, 'we know
they have refuse us.' 'Why, how did you know that? Did they say
no to you?' 'They did not say no. But all the time we visit in their
office, no one ask us to sit down.' "

Some women at the party wept as they listened to this tale.
"This can't go on! It's not decent!" But though the bulk of
American opinion, according to the polls, was favorable to the
Loyalist cause, Washington was silent, sitting on its political

hands as fascist bombs rained down upon Spanish cities from foreign planes. From Capitol Hill apologetic messages filtered through subterranean channels. "This is a political year. . . . Because of a certain religious voting bloc the government is unable to render assistance at this time."

In New York, frustration, sorrow, and anger mounted with each fresh headline announcing a new Loyalist defeat. Many writers could no longer write, artists were unable to paint —the growing tragedy was so overwhelming that individual creative effort seemed puny and meaningless beside the details of the murder of a whole democracy which daily came screaming from the radio.

Each evening that I phoned, or saw, Nellie, we spoke of Spain. Our conversations were always the same, filled with helpless distress. Sorrow became monotonous; horror, too. One night on the phone we exclaimed together, in unrehearsed despair: "Jesus Christ, let's meet and screw."

In an attempt to conquer loneliness during this period, one went to the almost nightly mass meetings and rallies, one listened to fiery and accusatory speeches directed against Washington, one gave money when the chairmen called for collections, and one returned to one's room or apartment drained, sickened, unable to sleep. It was a time when one seemed to live on nervous energy. One's phone rang constantly. "Did you hear that President Roosevelt promised to send them some tanks?" "And I read where France is sending planes! . . ." But the rumors always turned out to be false. Artists donated more paintings to be auctioned at mass meetings, writers gave manuscripts of their novels, Hemingway addressed cheering audiences to raise funds for ambulances. Perhaps because the Spanish tragedy was so public and prolonged, to some Americans its traumatizing effect was even greater than that caused, later, when the world suddenly learned about the gas ovens of Hitler. The Fuehrer's underlings had managed to conceal their mass murders until the Allied armies overran the death camps, while the terrible details of the Spanish Civil War were printed daily on the front pages of newspapers.

As if the suffering caused by the Depression, allied with the nightmare of the Spanish betrayal, were not calamitous enough, another area of turmoil suddenly surfaced in New York. Burgeoning activities of local Nazi storm troopers appeared in Manhattan's Yorkville district, along East 86th Street. Flushed by the successes of their compatriots back in the fatherland, members of the newly formed German-American Bund marched in brown-shirted cadres through the upper East Side streets, right arms extended, shouting: "Heil, Hitler!" Many citizens were outraged by these antics, but the police declared they were powerless to stop the Bund rallies on the street corners. "They have the right to free assemblage and free speech, too."

As these street meetings grew in size and intensity, groups of Communists traveled by subway to Yorkville to protest, and if possible prevent, the brown-shirt rallies. Clashes occurred, which were quelled with difficulty by struggling police. One afternoon Lieber phoned me from his office while I was working in the quiet of my apartment.

"Albert, the fascists are going to hold a big meeting this evening in Yorkville. We've got to appear and display our strength." I had never taken part in a demonstration, or counter-demonstration, and when I replied that I'd planned to work all evening on the novel I was writing, Lieber raised his voice over the phone. "It's your fight, too! Do you want Hitler's philosophy to take root here?" It is always a waste of time to answer a self-righteous man in his anger. Lieber's voice rose to an excited pitch. "Listen, don't you feel *anything* about what Hitler is doing to the Jews?"

Of course I did. His query was insulting. Although with

effort I remained silent under his insolent attack, his words nevertheless made me feel guilty. "All right." I gave in.

That evening I rode the subway to 86th Street. When I climbed the subway stairs and emerged on Lexington Avenue I saw the mass of people and the police. Wooden barriers had been set up; additional police on horseback were stationed on the corners. I looked about, seeking Lieber's face in the crowd; we had agreed to meet in front of the florist's shop on the southeast corner of 86th, but the police were shoving people back behind the barriers and I saw at once it was impossible to locate anyone in this crush. I heard shouting.

"They're on Third Avenue!" "Let's stop that fascist meeting! . . . "

Though the mounted police, maneuvering their horses, managed to squeeze some people back onto the sidewalk, a crowd overturned the barriers and surged east toward Third Avenue where the brau houses stood in a row on 86th, like a section of Berlin. The crowd began roaring hoarsely. "No storm troopers here!" "Down with Hitler! . . ." Leftists carrying anti-Nazi signs were joined by members of the Jewish War Veterans wearing overseas caps and bearing American Legion banners. Suddenly in the distance, under the Third Avenue El, I glimpsed the brown shirts' swastika banners. A bigger roar went up.

"Down with fascism!" "Destroy Hitler! . . ."

Caught in the churning crowd, I was swept along toward Third Avenue where I witnessed a speaker in a Nazi uniform haranguing listeners over a public address system rigged atop a panel truck. The truck was guarded by about twenty men in storm troop uniforms who stood facing the audience, their stolid faces upraised—the scene seemed an illustration cut out of a German magazine. In the din the speaker's voice blurred intermittently into the clamor of the crowd. Looking along the row of stores down Third Avenue, I saw the frightened faces of

Jewish merchants staring from their windows. Suddenly the volume of the amplifying system on top of the truck increased and the words shot out above the heads of the crowd.

"True Americans, rise up! . . . Down with Zionism! . . ."

From the upper windows of tenements lining both sides of Third Avenue onlookers stared down; while some were silent, others began shouting encouragement to the brown shirts.

When the police on horseback appeared from Lexington Avenue, their arrival inaugurated a series of struggles along the sidewalks. Horses reared up, clubs were raised above the crowd; as blows rained down, a new cry went up:

"Cossacks! . . . Down with the cossacks! . . ." Only two blocks from silk-stocking Park Avenue, one now heard the cries of Union Square. "Bastard cossacks! . . ." As a detachment of brown shirts moved south on Third Avenue there was a crash of glass—the windows of a jewelry store and a haberdashery had been broken. Nearby, storm troopers were overturning a corner newsstand; wheeling around suddenly, I saw the trapped, terrified face of a helpless little Jewish news dealer as the brown shirts, ripping magazines from his racks, screamed, "Juden, Juden!"

The demonstration didn't last much longer after that. Police reinforcements arrived in vans and the officers, swinging clubs, went after everyone. Soon both brown shirts and protesters had scattered down the side streets.

When I returned to my apartment the telephone was ringing.

"Were you there?" Lieber demanded.

"Yes."

"I didn't see you."

"I didn't see you, either."

He calmed down over the wire. "I hope you didn't get hurt. I was almost run down by one of the horses."

"I haven't got a scratch."

"Good." He laughed grimly. "It's happening here now." He hung up.

I tried to get back to my novel, but the disturbance on 86th Street had shaken me. For two days I sat around my apartment without working, then wrote a story. I set the piece in Chicago, under the Lake Street El. The main character was a short, stocky news dealer who operated a newsstand adjoining one of the metal El posts. He was my father, and I was a thirteen-year-old kid coming from high school one afternoon to relieve him at his newsstand. As I passed a poolroom on my way to join my father, several hoodlums emerged from the doorway to taunt me, shouting obscene remarks about my older sister. The rest of the story wrote itself, and I sent it to Lieber. He instantly submitted it to *Harper's,* and the next day received a telephone call from one of the editors.

"We're very interested in Halper's story, 'Prelude.' However, we'd like a few changes."

"What changes? Why?"

"It's a little too—strong, we feel. We've never published a story dealing with anti-Semitism here before. I don't believe any national magazine has."

"Don't you believe it exists here? Anti-Semitism?"

"Yes, of course. But the incident the author describes seems overly—violent."

"Were you at 86th Street the other evening?"

"I read about it in the *Times.* Well, I'll call you back in a few days and let you know. As I said, we like the story but somehow we don't believe things like that could happen in an American city."

Lieber phoned me to report the conversation he had had with the editor. He was discouraged. "I guess I'll have to give it to the *New Masses.* I'll wait a few days."

Two days later the *Times* reported an incident which had occurred the previous evening on the lower East Side. Two men entered a small basement print shop and, holding the Jewish proprietor helpless, had scratched a swastika into the flesh of his chest with the point of a pocket knife. The story appeared on the front page. Lieber phoned *Harper's,* which still held my story.

"Well, can it happen here?"

George Leighton, my friend at *Harper's,* had answered the phone. "They've decided to publish the story."

Well, I had sold it. But this experience again hammered home the point that, either as combatant or spectator, it was useless to tell myself I could insulate my work from the conditions that prevailed in my time.

What Do You Think of the Pact?

Each morning when I left my apartment on 30th Street for breakfast, the city was already humming and alive. In nearby loft buildings the manufacturers of women's bathing suits, bras, and slips had their staffs working at machines. Trucks were drawn up outside waiting to haul cartons of merchandise. The side streets were jammed with traffic. Errand boys were carrying parcels into buildings. I made my way toward Fourth Avenue to my favorite cafeteria on 28th Street, the Belmore, the one patronized by shipping clerks, office workers, and cabdrivers. At nine-thirty in the morning the large cafeteria was more or less deserted, with only a few tables of cabbies sipping their coffee. I entered and approached the long service counter to give my order for the thirty-cent breakfast special—grapefruit, one egg, buttered toast, and coffee. During this quiet hour I always had a table to myself, and as I started on my grapefruit I watched the manager's assistant, a woman in a white dress, place a fresh rose in the slim vase on every table.

The Belmore Cafeteria was the cabbies' Montparnasse cafe; I heard them discuss their earnings, their enemies the traffic cops, and weighty international political events. "Yesterday was lousy, I only made a pound." "So when this mick cop wants to give me a ticket in front of Grand Central I says, 'Is it my fault the light turned red when I was wedged between them two big trucks?' " "This Hitler, he thinks he owns the world but take it from me he'll burn his ass sliding into home plate." "And that Mussolini guy, what the hell's he doing in Africa? . . ." The cafeteria manager, not a lover of cabdrivers, made the rounds and paused at my table, lowering his voice as he uttered a complaint from the corner of his mouth. "Why do they take up room here? For a five-cent cup of coffee! They think they're philosophers but take it from me they're the scum of the earth. . . ."

When I returned to my apartment the mail was waiting in my mailbox in the vestibule—additional appeals for money for Spanish refugees, for labor defense committees, for assistance to striking miners. If your name was on one list, it was on them all.

Whenever I phoned Lieber about a manuscript or the sale of translation rights, as soon as he gave me the information I sought, he plunged into a political pitch. "Did you see in today's *Times* where Franco's army is only *thirty* miles from Madrid? The masses here must be aroused! I wish you would get more active, Albert, be really involved," he pleaded. His words always irritated me but I kept silent. One day, when Lieber was pressing too hard, I made him a proposition.

"I'll make a bargain with you, Max. Want to hear it?"

"Certainly." His voice was eager. "What bargain?"

"The day Hemingway and Faulkner join the Party, I'll take out a card, too." He didn't think that was funny. But it silenced him for a while.

As for Spain, the bloody struggle there after three terrible years was reaching its terminal phase, like a shriveled old man choking and dying in a hospital. At the end the Loyalist side was bled white, the cities were in ruins, and the politicians were still quarreling among themselves as the fronts collapsed. Franco marched triumphantly into Madrid. Accompanied by bugles, braids, and banners, he announced a new epochal era for Spain. Intellectuals began streaming toward the borders while the hungry masses cheered the victors, lifting up cupped hands for bread. As the Caudillo bowed and smiled, firing squads were already shooting truckloads of citizens in the cemeteries. Overhead German and Italian planes showed off with elaborate maneuvers. Hitler and Mussolini sent warmest and fraternal greetings to the captured city. In years to come, Eleanor Roosevelt was to say sweetly: "Looking back, I think my husband and our government should have sent some kind of help."

In New York, the final collapse of the Loyalist fronts came as almost a relief: many people turned to each other as if living in a surrealist dream. Nellie phoned me and in her anguish said, "I've been on the verge of vomiting all day." But this blow was soon to be followed by another.

One morning the announcement of the Nazi-Soviet Pact splattered across the front pages of newspapers like black blood. At first the comrades refused to believe the headlines. How could this be true? It was "another capitalist plot to divide the workers." The report of the pact in the press was so monstrous it was obviously a fake. Comrades and fellow travelers rushed to the phones to call one another. "Did you see the latest capitalist lie in the *Times*? . . ." "The American press has become fas-

cist! . . ." "Of course tomorrow morning Moscow will denounce
the whole thing as false. . . ."

The following day *Pravda* pronounced, in solemn and
reasoned phrases, the wisdom and sound "historical dialectics"
of "this political move with our new friends to the west." Everyone, including the State Department, knew that soon Poland
was to become a walnut between the nutcracker of German
panzer divisions and the legions from the steppes.

In New York, the Party leadership struggled valiantly to
keep the rank-and-file membership in line. There were hastily
called cell meetings, to "explain everything." But following the
first bulletin from *Pravda,* members began resigning with the
rapidity of autumn leaves falling in a three-day windstorm. As
they thought of Hitler's persecutions of their co-religionists,
many Jewish comrades tore their cards to bits or set them afire.

The day after the announcement of the pact, I went to
Lieber's office to discuss a manuscript of mine. The meeting had
been arranged a few days earlier. As I opened the door I heard
voices; there was another client in his inner office. His secretary
was not present in the outer office, doubtless gone out for her
usual morning coffee break. I cleared my throat audibly, but because Lieber and his visitor were speaking so animatedly they did
not hear me. I sat down in the outer office and waited.

Beyond the thin glass door they were discussing the Nazi-
Soviet Pact. The client seemed almost in tears, and Lieber himself was speaking in a tone of distress I had never heard before.

"But we must be patient," he was pleading, "we must
have faith in the Soviet Union and what it stands for. . . . After
all, Moscow knows what it's doing. . . . Stalin has a plan, a
design that will benefit the masses everywhere. . . ."

"But a coalition—with the Nazis?"

"I know, I know. . . . But for God's sake we must trust,

must be patient . . . until we know the reason behind it. . . ."

"But with the *Nazis?*"

Then I recognized the visitor's voice. It belonged to a writer whom I shall call Oscar Plotzman, a writer who had written for the *New Masses* years ago, before going to work in the dream factories of Hollywood. I had met Plotzman several times in Lieber's office and I knew he was Lieber's close friend as well as a client.

"I admit I, too, was a little confused at first," Lieber was saying, his voice none too convincing but struggling to reach a tone of earnestness. "But one can't lose faith in the Soviet Union. Wait, wait awhile, and I'm certain everything will become clear to us." There was a silence. "I beg you, don't do anything rash. Please, as a personal favor to me! Look, we've known each other for years—aren't I your friend?" Following a pause, a sigh came from beyond the glass door.

"Okay, Max. I know you're my friend. This has knocked me for a loop, but I have faith in Stalin."

Lieber laughed with relief. "You think Stalin is stupid? A great Marxist, like he is?"

They came out of the office together, smiling, and saw me.

"I just got here," I said. Plotzman extended his hand warmly to me. "How's California?" I asked.

"Fine, fine," he smiled. "It's been years since I saw you, hasn't it? I'm married, have two children now." Lieber was beaming.

"Wonderful," I said.

"When are you coming out to work in films? We're making some good pictures, you know."

"He's working on a new book," Lieber explained cheerfully. "Maybe he'll make the trip west some day."

"Fine. When you finish it, come out to the coast." Plotzman pressed my hand. None of us knew then that one day he would be blacklisted, would do time in jail. Lieber walked Plotzman to the door and out into the hall toward the elevator. When he returned we went into his office and conferred about a few possible changes in my manuscript. We were business-like during our discussion, but when our conversation was over Lieber suddenly looked tired.

"What do *you* think, Albert?" he said, turning to me.

"About what?"

"About the pact."

"I don't know. It came as a shock."

"But what do you *think* of it?"

He was totally unaware how desperate and pleading his expression had become. He wanted me to say I had faith in the Soviet Union, in Stalin. He was at my mercy, all his defenses down. But I could not bring myself to move in for the kill.

"I don't know, Max. I really don't know."

At that moment his young secretary returned. Poking her head into the inner office, she greeted me with a good-morning smile. "I'm back." As she sat down to her typewriter, I left.

The turmoil, the wavering in the Party ranks, didn't last long. After numerous cell meetings and the hurried publication of spiritedly written "scientific dialectical" articles in the *Daily Worker*, the membership discerned the great wisdom in Stalin's move. Even many comrades who had torn up or had burned their cards returned to the fold and humbly apologized for any "totally unwarranted bourgeois doubts" they had temporarily harbored "in a brief moment of confusion."

Three
Black Writers

During the thirties the relationship between the white and Negro intellectuals was, on the surface, relaxed. The black nationalist movement had not as yet been really launched—in fact it was in its infancy—and whenever white and black intellectuals met to discuss art or politics it was a meeting without anger. That would come later. In the thirties I knew three black writers: Claude McKay, Langston Hughes, and Richard Wright.

I knew Claude McKay because I had met him at a party where we talked about Jean Toomer and Eric Waldron. He said he rarely met anybody who knew the work of either Toomer or Waldron, and he started calling me up and asking me to his Harlem gin parties. I knew Langston Hughes because he was Lieber's client. We had met frequently in Lieber's office and Lieber used to invite us both as weekend guests to his Bucks County farm. I knew Richard Wright because he and I worked in the same Chicago Central Post Office—though at different times—and when Wright came to New York to live, a mutual friend arranged our first meeting. All three of these men are very much dead now.

I don't remember just where Claude McKay lived in Harlem but I recall he moved often. He resided for a time, I believe, in one of the side streets off St. Nicholas Avenue. When I climbed his flights on my first visit there I saw all the duplicate and triplicate locks on the doors as I made my ascent. It was wintertime and the halls were cold.

When I opened the door to McKay's flat I recognized the familiar heat coming from a gas oven. There were about ten guests present, two of them white, a man and a woman, and I saw everybody had drinks and was having a good time. McKay came over, smiling, and introduced me to the others. Then he said, "Have a hard time finding this place?"

"There's no number on your door downstairs."

He laughed. "No numbers anywhere on this street. That's to fool the collectors. The mailmen already *know.*"

McKay was originally from Jamaica. He was very dark skinned with finely cut, almost Oriental features. He had quick, observant eyes and spoke with a slight West Indian accent. He had gone to Kansas State College and after that had worked as a dining car waiter, writing in his spare time. Eventually he published a talented book of poems, *Songs of Jamaica,* and was immediately taken up by the white literary partying set. He began contributing to the literary magazines, among them the *Liberator* which was the forerunner of the *New Masses,* and, riding the crest of his popularity, lived for a time in England where he met George Bernard Shaw, the Webbs, and other elite Socialists. Then he journeyed to Moscow, where he was wined and dined profusely. All this he told me later. By the time I first met him he was no longer being wined and dined by anybody.

He was employed by the Federal Writers Project, for a while, which meant he could meet his rent and eat sparingly.

As such gatherings go, it was a nice party that night. Once again McKay began to talk to me about Toomer and Waldron. He spoke mostly about Waldron, I recall, possibly because Waldron was a West Indian like himself. When I remarked that Eric Waldron's *Tropic Death* was a very fine and powerful book of short stories which had been cruelly neglected and forgotten, McKay's face lit up. "We ought to form a committee and resuscitate that book!" he said. I laughed, saying I was not a press agent but would try my best to help. Our conversation about Waldron came to a close when someone knocked on the door, and in walked Zora Neale Hurston, who was greeted by McKay warmly. McKay introduced her to those people at the party she hadn't met before. He made her a drink, someone gave her his chair, and she quickly became the party's center of interest.

Zora Neale Hurston was a slim, attractive young woman in her late thirties at the time I met her. She was a wonderful conversationalist, with a wickedly sharp wit. Among the jobs she had held in New York was that of private secretary to Fannie Hurst, the novelist. Her duties enabled her to meet many white people in Miss Hurst's circle, some of whom she did not especially admire. She was a skillful mimic, and her repertoire of imitations set the party in an uproar.

The gin flowed that night. McKay didn't believe in serving food, or maybe he couldn't afford to that evening, for all Zora Neale Hurston could scrounge in his kitchen later was a half a loaf of bread and a few thin pieces of baloney. When the party broke up, someone said he had an old car downstairs at the curb. We left McKay waving to us from the top of the stairs. Out in the cold night air about ten of us piled into the car, whose owner delivered several of us to the nearest subway station.

I never saw Zora Neale Hurston again. She had several fine stories published in *Harper's,* I believe, and had one or two novels to her credit. Like McKay, she was taken up for a time by white people who gave parties; and though she was invited to many literary salons downtown I'm certain she never unsheathed her sharp wit for these hosts and their guests or treated them to the mimicry she displayed at McKay's place that night. Again like McKay, she later experienced a diminution of her literary output, and in the literary jungles of Manhattan she soon found herself neglected, then forgotten. Years later she died in poverty in a southern city, her partying days over, her books out of print.

I saw McKay after that party for almost a year, off and on. Our meetings were always very friendly, and I soon had the good sense to bring a bottle with me whenever he phoned to tell me he was having some friends drop in at his place. The parties were fine, but not as fine as the first one. Soon the intervals between our meetings lengthened, then when McKay phoned me to drop by I sometimes made excuses. Parties—white or black—have a tendency to repeat themselves. Later, when I invited McKay to my place when I gave a small party, he said he couldn't make it. I called him a second time. He was cordial over the wire, but he happened to be busy again. This is not unusual in New York and I was not offended; one meets people at parties, one feels friendly toward them for a while, and as time passes one does not meet with them any more.

At the time I knew McKay he was not writing well or much. I sensed he was at the end of the line—a terrible and tragic period for a writer. Lacking sustained encouragement, he was a talented man born too early, functioning in an era when genuine Negro literary ability was a cultural curiosity. If he were alive today, he would most certainly be a major figure among black intellectuals. But during the time in which he lived, when only the singer Paul Robeson and the dancer Bill "Bojangles"

Robinson were popular Harlem personalities, McKay must have lost heart. Before he died in 1948, he had converted to Catholicism, repudiating his articles in the *Liberator* and his Marxist beliefs.

Langston Hughes is difficult to write about—difficult because he was a wonderful, warmhearted, and generous man who in my opinion was an embarrassingly minor talent. I liked him but I could never read his work. Because of his subject matter, black life, I demanded stronger stuff from him, but he never delivered—not to me anyway. Only in his first two slim volumes of poetry—*The Weary Blues* and *Old Clothes to the Jew*—did I feel a true emotional core to the man.

He and I used to ride in Lieber's car to our agent's Bucks County farm. Lieber was always in a good mood on these trips because he had gotten away from his office for a couple of days. Hughes and I looked forward to these weekends in the country. A jaunty host, Lieber prided himself on being a gourmet cook and, sitting in the large living room of that old stone house with its great fireplace, Hughes and I watched him painstakingly putting butter and chopped onions on top of the steak after taking it off the coals. While eating the good food and drinking red wine, we would discuss writing and politics, subjects we beat to a pulp visit after visit. Though a good conversationalist, Hughes was, like myself, more or less a listener out in Bucks County because Lieber, away from his office, loved to play the role of paterfamilias after dessert, relating stories, some of them not too complimentary, about editors and publishers, and writers who had left his stable. Lieber loved being an agent, especially now that he was a prosperous one; and he was excusably pompous upon occasion, reminding us of his foresight in acquiring unknown writers of talent who had been turned down by other agents, who later became established literary figures. Hughes and I, having heard this monologue before, listened with amused and friendly tolerance. When Lieber had talked himself out, Hughes would sometimes, in his modest way, take over, spinning off stories and anecdotes.

Langston Hughes had traveled practically all over the world. He had met almost everybody. His brown skin had been his passport to everywhere. He described his stays in Spain, Mexico, and the Soviet Union, telling us about the writers, artists, and musicians he had met in those countries. He was especially fond of Carmel, California, where he had lived for some time. Like McKay and Zora Neale Hurston, he had been taken up during the beginning of his career by white people, notably the Carl Van Vechten salon. But when I met him that phase of his life was over. As a literary craftsman, he was very skilled in many areas. He had written an early, awkward play, *Mulatto,* in which Leon Janney, a white actor, had acted the leading role, and it had had an extended Broadway run.

"You must have earned a lot of royalties on *Mulatto,*" I said, "with a run like that."

Hughes gave me a wan smile. "No, the tickets sold cut-rate most of the time." During the early thirties, I remembered, you could purchase a balcony seat for a Broadway play for fifty cents, which meant a minuscule royalty for the author. Hughes said that despite the play's lengthy run, he had collected only about $5,000 from it, a paltry sum for a long-run Broadway production.

Hughes was one of the most prolific clients in Lieber's agency. He turned out poems, fables, novels, an autobiography, collections of short stories, plays, and musicals. He also made the lecture tour circuit, and was popular as a platform performer reading his poems.

The trouble with Hughes was that everybody loved him. He was too sweet, too warm, too generous. He lacked enemies—always a sign of weakness. Even during the disgraceful McCarthy hearings when he was under pitiless harassment by the Senator's committee in Washington, he did not lash back at his tormentors. When he died, countless people—black and white—openly wept. They remembered his numberless acts of kindness, his warmth, his smile. Memorial meetings were held in his honor, and a movement was started to name an off-Broadway theater after him.

Richard Wright was unlike McKay and Hughes in every respect. He was powerful, unflinching, tenacious, self-confident —and he made enemies. When I first read his poems and short stories in the *New Masses,* I did not think he had much talent, regarding his work as dull Party-line writing. But when I began reading his *Native Son* I realized at once America now had a startling new major writer. No one, I felt, had ever handled Negro material so forcefully before, with such true skill and soaring accuracy. I finished the book feeling excited, over-whelmed, and a little jealous.

Soon after I read *Native Son* my phone rang; it was Walt Carmon, whom I had met in Moscow. He and his wife Rose had returned from the Soviet Union several years ago and we had kept in touch, seeing each other occasionally.

"Hey, do you want to meet Richard Wright?" Walt asked.

"Sure," I said. "When and where?"

"I'll call you back; I saw him last night. We were talking about Chicago writers—Nelson Algren, Jack Conroy, and you. When I said I knew you and that you were living in New York he said he'd like to meet you. I'll call you back after I get in touch with him."

We met a few days later, at the appointed place under the big clock of the old Central Savings Bank on the corner of Fourth Avenue and 14th Street. Standing there, I saw Walt and Wright coming toward me. Wright was a little under medium height, solidly built, with a pleasant face. As we shook hands, I sensed at once that under that smooth exterior a powerful dynamo was humming day and night. We appraised each other briefly, somewhat like contending prizefighters, then we both smiled. It seemed like a good beginning.

The three of us walked to a luncheonette across the street. We had a lengthy lunch, during which Wright and I talked about Chicago, the night shift at the Post Office, and Raklios' lunchroom across the street on Jackson Boulevard where the night-shift employees ordered their hamburgers, apple pie, and coffee. We agreed that the big Post Office had been like a prison, recalling the dust from the mail sacks floating in the air and the supervisors constantly walking the long aisles of mail cases.

"You wrote a piece on the Chicago Post Office in the old *Haldeman-Julius Monthly,* didn't you?" Wright smiled. "A lot of us clerks had a copy of that issue in our back pockets when we were throwing the mail. The supervisors saw it and didn't like it." He laughed.

"*Native Son* will be a landmark," I said enviously. "I'm sincerely jealous." Wright looked pleased. "What hit me between the eyes was the setting, the South Side scene," I continued. I told him that one of my former jobs had been as a sort of junior advance man for the R. J. Reynolds Tobacco Company, trying to promote a product, a chewing tobacco plug called Apple Sun Cured, to the Negro trade on the South Side. "I used to go into those candy stores and poolrooms on State and 31st and I was scared stiff in those all-Negro hangouts. I knew they didn't want to listen to my spiel about Apple Sun Cured chewing tobacco. When they listened in stony silence I wanted to run. I worked at that job for two months, then quit." Wright laughed again.

"What part of Chicago were you born in?" he asked.

"Around Lake Street and Ashland Avenue."

"That's all black territory now," Wright said with a smile.

"It was always a bleak section of Chicago and you can have it."

I wanted to discuss *Native Son* further, but hung back. I had felt, while reading the novel, that the trial scenes were overlong, with their set speeches, which could have been cut drastically; they had caused the book to drag for me, a major flaw in the novel, I thought. But I said nothing to Wright about it. Years later, reading *The Stranger,* I admired Camus' skill in condensing the trial scenes in the last half of that novel. In some way these two superb books, so utterly diverse in conception, were oddly similar philosophically, both heralding the arrival of the urban anti-hero in modern literature.

"Say, *Native Son* is being made into a play," Wright told me. He didn't look too pleased. "I'm working on it with a professional playwright, Paul Green, but it's difficult to write with another person and make him see what you think ought to go into the play."

"You ought to play the part of Bigger," Walt, who was sitting next to Wright, said.

"Oh sure, oh sure," Wright laughed. "It would close after the first night." *

---

* One day, when Richard Wright had already been living in Paris for several years, I saw a notice in a New York newspaper on the film *Native Son.* The item noted that the picture had been recently produced in a large South American city (Buenos Aires? Rio?), had been bankrolled by a wealthy Latin patron living in France, and was now being shown in a small Manhattan art theater. I didn't see the film during its first run, which lasted only one week; it received extremely poor reviews, and the management abruptly terminated its run. Anxious to view it, I waited for it to appear in the second-run art houses. Then one day I saw in a small ad in the *Times* that *Native Son* could be seen in the Irving Place Theater, the famous old burlesque citadel near 14th Street which had

When we started on our dessert, Wright told me he had an old novel in his trunk, a manuscript about the Post Office that he was holding in reserve. "Just in case I run dry," he smiled. I hesitated, then advised him not to publish it. I had been in somewhat the same situation some time ago, I explained. It was during the year following my return from my Guggenheim in Europe, when I hadn't been able to complete much work because I felt stale. Because my previous books had sold well, Viking Press had suggested that I agree to the publication of my old novel, *Windy City Blues,* the one they had turned down three times several years ago. This offer had rekindled my enthusiasm for the manuscript, and Viking drew up a contract and Lieber arranged for an advance. Then I began to read the manuscript after the lapse of years. Rereading the novel forced me to kill the deal. It was a good book, it had many good things in it, but it should have been published as a first novel several years ago, not now. I was firm about not publishing it, and Lieber tore up the contract.

Walt and Wright listened in silence. Then Wright smiled. "I think you did right. It's something to think about."

When we finished lunch, Wright insisted on paying the

---

been closed during the puritanical La Guardia administration and turned into a movie house. I went to see it, alone.

Inside the theater, I saw there were only four other patrons in the entire house. When the film started, to my surprise Richard Wright was playing Bigger Thomas, the lead role! He had dropped about thirty pounds and, though surely by now in his middle or late forties, he appeared extremely young. He looked like Bigger Thomas. And he wasn't a bad actor! In the huge, darkened, almost deserted theater, I watched his performance with amazement. It was a crudely made film, with many amateurish touches, but it somehow had a curious authenticity, an odd power. The end of the film was awkward; as the picture unfolded it seemed to fall apart: and yet, to me, the book was *there*. As I left the theater, following the other four ticket purchasers outside, I approached Fourth Avenue, under the clock of the savings bank where I had first met Wright.

check. As I offered half-jokingly to split the check he looked a bit nettled. "I told Walt I wanted to meet you, didn't I?" I gave in. Walt said something about Wright's prosperity from *Native Son*'s royalties and we all laughed, but I knew then Wright and I would never be friends. I had unintentionally rubbed him the wrong way about the check, perhaps even insulted him in some mysterious racial way. We walked for several blocks together, talking amiably about a number of subjects—movies, books, sports. When we reached 18th Street we separated, Wright and I shaking hands, both saying that as old Chicagoans we ought to keep in touch. Just before he turned away he suddenly said, "It was nice to meet you." "It was nice to meet you, too." We both meant it. Then he and Walt walked east, while I turned north toward my apartment.

Native Son, a book-club choice, continued to sell very well, and I was glad Wright was going to make enough money to insure his financial independence for a long time. When it was produced on Broadway with Canada Lee in the lead role I went to see it, and I thought the dramatization was a good job; Canada Lee was fine in it. After that, Wright wrote *Black Boy,* another very good book. It, too, was a book club selection, and now he was, deservedly, popular and prosperous.

After our initial meeting I didn't see Wright for a long time. During that interval my relationship with Nellie deteriorated, and we finally parted. Our breakup, for which I assumed the blame, came over my continued reluctance to marry a woman I feared would attempt to run my life; our parting was extremely painful. Nellie married another man, a New Englander; she gave up her literary agency and moved out of the city. Soon afterward I also married, had a son, and moved across the river with my wife and child to Brooklyn Heights.

One afternoon, unable to work well, I was out walking, killing time amid the fine old streets near the river, when I saw

Wright strolling toward me. We greeted each other and shook hands and said, practically with one voice: "What are *you* doing around here?" I explained I lived nearby; Wright said he was now living in a garden apartment on Middagh Street, only a few blocks away. His house was owned by Carson McCullers and had a fluctuating population made up of W. H. Auden, Tennessee Williams, Paul Bowles, Gypsy Rose Lee, Truman Capote, and others. When I looked surprised over his living there, he laughed. "I leave them alone upstairs, and they leave me alone downstairs." Wright had put on weight and looked prosperous. We walked along the quiet streets for a while, then separated, and went back to our desks. He told me he was married and had a small daughter.

After that we ran into each other occasionally in our walks around the Heights. Once Wright confessed he was having trouble writing his new book; I said I was having difficulty with my work, too. We agreed we had both reached that period of our lives when writing was becoming tougher instead of easier. We took solace in noting that Hemingway hadn't had a book published in many years, and the same silence had come upon Faulkner. But the solace to be got from these remarks, we knew, was mere whistling in the creative dark. During our walks we never discussed politics. I had heard the rumor that Wright had broken with the Party; his breakaway was not publicized and very few people knew about it.

For some people Brooklyn Heights is a wonderful place to live. Formerly a fashionable area of Brooklyn, it still has fine old houses, small quiet side streets where bankers and shipping magnates organized a secluded, gracious social life a century ago. From the head of Montague Street the panoramic view of Manhattan is breathtaking, with sweeping vistas of skyscrapers, the Battery, and the harbor. Yet despite this lush, even dramatic setting, there is a drowsy, somnolent air about the area that to some people is enervating. One day Wright told me he was moving to Greenwich Village with his family. He had had enough of the quiet, sedate Heights.

The next time I saw him was at a party in Manhattan. He had come alone, without his wife, whom I had never met. He looked at peace with himself and relaxed; he told everybody at the party he was moving to Paris with his family and that his wife was at home packing suitcases. "Is this a permanent move?" someone inquired. "It is," he smiled. During that evening there was the usual flow of conversation, until a guest suddenly remarked, in a self-righteous tone, that in these times a person had to stand up and be counted on the issues of the day. "You just have to," the guest said. It was the type of statement that always makes you cringe inside, but when a fool utters it you only waste your energy bothering to make a reply. Wright cut the guest down to size by saying blandly: "My mother used to tell us, 'You don't *have* to do anything but die.' " I thought it was a simple and wonderful statement. Soon after that Wright glanced at his watch, smiled, and left.

A few days later he departed with his family for Paris. It was the most unwise move he ever made. Someone told me he had gone through a bitter experience of discrimination trying to rent a bigger apartment in the Village. This enraged him, perhaps further fueling his furies to the point of wanting to clear out of America.

Nevertheless, I was surprised that a writer of Wright's talent and perception had decided to pull up his roots and leave. Hadn't he witnessed the plight of émigré writers and painters in New York who had fled from Hitler and Pétain during the war years? Didn't he know that the quality of their creative output worsened, or in some instances even ceased entirely? That such writers as Ernst Toller, Stefan Zweig, and others, unable to function here, had committed suicide in a friendly but foreign land? That perhaps only Henry James, who had labored for decades to become a professional Englishman, had finally succeeded in surmounting the psychological obstacles all creative émigrés face?

Wright's exile, it seemed to me, bore a connection with his limitations. In politics his instincts were absolutely fine and true. When he realized that the Communist dictatorship, to remain in power, always put its intellectuals into a creative straitjacket, he quit; that move cost him friends he was once close to. He parted, for example, from Paul Robeson, a sincere but politically naive man. He went to Africa and met Nkrumah, and returned disillusioned and bitterly critical of the political machinations of that black leader. In the book *The God That Failed,* Wright contributed one of his finest pieces of writing, an autobiographical article describing his arrival at, and final withdrawal from, the Communist camp.

But his anger and uncontrolled furies finally led him down a strange street—flight from the only roots he was ever to possess. Fleeing America, he found a temporary solace in the company of Frenchmen, or in American émigrés like himself. In middle-age, he soon became as rootless as the thousands of other restless transients living on both sides of the Seine.

The quality of Wright's writing deteriorated rapidly in France. His travel book on Spain is an embarrassing volume to read. Succeeding books were poorly constructed and lacking in any originality. To my surprise, his old Post Office novel, *Lawd Today,* which he had told me he was holding in abeyance "in case I run dry," was finally published, posthumously—why hadn't he specified in his will that the manuscript be destroyed? When *Lawd Today* appeared it was ignored by the critics and its sale was small.

When Wright died of a heart attack in Paris, at fifty-two, I wasn't surprised. As I read the news item on his death, I recalled the day I had first met him under the big clock of the Central Savings Bank on 14th Street. I remembered my first impression—that under that pleasant exterior a powerful dynamo was humming day and night. Having earlier sparked his creative drives, it had finally overloaded his righteous hates.

No, Wright and I were never really friends. Our meetings, after that first one on 14th Street, were politely cordial, nothing more. Though we were fellow writers, struggling with our separate working problems, this common condition was not sufficient to propel us beyond the boundary of a casual relationship. But in the occasional guarded looks we gave each other as our paths crossed, I sometimes felt we had been on the edge of a friendship, a friendship that never materialized. Why was that —why? I suspect the problem was racial. It was against Wright's nature to be a "whitey" lover. Just as it was against mine to be a "spade" lover. Fine. But why couldn't we both have been, simply, *men?*

Wright fled to France, to escape America—but America, with all its agonies for a black man, remained in his blood. Wright's mediocre books will be forgotten. But with *Native Son* and *Black Boy,* his claim to enduring literary fame is definitely assured.

The End of an Era, and the Beginning of Something

The Depression ended with America's entry into World War II. What Franklin D. Roosevelt and Congress failed to accomplish in their attempts to end mass unemployment by passing radical social legislation and inaugurating large make-work programs, the attack on Pearl Harbor by the Japanese succeeded in doing by causing American wartime payrolls to bulge and by spurring industrial production to record-breaking heights.

With the end of the Depression, the thirties came to a close. The left-wing press suddenly ceased its attacks on President Roosevelt and capitalism, calling for an all-out effort to defeat Hitler's war machine which had hurled itself deep into Russia. Now the *Daily Worker* no longer called President Roosevelt a social-fascist but, instead, ordered its cartoonists and writers to portray the President as "our great democratic leader" of the "great American masses dedicated to smashing the slimy fascist foe."

All were comrades-in-arms now. Only those writers who were working on unfinished proletarian novels about dust bowls or strikes in southern coal mines, which they were certain the editors of the *New Masses* would have endorsed, felt let down.

And as if obeying a referee's whistle in some colossal football game, protesters against the "system" stopped advancing upon the goalposts of Union Square. Overnight the banners and placards were put into cold storage; the parade leaders called off the show. With a brooding glance at the sudden emptiness of the 14th Street gridiron, the cops on horses and motorcycles, recalling the glories of the past when they had struggled against the surging demonstrators, regretfully withdrew. Now all they had to look forward to was the staid chore of directing traffic and giving out parking tickets.

It was, indeed, the end of an era.

In time, World War II itself came to a close, with all its terrible bloodletting, heroism, treachery, and sacrifices. Stumbling on spindly legs, the survivors of Dachau and Treblinka were set free, and wept; and a shocked world gave them hot soup and chocolate and clothing. Then America, the holocaust behind her, set about in earnest manufacturing washing machines, automobiles, and suburbs for the affluent age ahead.

And during this upbeat period writers continued to finish books for which their agents obtained fresh contracts. Lieber had married again, for the third time; his new wife was an attractive, quiet blonde girl, and he looked very happy whenever I visited his office. It was a good time for writers and publishers; with the war over, the new paperback revolution became a source of additional royalties, and publishers increased their advances. In this pleasant aura, Lieber and his wife Minna came to our apartment in Brooklyn Heights frequently for dinner, and Pauline and I and little Tommy in turn visited the Liebers at their apartment on the upper West Side. Bread was broken during these meetings, and we toasted each other. We were all older now—with the bad times of the Depression behind us. Yes, the era of the thirties was dead—that decade was buried forever.

Then one day a man named Whittaker Chambers, whom I had met once in my life—on the southeast corner of 14th Street and Fourth Avenue—accused Alger Hiss, whom I had never met, of belonging to an underground Communist apparatus, and suddenly the thirties returned with full force for me.

A Visit
from the Boys

I was coming up the stairs to our third floor apartment in
Brooklyn Heights when the phone rang. It was late afternoon,
about five-thirty, and I had just put in a day of writing in a small
rented room where I went each day to work, like a man going
daily to his office. Tommy was alone in the apartment—Pauline
was borrowing a cup of flour from a neighbor downstairs—as I
entered the doorway.

"A man is calling, it's for you, Daddy!"

I took the receiver from his small hand and heard a pleasant, even voice.

"Is this Mr. Halper?"

"Yes."

"Albert Halper?"

"Yes."

"This is Mr. Smith calling, from the Federal Bureau of
Investigation. I'd like to drop over and see you."

"When?"

"This evening. At seven-thirty. Will you be home?"

"Yes—but why?" My heart was pounding.

"I'll tell you when I see you." He hung up.

When Pauline came in, with a cup of flour in her hand, she said: "What's the matter? You look pale. Are you ill?"

"I'm all right." Tommy was watching me. I managed to laugh. "Go into your room and read your cowboy comics for a while."

"Will you come in my room later and listen to me read?"

"Sure." He left.

"What's wrong with you?" Pauline asked.

"The F.B.I. just phoned. A man is coming to talk to me this evening. At seven-thirty."

"Why?"

"I don't know."

She put the cup of flour down, worried. "There must be some mistake. You didn't do anything wrong." She glanced at me questioningly—had I hidden anything from my past?

"No," I said, reading her thoughts. "I'm clean."

"Then why?" She still looked distressed. The cold war had begun, along with political exhumations of the thirties by Congressional committees. But what had that to do with me? My brain was ticking fast.

"Let's eat early. Then take Tommy to your sister's and don't return until I phone you at Dina's and tell you the man has left."

"All right. Call me as soon as he leaves?"

"Yes. Of course I will."

We ate in silence and then she took Tommy by the hand. "I'll be waiting for your call," she said.

After they had left the apartment I glanced nervously

about the living room. What "incriminating" articles were in the apartment? Nothing. Then I turned toward the bookshelves. Going to them, I removed volumes of Gogol, Chekhov, Tolstoy, Babel, Turgenev, Goncharov, and others, carrying them out of sight into the bedroom. Though these were circulated freely in all the public libraries, I did not want my own collection to look too "Russian" when my visitor entered the apartment. I thoughtfully placed the *New York Times* on the coffee table, also a copy of the *New Yorker*. In the kitchen I found a copy of *Woman's Day* that Pauline had brought from the A&P. I carried it into the living room, placing it next to the *New Yorker*. Then I waited.

At seven-thirty sharp the doorbell rang. A few moments later two clean-cut American types in their early thirties entered —I had expected a single caller—and the first displayed his credentials and said quickly, "You know Maxim Lieber and Whittaker Chambers, don't you?" It was a well-prepared trick, coupling the two names together immediately, and it worked.

"Well, yes—Mr. Lieber is my literary agent. But I met Chambers only once, a long time ago. . . ."

"But you know both of them, don't you?"

"Well, yes. . . ."

"How long have you been acquainted with Mr. Lieber?"

"About twenty years. He's been my literary agent during that time."

One of them, the second one, the blond, was already taking notes on a piece of paper; while he waited for my answers he managed to move casually near the bookcases, where I noticed he was scanning the titles.

"What's the reason for this visit?" I asked the first one, the short one.

"We're engaged in an investigation. You've read the

recent news items about the charges of espionage Mr. Chambers has brought against Alger Hiss?"

"Yes. Last week. But what's that got to do with Lieber, or me?" But even as I spoke, I felt, deep inside me, that Lieber might be implicated in some way. I warned myself to stay cool, not to become rattled. All I had to do was to answer their questions truthfully, just answer briefly and to the point.

"Did you ever hear of the American Feature Writers Syndicate?"

"No."

"Weren't you an officer of the American Feature Writers Syndicate?"

"How could I be an officer if I never even heard of it before this evening?"

The first one, the short one, opened a large envelope and showed me a photostat copy of a legal document—incorporation papers enumerating the list of officers of the American Feature Writers Syndicate. Lieber's name was among them; two other names were totally unknown to me. Mine was a fourth name.

"Is this your signature?"

I looked at the name near his index finger. It certainly was in my handwriting. "Yes," I said. "That's my signature." I was sweating a little now. "What is this syndicate?" The two glanced at each other without speaking. Then the short one said:

"Did you give Mr. Lieber power of attorney in money matters?"

I thought a moment, trying to remember. "Yes. For one year, when I lived in Europe, so that he could sign literary contracts for me while I was traveling through different countries."

"Never for use in the American Feature Writers Syndicate?"

"How could I? I never heard that name before this evening."

"Yet this is your signature on the filing papers?"

"Yes."

"Then how do you explain this clause, in the filing papers which you signed, granting Mr. Lieber the power of attorney in financial matters for this syndicate?"

"I can't explain anything."

"You're saying this is your signature, but you don't remember signing this document?"

"That's correct. I have no memory whatsoever of signing it or granting Lieber power of attorney for the syndicate." I was very nervous now. The interview was starting to resemble a chapter out of a book by Kafka. I watched the short one, who was evidently the spokesman for the team, open a large envelope and take out about twenty-five photos of assorted sizes. He passed the photos to me, one by one. Two of them were of Maxim Lieber; in one of them Lieber was smoking his pipe, with his jacket removed.

"Who is that?"

"That's Lieber, my agent."

He handed me the other photos. Many of them were candid camera shots, taken when the subjects were boarding planes or buses and did not know they were being photographed. I did not know any of them; they looked like Americans, with the exception of a young Japanese male.

"I don't recognize any of the others," I said.

He put the pictures back into the envelope. "You wrote for the *New Masses,* didn't you?"

"Yes, I did." The second one, the blond, began taking notes again. I continued: "I contributed to the *New Masses* during the thirties, along with Hemingway, Thomas Mann, Granville Hicks, Edmund Wilson, Sherwood Anderson, and a lot of other writers." My heart was pounding harder. "It was a time when the literary and social climate was different than it is today.

It was during the Depression, when artists and writers were concerned. . . ." I stopped talking. Suddenly I realized these two men had been small children then, unaware of what had been happening during those years. From the studied, impassive looks on their faces I knew they didn't know what the hell I was talking about. Shit! Why did I have to defend myself before *these two* anyway? Or before *anybody,* for that matter? I clamped my mouth shut.

They questioned me intensively for about thirty more minutes. Did I know so-and-so? No. Did I ever meet another so-and-so? No. Did I remember Miss Nellie Hampton, who had been Lieber's secretary at one time? A shiver went down my spine. They asked the question again, looking at me closely.

"Well, yes. I remember she worked in Lieber's office for a year or so." I had to force the words because my throat had become a bit constricted.

"Did you know her well?"

"I saw her every time I went to Lieber's office on literary business."

"Do you know where she can be reached at the present time?"

I hesitated. "I heard she got married and moved to another city."

The blond one was writing rapidly. "Do you know the name of the city?" the short one asked.

"No. It's been many years since I last saw her."

I noticed toward the end of the interview the short one, who had done practically all the questioning, had let up on me a little; the softening of his tone was almost imperceptible but I had felt it. Perhaps it was because I had answered all his questions.

"What's this all about?" I asked. "Don't you think I ought to know, even an inkling?"

He glanced at the blond, very briefly. "I guess I can tell you. You'll read about it in the papers soon. We have reason to believe that the American Feature Writers Syndicate was a cover for an espionage apparatus. The filing papers list Mr. Lieber's Fifth Avenue office address as the address of the American Feature Writers Syndicate." He looked at me steadily. "I'm not at liberty to say anything more at this time." I was silent. He placed the notes of our conversation together with the photostat copy of the filing papers into a large envelope and stood up. "You might be called to Washington to testify in court when this case comes to trial. Can you be reached here?"

"Yes. This is my home."

He motioned to the second one and they turned to go. At the door, in a move that I recognized later as being rehearsed beforehand, the blond one turned and said: "Were you ever a member of the John Reed Club, or the Communist Party?"

"No. Never."

Then they left.

After they had gone I went to the bathroom and drank a glass of cold water. I felt wrung out. Returning to the living room, I stared at the empty chairs in which they had just been sitting. I began to pace the flat, debating whether I should phone Lieber to tell him of the visit the F.B.I. had paid me and ask him about that cover business. I decided against that move—better to wait and let my thoughts cool.

Pauline returned to the apartment after I called her at her sister's. She looked at me anxiously. "What was it all about?"

I waited until Tommy went into his room to play with his toys. "It's about Lieber. They said he was engaged in espionage activities. They said he used his office for an apparatus cover."

"But where do you come in on this?"

"They said I signed the incorporation papers for this

cover. They showed me a photostat copy of my signature. I admitted it was my handwriting.''

"What? How is that possible?"

"I really don't know.''

A Friendly Call

I didn't phone Lieber that evening, nor the next day, nor the next. Every morning I went to my small rented room where I worked away from home, lay on the cot, stared up at the ceiling, and thought. How had my signature come to appear on the filing papers? It was my handwriting, all right. I did not believe the F.B.I., or anyone else, had forged it. It was my handwriting, no doubt about that.

I lay on my back facing the ceiling for hours, thinking back over the past, trying to recall if I had ever signed any papers like that. The thirties, in my mind, were so deeply embedded in the shadowy past that only the major events of that era returned to me at first—my sojourn in the Bronx, Hedda, my first story in the *American Mercury,* Louis Adamic, my year in Europe, Nellie, and a few other recollections. The name, American Feature Writers Syndicate, meant nothing to me. Yet I felt, somehow, I had signed the papers. But how—when? That signature was certainly mine.

I was unable to work in my rented room. Day after day I lay on the cot, thinking. Why couldn't I pierce the curtains of the past? Had Nellie been in the apparatus? I felt certain she hadn't. I suddenly recalled how she had warned me against becoming "involved" with Lieber; and I remembered her troubled, frightened expression and how I had ignored and laughed at her concern at the time. No—she was innocent. I sat down and wrote her a letter informing her about the F.B.I.'s visit to me and their apparent search for her; but I realized I did not know her address or even her married name. I took a chance and addressed the letter to an old girl friend of hers, a former schoolmate I had once met fleetingly on a street corner with Nellie. I typed on the envelope: "Please forward, urgent." I waited for days, but received no reply.

In my small rented room I continued to sort my memories, trying to seize on the vital one. I have always been skeptical when reading accounts of witnesses in a courtroom who testify they did not remember a face or an incident, then, after days or weeks during a long, drawn-out trial, they suddenly stated they recalled the face, or incident. This always sounded fishy to me.

But one day, after lying on my cot for hours, the curtains of memory finally parted and I recalled that for a brief time during the thirties—perhaps for a month or two—some new lettering had appeared on Lieber's outer office door. "You going into another business?" I remembered having inquired jokingly. "No." He had punched me playfully on the arm, laughing. "I'm handling some foreign authors, for French and British magazines. I'm running a new literary outlet out of this office, that's all." In a few weeks the lettering had been removed from the door and I took no further notice of it—evidently the new venture had not proved profitable and Lieber had discontinued it. Though I strained my memory I could not recall the words on the door. But that was it—it had to be it! Then with a rush I remembered that a short time before the new lettering had appeared on the door Lieber had phoned me, asking me to drop in to discuss a manuscript I had sent him. When I showed up at his office and our little conference was over, he had mentioned, casually, he wanted someone to act as a witness for a literary contract and would I sign the papers for him? I had moved to his desk and had taken the pen he had offered me, and now I suddenly remembered his too casual, almost too offhand air.

"What's it for, a sale to the movies?" I had jested. I had flipped the close, single-spaced typed pages, not bothering to read the long paragraphs of legal jargon; I had signed similar closely-typed contracts for my own books, rarely reading the complicated wording, having complete faith in my agent. Lieber had laughed.

"I wish it were a movie sale. It's just a contract for a new author, someone you never heard of. My secretary is ill today, or I'd have her witness it." I bent over the "contract" and signed the papers. That had been it! And as I returned the pen to Lieber, two young men entered the office and Lieber, smiling, introduced them to me. I couldn't remember their names or faces, but somehow they hadn't struck me as being writers. Escorting me to the door, Lieber had thanked me for witnessing the document while the two young men had remained in his office.

Now, recalling that incident, I suddenly felt like an animal caught in a trap. I felt certain I knew, at last, why Lieber had kept after me during all those years to join the Party. When Lieber had been approached by his superior in the underground for a literary "name" on the letterhead of the American Feature Writers Syndicate, he had thought of me, feeling I was due eventually to drop like a ripe fruit into the Party basket where my silence would be assured once I was in the fold. His frequent flashes of temper, his increasing nervousness whenever I had laughingly brushed aside his numerous requests that I take out a Party card, now fitted into the design! I had been used—

with the hope that his really genuine interest in me through the years, his "investment" in me, would pay off some day by my "deeper involvement." I lay there sweating, in my room.

The next day I heard from Nellie. She was living in a town in New England, with her two small children. She wrote that her marriage had failed—she was divorced. "The F.B.I. rang my bell yesterday. No, Al, I never was involved with that cover in Max's office, though I suspected he was up to something non-kosher. And you're absolutely spotless, so why worry? As I said, my marriage flopped, so here I am, getting fat and gray, but I have two marvelous kids, so maybe it was worth it. Only thing is, last week I went to see a doctor about a lump on my breast, and he says he thinks it's cancer. But don't worry, Buck, I think he's wrong. And I'm glad you've got a family. All my best. Nellie."

I read her letter a dozen times, over and over. I didn't show it to Pauline.

I didn't phone Lieber for a few more days; I still felt trapped. I couldn't muster sufficient energy to make the call. Whenever I thought of my signature on that document and my predicament now that the witch-hunts were on, I sweated. It was my handwriting, all right. I saw myself at the coming espionage trial, the Federal prosecutor hammering me with questions about my past, accusing me of being a member of the Chambers-Hiss underground cell. I saw my writing career being smashed to bits, my life lying in ruins.

"There must be some mistake," Pauline kept telling me. "Lieber wouldn't do a thing like that to you. He's not only your agent, he's your friend."

"He did it, all right."

"But you're not certain. You have no proof. Why haven't you talked to him? A man is innocent until he's proven guilty, isn't he?"

"Okay," I said.

I phoned Lieber, and went to his office the following day without telling him on the phone the reason for my visit. He seemed relaxed and innocent when I began talking to him and at once I was assailed by doubts.

"Max, the F.B.I. visited me recently. They mentioned something about the American Feature Writers Syndicate and they showed me my signature on the papers filed for registration for the outfit. They said you were involved in it, with Whittaker Chambers, and that it was an underground apparatus cover."

His control over his facial muscles amazed me. He kept an innocent smile, and seemed only slightly interested. Had he expected my visit? "What syndicate? What cover?" He spread his arms like an actor in a comedy, in a gesture that ridiculed so fantastic a statement as the one I had just made. But I knew at once he was acting.

"Max, did you get me to sign that document under the subterfuge of its being a contract for a literary property, a literary sale?"

He spread his hands again, still smiling. "What document? What contract?"

I tried to nail him down. "Max, was this syndicate a cover? Please answer yes or no."

He continued to smile innocently, still under absolute control. "What syndicate? What cover?"

I asked the question five or six more times, rephrasing it each time. He continued smiling, and wouldn't give me a yes or no answer.

"For the last time, Max, please give me a definite answer."

Again he smiled, but this time he didn't bother to follow through with his routine reply. He merely spread his hands pleasantly again.

I left.

Good-bye
to Something,
to Somebody

When I returned to the apartment after seeing Lieber, I felt ill. Pauline was concerned.

"Shouldn't you see a lawyer?"

"Why? How can a lawyer help me? If they call me to Washington to testify, I'll go. I've answered all their questions already. I could tell my answers told them nothing. But if they want to interrogate me again, I'll make the trip."

I waited a few days, then wrote Lieber a letter. It proved to be a difficult letter for me to write. For years he had been a close friend, much more than an agent to me. He had helped me enormously, had encouraged me at a time when I had needed the warmth and friendship he had given me. You don't junk an old friend like that without pain, without agony. I wrote three drafts of a longish letter, each of which I destroyed. Finally, I typed a simple note thanking him for all he had done for me, adding that I was quitting his agency. I didn't tell him why I was breaking off a twenty-year relationship. He knew. I mailed the letter.

When he answered with a long, scurrilous letter, denouncing me for being an ungrateful client, a false friend, and a cheap writer without talent, I remembered the abusive letter he had written another departing client, the man who had been raised in Hell's Kitchen and whom Lieber had labeled a hoodlum, a gangster. I reread Lieber's letter calmly. It was so insulting I did not show it to Pauline, though she begged to see it. I put it away in my file, thinking, "Well, that's the end of a relationship." And then I waited, for the Chambers-Hiss trial to begin.

The specific charge brought against Alger Hiss was that he had committed perjury in testimony given before a federal grand jury in 1948. The public soon learned, however, that the case held far greater implications than the usual prosecution for perjury in an ordinary civil or criminal proceeding. For if Hiss were guilty of the perjury as charged, he was *ipso facto* guilty of espionage—guilty specifically for the delivery, ten years earlier, of secret and restricted documents of state to a foreign power. Because of the statute of limitations, the prosecution could not indict for the more serious charge, but somehow, as the trial progressed, with Chambers' testimony piling up, the lesser charge took on an awesome significance. Journalists from all over the world jammed the courtroom, taking notes, sending home their dispatches. In the current cold war climate, this was prime news.

Each evening I pored over the lengthy detailed reports of the trial. I bought all the newspapers, wondering when Lieber would be called to appear as a witness; and I sweated waiting for them to call me, too. The journalistic accounts of the proceedings, day after day, were chilling, fascinating.

Chambers testified under oath that he and Hiss had been friends, dear friends over a lengthy period. At a pre-trial confrontation, Hiss had steadily denied this; he said he had never met Chambers but later, under firm questioning, he admitted he had met Chambers superficially once or twice, when Chambers had a different name.

In court Chambers continued to detail his alleged warm friendship with Hiss; he described the lengthy, philosophical discussions he and Hiss had had about politics, he mentioned the color and design of the rugs in the Hiss apartment, he told of Hiss's intense interest in bird-watching, of auto trips the Chamberses and the Hisses had taken together on weekends; Chambers constantly sprinkled his descriptions of his relationship with Hiss with intimate and friendly details and touches.

At the pre-trial confrontation, Hiss had demanded to see Chambers' teeth, which had received a great deal of dental repair since the thirties. When Chambers obediently opened his mouth, Hiss declared triumphantly: "This man whom I knew under a different name had terrible teeth." Reading this account, I suddenly recalled that during my first and only meeting with Chambers on 14th Street, when Chambers had smiled at something Sender Garlin had said, I had seen his stumpy, defective teeth. Chambers calmly and patiently explained at the pre-trial confrontation that his teeth had received major attention some years earlier.

Hiss employed the finest lawyers to defend him. In court he acted with a cool personal dignity. Because of his lean, quiet, unassuming, Ivy League appearance, and because several high government officials who had known him in the past had come forward as character witnesses in his behalf, it was difficult for some people to feel he was guilty of the serious charge put forth by the prosecution, even though he refused to take a lie-detector test. Yet one noticed a certain telltale weakness in the photos of his face in the newspapers, a cornered weakness that riveted one's glance upon the eyes and mouth. And the mounting testimony of Chambers, the continued divulging of details concerning his alleged friendship with Hiss, was most damning.

The aroused left-wing press, the comrades, had immediately swung into action, stating that Chambers was a liar, a psychopath. The character assassination of the chief witness was sustained and continued with increasing virulence during the two trials—the first having ended with a hung jury, eight jurors voting Hiss guilty, four, innocent. As the second trial progressed, leftists shouted that Chambers was a homosexual—someone had witnessed him placing a hand on the shoulder of a young junior editor of *Time,* where Chambers had been a senior editor. Chambers was a diseased person, the left cried. A psychiatrist who sat in the crowded courtroom (he was later identified as a friend of the Hiss family) declared that Chambers on the witness stand exhibited symptoms of paranoia. And the comrades shouted that the typewriter upon which Mrs. Hiss was purported to have copied State documents, one of the most damning pieces of evidence exhibited by the prosecution, had been purposely manufactured by the F.B.I. and was a fake.

During all this courtroom turmoil Hiss kept his composure. He told everyone—the press, the public—that he would be found innocent of the charges brought against him. It was all a big mistake. Each day his prominent lawyers labored hard for acquittal; they explored every legal avenue in an attempt to get their client acquitted. The jurors, in a unanimous vote, found Hiss guilty in the second trial.

I was never called to Washington, nor was I ever revisited by the F.B.I. Nellie Hampton was never called to Washington, either. Sitting in my Brooklyn Heights apartment, I had fol-

lowed the two trials avidly, rereading the testimony, the rebut-
tals, the summations, scanning everything I could see pertaining
to the case.

Lieber did not appear as a witness at either trial. Pleading
self-incrimination, he refused to testify concerning his alleged
relationship with Chambers and Hiss and the apparatus. Reading
about his refusal to testify in the sensational Chambers-Hiss case,
Lieber's clients began phoning his office for facts. His secretary
said Lieber was not available for comment. When pressed, she
replied that he was out of the city. No, she added, she did not
know when Mr. Lieber would return.

During Lieber's absence from the city, the trial had
dragged on, with the apparatus in which he was alleged to have
been involved mentioned frequently. Reported to be holed up
somewhere in New England, Lieber could still not be reached by
his clients, who had stories to sell, book contracts to negotiate.
Soon writers began to abandon his agency, the agency he had
spent twenty years of his life building up. While living in an
unknown locality in Vermont or Maine, Lieber meanwhile suffered a severe heart attack.

At last, with Hiss found guilty, Lieber returned to the
city a sick and beaten man. The roof had fallen in on him. His
agency was in ruins, and a writer who visited him told me he now
sat in his office alone surrounded by the photos on his walls of
departed clients, while his phone did not ring.

Later I heard he attempted to sell the remnants of his
agency but found no takers. Finally he closed his office and
moved with Minna and his two small children to Arizona to
regain his health. While in the Southwest he suffered a second
heart attack. When he had recuperated some of his strength, he
moved to Mexico City where another writer who had seen him
there told me he was kept under surveillance by the Mexican
police.

One night he packed his bags and, with his family, made his way furtively to the east coast of Mexico, toward a Polish ship in the harbor, and when the boat left Mexico, Lieber, Minna, and the two children were unlisted passengers on it. Upon his arrival in Poland, his health broken, no longer young, Lieber was offered a job in a state publishing house. These bits of information reached me gradually, through the grapevine of mutual friends, ex-clients, writers, and publishing people in New York.

I made no further effort to keep track of Lieber after that, but when additional snippets of news about him reached me I listened and filed them away in my mind. One day an acquaintance of mine, a writer, passing through Warsaw on an assignment, met Lieber there. Upon his return to America he told me Lieber was now old and gray and thin, his duties in the state publishing house frequently interrupted by hospital visits. He said Lieber had buttonholed him, asked him about people in New York, even inquired about me, and protested his innocence. He added that Lieber and his family lived in an extremely modest apartment in Warsaw.

Warsaw. . . . Hearing that name from my friend's lips, I suddenly recalled the journey I had made many years ago to Moscow, passing from the west and stopping in the Polish capital. It had been a one-day stopover, and in the afternoon, at dusk, I had wandered through its gray Pilsudski streets. That was still before World War II, before the Nazi-Stalin Pact, before the blitzkrieg, before the mass murder of Jews who attempted to defend themselves in the Warsaw sewers and cellars. During that night of my stopover I had seen the painted prostitutes standing in the doorways, watched the soldiers in their long campaign coats pick them up, heard the troikas rattling past on the cobblestones. Later, walking through the large Jewish section, I had seen kosher salamis hanging in shop windows, observed men and women drinking hot tea and talking with elaborate gestures at tables. All those people later met their death somewhere in the streets and cellars, or were massacred in Auschwitz, Treblinka. Even as I had walked the evening streets in 1935, I had felt, somehow, it was a doomed city—in France, politicians were already shouting, "Why should we die for Danzig?"

And now the Polish People's Republic had come to power, its "democratic" regime rolling along. With its intellectuals muzzled, its best movie directors working in Paris and Hollywood, its bureaucrats broadcasting daily pro-Arab, anti-Israeli manifestos, it constantly reminds the population they are heading for the Marxian sunrise. And somewhere today in that superhappy Leninist land, Maxim Lieber, my old and dear friend, my confidant, my sustainer, sits in a state publishing office, hopefully near a window, and edits or reads proof in Polish for some correctly oriented novel which will please the establishment he now serves.

Final Curtain —
Is This Where
We Came In?

The summer afternoon had gradually faded and the light had gone from the windows. Up the hall, in her room, Lorna was still painting. With memories of the Chambers-Hiss trial still vividly in my mind, I had forgotten, momentarily, the scenes of the thirties which had preceded them—my stay in the Bronx, the cold water flat on East 11th Street, the public baths, and all the rest. Then Lorna came into the room and in the dim light—I hadn't switched on the lamps—asked what I wanted for dinner. I replied, "Anything you have in the house. I'm not hungry this evening." She departed, releasing my memories again.

Before the telephone rang for me in the early afternoon I had thought I had about forgotten the thirties. It was a stupid assumption because you never forget your youth. It's always somewhere in your blood—the rooms you once lived in, the stories you had to write and destroy before you learned your craft, the novels you published which some people praised and you thought were good, too, but which, now, you never reread to see if they are still good or not.

While waiting for Lorna to call me for dinner, I sat in the gathering gloom—and found it impossible to keep back the flow of memories which had erupted in my mind as though rediscovered in a suddenly unlocked attic trunk. Again, I recalled the political arguments in the cafeterias, turbulent demonstrations in Union Square, relationships with former girl friends followed, later, by the unnecessary painful quarrels. Too, I thought of the sincere, ardent leftists I had known in the past—many of them, middle-aged now, still loyal to the Party line as the years roll by, steadfastly ignoring the bloody daggers hidden under the political blankets, refusing to believe the documentation of the purges, the mass deaths in the labor camps, the terrors behind the Stalin myth. Yes, these people, I told myself again, always needed the warmth of the Party, as children need the warmth of a mother's lap. But in 1938 the fatal knock on the door at midnight wrenched both Dinamov and Tretyakov from that warm lap, and gone now are Dinamov's steel teeth, and Tretyakov's fierce, hammy slogan, "Art is a weapon!" Only Brecht, sitting silently, with thin lips curved in that mysterious German Buddha smile, with an ode to Stalin to his credit, had escaped the holocaust—while Isaac Babel, the Soviet's finest writer, disappeared in the labor camps along with Prince Mirsky, Boris Pilnyak, Osip Mandelshtam, and all the others. . . .

Sitting in the faded light of the apartment, in the New York dusk, I failed to hear Lorna walking up the hall again. My memories had finally sifted to Nellie's death, to her last letter to me. ". . . Al, I gave my children your address. I told my two kids that if they ever got into trouble or needed a friend to get in touch with you. . . ." I had waited, but as the years had passed her children never contacted me, which meant the relatives who had adopted them were discharging their responsibilities honorably. Suddenly I heard Lorna's footfall in the hall. Lorna stood before me in the half-dark, knowing I must be thinking of the past.

"Dinner is served," she said softly.

I followed her up the hall and into the living room where we eat our evening meal. Two candles were lit on the table, as though for a festive event.

"I thought I'd make this evening lively," Lorna said, pouring the California wine.

"Why?"

"I don't know. Something in your face—you were miles away, looking so thoughtful."

We sat down to eat, and she turned to me again. "Are you going to call Lieber?"

I thought a while, then shook my head. It was not a painful decision to make. For I knew if I phoned and met him it would be an awkward moment—the initial glimpse of each other over the abyss of sixteen long years, followed by the first look into each other's eyes, followed by a greeting and a dishonest handshake. No, I wouldn't call him.

Yet, though he had betrayed me, I was somehow half-grateful he had phoned. We had lived through the thirties together, he and I, and as I remembered that difficult decade I was filled with nostalgia. Despite the Depression, despite the poverty and hardships we had experienced, despite even the bloody, tragic sacrifice of Spain, they had been wonderful days—days when I was young and working well.

And if today fewer people recognize my name, or know

my work, that is acceptable to me, too. Because in middle age, and older, as the years go by one watches the current "classics" successively fade into the woodwork; and then one begins to hope that if one's own writing has been good, perhaps one's contribution during the thirties will one day find its way into the flow of the mainstream.

Epilogue

And so the curtain descended on a part of my life, perhaps the most vital part. But behind that curtain the scenes kept changing, new dialogue had to be written and spoken to fresh audiences. I continued to write short stories and novels. But with the passing of the years somehow the work grew harder, the space between publication days lengthened. Why was that? I looked around and saw that most of my literary contemporaries had also slowed down. Some of them had slowed down completely, disappearing from the scene—and their absence often gave me a shocking sense of loss. Though only a few of them had been major talents, all had been serious writers who, without waiting to reach the age of retirement, had sighed wearily and laid down their tools. What were their thoughts during their new, terrible leisure? I had read statements by some literary critics who declared most American writing talents were short-lived. Was this true and, if so, why did this condition prevail? Did American writers indeed burn themselves out early? I remembered that Hemingway, Fitzgerald, Faulkner, and a few other important writers had completed their best work by the time they had reached their mid-thirties; but was this not also the case with European writers, with a few exceptions? Weren't the best efforts of E. M. Forster, Thomas Mann, Joyce, Camus, and others the fruit of their early years? The exceptions belonged to a bygone age—Dostoevsky, Turgenev, Hamsun, Hardy, Conrad, Baroja, who continued to produce major work during their middle and late periods. Why was that? . . . I thought a good deal about this in my own worried middle age.

On a moody afternoon weeks after Lieber's unexpected telephone call, unable to write a decent sentence or even to type a simple phrase, I ticked off in my mind the names of people, now gone, whom I had truly admired, and a few others whom I had despised. Thinking of departed friends and acquaintances was not a habitual pastime of mine, but for an hour I indulged myself in it. I started with Kenneth Fearing whom I hadn't seen since he had moved out of my digs in East 11th Street. Why did he come to mind, though we had never been really friends? He had died of lung cancer, and his half-wry, half-cynical face hung before me for a few moments. I recalled George Leighton, my good friend up at *Harper's* who had passed away, unemployed, broken after holding down a series of unsatisfactory editorial jobs on other magazines; toward the end, unable to finish a fine, well-researched manuscript on the colorful history of world fairs, he had phoned me often to relay his deep despairs. I hadn't heard from him for some time, then one day I saw his obit in the *Times.* And I remembered William Rollins, whom I had known only slightly, his work now forgotten, suddenly dying much too early after I'd seen him at a cocktail party. His novel, *The Shadow Before,* had been praised by many critics; it was a bad novel, but he was a fine, sensitive person. Another face flashed before me, quickly, the face of Sol Funaroff, the youthful Communist poet whose vibrant work smacked too much of Blok; he'd also died too early, from heart disease contracted from a poverty-stricken boyhood on the lower East Side. I recalled his look of left-wing pride, his fiery eyes. Then there was the amiable, food-loving gourmet Pierre Loving, plump, talkative, a sound critic, who dropped dead in Washington of a heart attack during World War II while working for the government. And there was Joe Freeman who, the only time I ever met him, I instantly hated, carefully nursing his self-inflated literary reputation, his oily baboon face peering at me over a luncheon table. As the prime literary critic and hatchet man of the leftists, Freeman somehow managed to chill and dominate fledgling "proletarian" writers who yearned to appear in the *New Masses*. And during Boris Pilnyak's ill-starred visit to America, Freeman was the interpreter, agent, and Party watchdog for the unwary, doomed Soviet writer, staying at the talented Pilnyak's hotels, accompanying him to Hollywood, guiding and subtly directing his every move. When Freeman died, the *Times* obit, written by a man who had never known him, was very flattering.

Alone in my room during that moody afternoon, unable to work, I remembered other good friends, and a few who had not been friends. It was more pleasant to recall Josephine Herbst and her little stone house in Bucks County, Pennsylvania. A great talker, a fine wit, Josephine had traveled the world over, had known all the Paris crowd during the expatriate twenties, had journeyed to the Soviet Union in the thirties where she had met Lunacharsky, the minister of education. When Lunacharsky was executed in the purges, she told me: "I'm still sympathetic to them but they shouldn't have done it; he was a fine, intelligent person." When discussing personalities her comments were always acute, always fair. In Spain she had gone to the Loyalist front as a correspondent and upon her return to the United States had harangued big crowds at rallies for fund raisings. "Albert, it's not difficult to be a good speaker. You just stand close to the microphone, look over the heads of the crowd and keep shouting. It's just a trick you learn." Though there was never any trickery in what she had to say to them. One of her good friends in Bucks County had been Nathanael West, who had shown her his manuscript of *The Day of the Locust*. Discouraged, West simply couldn't finish the book satisfactorily. "Please read it, Jo," he asked. She told him she didn't buy the violent ending but, unable to find another ending, he sent it to his publisher, who printed it. Living alone after her divorce, from John Hermann, the writer, Jo kept a shotgun behind her door, "for snakes." She lived in that little stone house for about forty years, staying occasionally in New York, and died in abject poverty. A crowd came to pay her homage at her funeral.

Another face floated before me, Tess Slesinger's. One of Elliot Cohen's *Menorah Journal* writers, young, talented, she was extremely attractive and witty, and there were those who thought she would become another Dorothy Parker. She had no agent, so I brought her up to Lieber's office, and we three stood talking and joking, and soon Tess began sending Max salable stories that landed in *Vogue,* the *New Yorker,* and other magazines. Then she sent him her first novel, *The Unpossessed,* which he didn't like because it razzed certain leftist intellectuals, but he sold it to Simon & Schuster. After it was published to rave reviews, he got her a Hollywood contract as a writer; she married on the coast, for the second time, and did high-priced scripts for the movies, and never wrote another novel or magazine story either. Still beautiful, witty, a heavy smoker, she died in 1945, at forty, of cancer of the mouth.

These were some of the faces of my contemporaries that drifted before me that day. No, I didn't think about them often; I'd found the present, with its usual writing problems, sufficient to engage my attention. During one period, like many writers, stale, restless, I had tried teaching. Urged on by Leonard Ehrlich, I joined the staff of the City College of New York as an instructor in writing for a few unhappy semesters. I stood before my open-faced students. What could I tell them about writing? I was puzzled as they stared up at me. I thought City College a fine school, with a huge, lively student body; but I was soon appalled by the illiteracy I encountered in my classes. The time was the late fifties, the early sixties, with the faint beginnings of campus turmoil. These kids, I found, had almost no writing ability whatsoever. Their spelling was atrocious, their grammatical errors frequently embarrassing. It shocked me to learn they hadn't even heard of Ring Lardner, Stephen Crane, Sherwood Anderson. Of course they had read Hemingway, Fitzgerald, Salinger, and some knew the work of Bellow, Updike, and Malamud. But their knowledge of American writing was really minimal; they had no fundamental literary roots, though some of them seriously professed the desire to become writers. Only two or three students displayed any eagerness or sensitivity about the feel, the meaning of writing.

Toward the end of my first semester, I found in my private mailbox a mimeographed sheet sent out to instructors by the college administration warning of student cheating. According to this communiqué, national research had shown that about 30 per cent of the student body cheated during final exams. "Do not sit at your desk. Walk up and down the aisles while the students write their examination papers. Report the names of cheaters." A few days before this communiqué, I had gone to the college book store to make a purchase. It was my first visit there. A huge, well-stocked store, it resembled an armed camp. Clerks were ultra-alerted. As I entered, I was instructed to check my briefcase in one of the many metal lockers before I passed a turnstile and was given a key. When I introduced myself to the check-out girl at the cashier's desk, she said softly, tactfully: "Major thievery is a problem here." A few days later I read an article in *Esquire* about this student pursuit; according to the article many students financed their college education by stealing and re-selling textbooks. They did so, apparently, with no feelings of guilt. A college education? Were these the idealists who harangued for revolution? Youth seeking the ultimate truth? Concerned young people who sought to cleanse the country of hypocrisy, cant, future wars, militarism, the R.O.T.C., and so on?

Well, I knew the thirties had their full share of phony leftists, phony idealists, phony intellectuals—all ostensibly yearning to save the world. Instead of quoting from the books of Mao and Che, they had spouted the phrases of Lenin and Stalin. During demonstrations in Union Square their obscenities directed at the police were stout; but they had not mastered the art of vehemently flinging the roughest four-letter words at the "pigs." The Molotov cocktail had not as yet been invented; the dynamiting and firing of libraries had not been fashionable, nor even been thought of. The thirties had been a stormy era; but its violence, highly verbal and exciting, had never quite made it to the precipice.

And where did many of those young truth-seekers of the Depression land? In the legal profession, in sales promotion, on Madison Avenue, and in the mass media where, affluent today, they wring their hands and say they do not "understand" their wild, long-haired children—those vocal kids who, soon enough, will confront the rock-bottom problems of their own incipient middle age.

In time and without regret I left the world of teaching. Curious, restless, weary of the solitary life of the novelist, I wrote two plays. To my surprise I sold them, and was hurled into the exciting, vulgar, demanding life of Broadway. Meeting my producer, I soon reveled in the collaborative turmoil about me, sitting in on readings, conferring with a director, viewing sketches for the stage sets. Having loved the theater since my youthful visits to the galleries of the Blackstone, the Garrick, and other houses in Chicago, I was thrilled to assist in the hiring of Lee Remick, Polly Bergen, and Ralph Meeker for my play, *Top Man,* the story of a young physician I had known who had aimed too hard for a quick success in medicine. The play flopped in Philadelphia. At the final night of our tryout there, before the curtain rose and the hidden audience was settling in their seats, the producer, an aging man of the theater—small and bald, a steady patron of Lindy's, an old intimate of Eddie Cantor, Paul Muni, Menasha Skulnik, and a host of others—made a sad speech, announcing to the loyal and melancholy cast that he "was closing Albert's fine play, for revisions. I'm storing the sets, you'll all be back again." Then he embraced me warmly before the actors, behind the curtain, and the play went on that night. But it was not revised and the cast sought other jobs, with Lee Remick going to Hollywood to become a star and Polly Bergen taking a singing stint at the Persian Room. *My Aunt Daisy,* my other play, was produced by Lawrence Langner of the Theater Guild, in Westport, with Jo van Fleet in the lead role, and it was a success there, but somehow it never reached New York.

All during that moody afternoon additional memories began crowding in. They shuttled back and forth, rapidly, from year to year, not following any consecutive pattern. Sections of time flew by like blurring railroad ties between tracks under a speeding train, racing past the way stations of my career, my life.

One day in 1945, Elliot Cohen, who was just starting *Commentary,* called me on the phone. We hadn't met or spoken to each other for almost fourteen years, having somehow drifted apart because of an unimportant and silly quarrel. Over lunch the next day he told me of his editorial plans for *Commentary.* He said he would like me to write a story for the new magazine. I said I would. We talked of the old days. We parted warmly, and I sent him a story, which he published, and we did not meet again for over a decade, when I spotted him walking alone on Fifth Avenue near 90th Street. He passed, not recognizing me, and when he was about fifteen feet away I called out to him.

"Elliot!"

When he turned, I saw that his eyes were glassy, unfocused. He finally recognized me, he smiled, and we shook hands. It was a chilly autumn afternoon, with the wind tearing down Fifth Avenue off Central Park. Elliot was wearing only a suit. Somewhere I had heard a rumor that he had been ill. As we began walking in the wind, he inquired about my work, my present marital status; he asked if I had any children. His eyes had begun to regain their old warmth. We talked and walked for a long time in the cold, windy sunlight; though his teeth were chattering, he didn't seem to notice it. At 79th and Fifth Avenue I saw the actress Eva Gabor waiting at the curb for a taxi; dressed in a long mink coat, she saw I recognized her and gave me the faint smile all so-called celebrities bestow upon their public and stepped into the cab that had stopped for her. Elliot didn't see her. His eyes had become slightly unfocused again, and I began to worry about him in the cold. I suggested that we turn back; and at 86th Street and Fifth Avenue we shook hands, before he headed west through the transverse that cut across the park to his apartment on the West Side. Turning after pressing my hand, he said, "Call me, Albert, call me." His teeth still chattering, he shuffled out of sight.

I never called him, or saw him again. And why the hell didn't I? Why? Shortly afterward he committed suicide by placing a plastic bag over his head. The Riverside Chapel on Amsterdam Avenue was jammed at his funeral. Men and women were standing along the side walls. In the crowd I saw people I hadn't seen in many years, the old *Menorah Journal* group of writers—Louis Berg, Charles Reznikoff, Herbert Solow, William Shack, and many more. There were also the younger writers whom I didn't know—Norman Podhoretz, Irving Kristol, and others connected less with the *Menorah Journal* than with *Commentary*. White-faced and choking, Lionel Trilling delivered the eulogy over the closed casket. People started weeping for wonderful, warmhearted, self-effacing Elliot Cohen. Sobs broke from women. As the rabbi intoned the *Kaddish* prayer, many people wept harder than ever. When the service was over I came out of the chapel with Lorna. Long black limousines were waiting at the curb. Louis Berg approached me, his eyes streaming tears. "Where's Kip Fadiman, why didn't he come? Please, ride to the cemetery with us, Albert." And Lorna and I got into one of the cars that became the cavalcade to the hillside cemetery in Queens where the old *Menorah Journal* group milled about the open grave until the rabbi arrived. . . .

And so this book ends here, fittingly, with Elliot Cohen. He had been my literary godfather and the godfather to so many others. It's not a sad ending, really—for wasn't he a truly intelligent, wonderful man? He was generous, he never betrayed one; and as he'd shuffled off into the transverse cutting across Central Park that chilly day I really meant to phone him soon. Really, I did. . . .